DEVELOPMENTAL COUNSELING

DONALD H. BLOCHER
UNIVERSITY OF MINNESOTA

SECOND EDITION

THE RONALD PRESS COMPANY • NEW YORK

This edition is dedicated to those special students who have helped so much to stimulate and discipline my thinking.

PREFACE

This text provides a broad and integrated structure for the practice of counseling. It is based on the premise that the professional
counselor's ultimate goal is to maximize human effectiveness, by
facilitating the growth and development of fully human beings.
Although primarily psychological in orientation, the book draws
extensively from other disciplines, particularly anthropology and
sociology. It will be of value to professional workers in a wide range
of settings, whether counselor, psychologist, social worker, teacher,
or dean. All will find it useful in framing the process of human
development and in establishing their roles in the encouragement of
such development.

A number of aspects of *Developmental Counseling* make it different from most books in the field. First, it presents a cohesive
description of the process of human development organized around
life stages and elaborated in terms of social roles and coping and
mastery behaviors. Since development is envisioned as a lifelong
process, this material may be useful to workers in settings ranging
from the nursery school to the geriatric clinic.

The book also deals with models of human effectiveness that help
the reader grasp the upper limits of human functioning. It offers
a systematic eclectic framework for designing developmental approaches that draws upon several sources of gain and allows the
counselor to shape his interventions in terms of his philosophical
commitments and personal resources.

Developmental Counseling is also unique in terms of the attention it gives to the roles of counselors as behavioral scientists and
as agents of environmental change. The book takes the view that
human development can often be facilitated by improving the
growth-producing capacities of human institutions. The counselor
is viewed as a behavioral scientist who works not only with individ-

uals as clients, but who also helps client systems such as families, classrooms, schools, and community agencies in their attempt to provide fully human environments.

Finally, the book presents an approach and a selection of material relevant to working in a changing society beset with social problems of unprecedented magnitude. It is geared to the needs of professionals attempting to work with the full range of human beings and human problems. In addition—and to make it as relevant as possible to today's society—new materials have been added to this edition to reflect recent developments in minority relations, roles of men and women, ecology and the environment, and so on.

I wish to acknowledge the invaluable assistance of Rita S. Rapoza in researching and generally assisting with the preparation of this edition.

DONALD H. BLOCHER

Minneapolis, Minnesota
April, 1974

CONTENTS

DEVELOPMENTAL COUNSELING

TOWARD
AN ECOLOGY
OF HUMAN
DEVELOPMENT

Alexander, the twelve-year-old hero of Ben Piazza's novel, *The Exact And Very Strange Truth*, comes to grips with one of life's ultimate realities when he reflects, "Peculiar how things can change so sudden. Things can be one way today and tomorrow be the very opposite. That is the exact and very strange truth."

A freckle-faced fourteen-year-old boy suddenly discovers that girls are not just soft boys. A sensitive sixteen-year-old has his ideals bruised by the realities of a cynical adult world. A blonde cheerleader gazes at an engagement ring with a mixture of awe and apprehension. A middle-aged machine operator watches his job being automated out of existence. An unemployed aeronautical engineer drives a taxi cab and waits for politicians to decide on national priorities. A distinguished professor approaches retirement with a growing sense of panic.

All of these people face change—changes occurring within themselves and within the world in which they live. Suddenly, the inevitability of change has become the only real certainty—the exact and very strange truth. Each situation of changing self and changing world is experienced as an isolated and cataclysmic event. Taken together, however, these experiences form the pattern and fabric of what we call human development. To the serious observer they form what Robert White (9) called "the study of lives."

How do human beings deal with change? How do they cope with stress and stimulation in their environments? Are the changes that occur in each life orderly and predictable? How is it that some people apparently achieve high levels of control and mastery over the course of their lives, while for others life appears to be a series of unmet challenges and unmitigated disasters.

These are a few of the questions that confront the counselor who, as Tyler (8, pp. 10, 17) puts it, believes that "the psychological purpose of counseling is to facilitate development." This point of view is one held by a growing number of people in the helping professions. Increasingly, teachers, school counselors, ministers, psychologists, social workers, and physicians have given up trying to adjust people to the demands of a kaleidoscopic culture and a sick society. They have begun to desist from prescribing non-existent panaceas for dimly perceived ills. Finally, they have restrained themselves from attempting to mold into their own images, individuals with vastly differing backgrounds, needs, and values.

Instead, these workers have started to shift their attention and their efforts to the task of helping others to become aware of and to learn to exert some degree of control over the course of their own lives, and to help society to learn to shape environments that can support fully human patterns of individual development.

Such professional helpers will hereafter be called developmental counselors for want of a better name. As we shall see, that label is not fully adequate. The concerns and approaches we shall examine in some cases go well beyond those that are traditionally associated with counseling and psychotherapy.

The developmental counselor intervenes, consciously and planfully, in other human lives to help change behavior and experience. The choice, of course, for any human being is *not* to change or not to change. All human beings change—and do so continuously—whether they will it or not. The one freedom that no living being can ever enjoy is the freedom to remain the same. All people change, psychologically and physiologically, within themselves and in their relationship to a changing outside world. Human freedom lies not in our ability to resist or to protect ourselves from change, but from our ability to participate as fully as possible in it. Freedom lies in helping to influence the directions, rates, and distances we travel through those change processes that we call development.

FREEDOM AND INDEPENDENCE

A major reality faced by developmental counseling involves the nature of independence. One of the most profound misconceptions to plague counseling has been that which tends to confound the nature of human freedom and independence.

Man is unquestionably a social being. His culture, his language, his very humanness arise out of his interactions with other men. In this sense, a truly independent man—that is, one who shunned all kinds of significant interactions with others—would be scarcely recognizable as human. Men are by nature *interdependent*. What we really mean when we observe that a person is "independent" is that he has spread his essential interdependence across a network of relationships and interactions with others. Conversely, the dependent person has constricted his legitimate needs for others into a few usually inappropriate relationships and so experiences vulnerability and weakness, rather than strength and security in his interpersonal life.

Developmental counseling does not have as its goal making people more *independent* in the sense of being more nearly self-contained. It does have as a goal helping individuals to build an appropriate network of growth-producing relationships through which they can enrich their own lives and the lives of others.

A basic assumption of developmental counseling is that human personality grows optimally out of healthy interactions between the growing organism and the culture or environment.

Cultural and social forces are clearly recognized as exerting very powerful influences over the individual and his development. Maximizing the individual's possible control over those limited aspects of his development in which such control is feasible is seen as one of the most important goals of developmental counseling.

The question of determinism versus free will is a complex philosophical issue that remains unresolved after many centuries of very serious inquiry and acrimonious debate. Since its extreme positions are almost entirely untestable, they tend to be of relatively little concern to the individual confronted with real and immediate decisions in a real and immediate world. Such people *experience* freedom, delusion or not, when they perceive alternative courses of action open to them and have available some kind of value system on which to choose among those alternatives. The *feeling* of freedom is a vital part of human experience and an active ingredient in human satisfaction. From this standpoint, then, human freedom is heavily a product of *awareness*. The feeling of freedom derived from a high level of awareness in direct experiencing is just as important to the convinced determinist as it is to the person who believes in free will. The existentialist Kierkegaard is once said to have remarked that the philosopher who creates a deterministic system is in the position of a man who builds a great castle and then goes to live in the adjoining barn.

No individual in any society is, of course, ever completely free, or probably ever really wants to be so. Wandering alone in an infinitely confusing maze is in one sense the ultimate in freedom—no prior constraints reduce the range of possible choices. It is of course also the ultimate in terror.

Many kinds of behavioral constraints and influences are present in every person's environment. As we have seen, for example, no human being has the freedom to remain the same. Human behavior is dynamic and, to a large extent, reactive. It is, however, possible—and perhaps even necessary—as Allport (1) said, to conceive of man as more than *merely* a reactive being who is completely the creature and victim of his environment. Even when man's overt behavior is completely reactive, the meaning that behavior has to him may well depend on the way in which he perceives it. Figuratively speaking, the rat in the Skinner Box may well chuckle about the way in which he has conditioned the psychologist to feed and care for him.

GOALS OF DEVELOPMENTAL COUNSELING

It is possible then to see developmental counseling as an attempt to help an individual to maximize his possible freedom within the limitations supplied by himself and his environment through increasing his awareness of the "here and now" aspects of his immediate experience and through developing cognitive structures by which to construe that experience.

Developmental counseling in this sense aims at helping an individual to become more fully aware of himself and the ways in which he is responding to the influences in his environment. It further assists him to establish some personal meaning for his behavior and to develop and clarify a set of goals and values for future behavior. Out of such awareness and understanding of his past learning experiences and present environment, an individual is better able to identify those influences that will best facilitate the future developmental directions and distances that are goal-oriented for him.

This is the sense in which developmental counseling is aimed at maximizing human freedom. It is philosophically devoted to such a concept of freedom while fully recognizing that for many people that freedom is severely limited. The opportunity structure within the society, the physical and emotional limitations imposed by previous learning and maturation, the immediate circumstances of the environment are all reality factors that restrict the freedom of each person. While it may be true then that most human beings have very limited freedom, it may be equally true that few of them are prepared to exercise the freedom that is potentially available to them.

Developmental counseling has a second major set of goals that runs parallel to those involved with human freedom. These goals cluster around the concept of maximizing *human effectiveness*. From a practical standpoint, effective human behavior can be defined as that behavior giving an individual *the greatest possible long-term control over his environment and the affective responses within him that are evoked by that environment.* The effective human being seeks mastery over those aspects of his environment that he can manipulate, and control over his own emotional responses to those aspects of his situation that he cannot master.

HUMAN EFFECTIVENESS MODEL

More will be said about the development of human effectiveness in Chapters 4 and 5. At this point it may be useful to sketch briefly a model for conceptualizing the relationship between developmental counseling and its goal of maximizing human effectiveness. The first dimension of this model deals with *roles and relationships*. People typically come to a counselor when they are experiencing difficulty in one or more significant areas of living. Perhaps the clearest way of looking at these areas is in terms of the roles in which an individual engages and the interpersonal relationships that are attendant to these roles.

Roles and Relationships

Individuals from infancy to old age are constantly in the process of entering new roles and relationships and modifying or casting aside old ones. Even a casual examination reveals the fact that there are great individual differences among people in the effectiveness with which they handle such roles. There are equally great intraindividual differences within persons in the effectiveness with which they operate in their several role situations (3, 4).

For example, the successful business executive may organize and control the operation of a gigantic corporation and at the same time be a notable failure as a father. A movie star may command the acclaim and adulation of millions and yet be unable to function adequately within any of a series of marital relationships.

Such differences are due to the fact that each role and relationship carries with it a peculiar set of demands, or expectations for behavior. These expectations are often formalized into duties, obligations, and responsibilities. Failure to cope with such formalized expectations usually incurs punishment or withdrawal of rewards that are anxiety-producing. Coping adequately with such demands is generally a necessary part of controlling the environment and consequently the rewards and punishments that it metes out.

To the extent that a developing human being encounters new roles and relationships in orderly and sequential patterns, he is usually able to handle them in reasonably effective ways. Most people, for example, handle progressively more complex and demanding roles of student, worker, citizen, spouse, parent, etc., in a fairly adequate manner. They have available at the necessary time an appropriate repertory of behaviors adequate to meet new demands.

Often, however, serious *discontinuities* between development and environmental demands occur. When these discontinuities arise, an individual may need help to acquire new, more effective behaviors.

The concept of discontinuity is an important one to developmental counseling. It is discussed in more detail in Chapter 6. If we conceptualize human development as the result of a dynamic interaction between a set of biological processes and tendencies unfolding within the physiological structure of the person, and the social and cultural forces impinging upon him from his environment, we can postulate that healthy growth and development results from some kind of optimal match between these inner and outer forces.

In very simple societies cultural influences may really act upon developing individuals at rates and in ways that closely approximate the biologically regulated processes which determine readiness for such experiences.

Preparation for productive work, for example, may proceed at the same rate that growth in physical strength and size gives the readiness for effective labor. As the child becomes physically able to perform work tasks in the family and society, he is given increasingly difficult and important responsibilities. Thus, he experiences *continuity* between his physical and vocational development. In simple societies, then, *biological clocks and cultural clocks tend to keep the same time.*

In complex industrial societies, however, there are many cultural clocks, none of which necessarily keeps the same time as the biological clocks that govern maturation. Indeed, the cultural clocks do not even agree with each other. The attainment of full adult status in an industrial society involves a complex set of legal, educational, and social regulations none of which are likely to be precisely attuned to the experienced needs of a particular individual.

In industrial societies, then, most individuals experience *discontinuity* between aspects of their development. At various stages, discontinuity is built into biosocial interaction processes. Entry into school, labor market, marriage, parenthood, or retirement are all examples of events that may be accompanied by severe discontinuities.

Developmental counseling is often the process by which individuals are helped to bridge discontinuities and enabled to proceed unhampered and undamaged along their development pathways. In practice, this bridging of discontinuities is essentially helping the individual to acquire an adequate set of behaviors with which to cope with the demands and expectations inherent in his new roles.

Coping Behaviors

The second facet of the effectiveness model involves the concept of *coping behaviors*. Coping behaviors are the specific instrumental acts by which the individual transacts with his socially structured environment. In any role situation a given set of behaviors will allow the individual to cope with—and, optimally, to exert mastery over—that portion of his environment. An important area of expertise for the developmental counselor involves helping his client to assess the role expectations that exist in the environment and to acquire a set of behaviors that well allow him to cope with them in ways that are goal-directed and satisfying *for him.* To some extent this is an exercise in personal problem-solving. It may involve the active tryout of new approaches, the learning of new skills and understandings, the making of important decisions, and the clarification of existing values.

Coping with environmental demands and expectations is *not* the equivalent of *adjusting* to them. For many developing individuals the role expectations that are most central in their environments may themselves be unreasonable, arbitrary, and capricious. Mere adjustment to the expectations of an irrational parent, an inhuman school system, or a racist society may well represent the beginning of an other-directed existence that deprives the individual of any chance for self-respect, positive identity, and personal meaning in his life.

At times the appropriate coping behaviors involve hard decisions to *resist demands,* to establish separateness, and to place commitment to personal values ahead of a convenient conformity.

Developmental Tasks

The developmental counselor is as much concerned with preventing growth-interrupting discontinuities as he is with bridging those that have already occurred. His primary role in this regard is as an expert on *developmental tasks.*

The third dimension of the effectiveness model has as its central focus the concept of developmental tasks. Facilitating human development consists largely of insuring that each individual has an opportunity to master the tasks that will equip him with the coping behaviors necessary for handling the central roles and relationships that are involved in his next stage of development.

A central theme in modern developmental psychology is the concept that human growth is orderly and sequential. This does not mean however that growth is inevitable. *Change* is certainly an inevitable and pervasive phenomenon in all human lives. Continued *growth* is not. A mounting array of evidence suggests instead that millions of people do not reach their full potentials for growth in many important areas. Cognitively, morally, and interpersonally many—perhaps most—human beings are literally "hung up" developmentally; unable to master the developmental tasks that will move them into more complex, highly differentiated and rewarding stages and sequences.

Human personality, then, does not simply unfold as the blooming of a flower. At its highest levels, development represents an exquisitely fragile set of mechanisms that require expert and timely interventions if they are to operate effectively.

The developmental counselor is an expert on these tasks in two ways. He is an expert consultant to the individual in identifying and locating those settings in which particular developmental tasks may be mastered. Educational tasks may involve the selection of courses or colleges. Vocational tasks may dictate seeking a new job or moving in a different direction within the same career field. Social tasks may involve joining an organization, or changing living arrangements in order to find new friends. For some individuals mastering key developmental tasks may mean abandoning safe and familiar settings and moving into new, less securely structured environments to seek out and test alternatives to those life styles with which they are most familiar. For some this may mean *leaving* family, job, or school to reach out into a new world of differing alternatives and opportunities.

Some developmental tasks may be mastered directly within the counseling situation itself. Both individual and group counseling situations involve opportunities to increase awareness of self and others, to experience more open and confrontive relationships, to gain confirmation and validation of self-concepts.

These kinds of developmental tasks are often best accomplished in individual and group encounters that occur within the context of counseling processes. Perhaps the clearest way to conceptualize this basic aspect of developmental counseling is through the psychological construct of identity formation.

IDENTITY FORMATION: A CENTRAL DEVELOPMENTAL TASK

The questions "Who am I?" "What do I value?" have confronted human beings in every age and under every circumstance. In one way or another these themes permeate most of men and women's important products. They are heard in their art, their religion, their music, and their literature. In centuries past, poets, priests, and philosophers helped some people to cope with the troublesome problems of values, ideals, attitudes, and understandings that are involved in establishing an identity.

In the twentieth century, at least, the struggle for answers to identity questions is more than an abstract philosophical exercise. The specters of racism, war, poverty, and social disorganization have worked to rob millions of people of the identity anchors crucial to their full development. Without such anchors and answers many people are unable to provide structure and organization to their own lives, or to attach realistic personal meaning to the events and experiences that confront them. Such individuals often are unable to commit themselves to purposes, take appropriate risks to achieve goals, or establish value systems that give direction and consistency to their own behavior. They are often unable to take responsibility for their lives or to accept the consequences of their own behavior. The term "identity structure" is used here to describe and explain the personality organization process that seems to give meaning and consistency to an individual's behavior and experiences. The identity structure is a psychological construct that embraces the whole constellation of self-referent ideas, attitudes, and emotions by which an individual knows himself. It goes well beyond these, however, to include the ways in which this self-structure is organized with respect to *important others*, groups, and institutions.

The construct of identity as used here involves more than what is usually described by the term *"self-concept."* Identity formation implies the development of many self-concepts, perhaps as many as there are roles and relationships involving the individual. The central role of values and interpersonal relationships in personality development is clearly recognized. The interdependence of the individual and his social environment is emphasized rather than obscured. Identity is a *psychosocial* rather than a purely psychological construct. Identity is the sense of *belonging to*, of *harmony with*, of *caring about* other individuals, groups, and ideals. Its opposites are *alienation, emptiness*, and *isolation*. The construct of identity has another important advantage as a frame of reference for conceptualizing important aspects of human behavior. Identity development can be seen as an active, ongoing process of interaction with environment. Preoccupation with the self-concept has led psychology to some extent toward a passive, almost narcissistic view of human personality development. At times it has seemed to imply that an individual discovers his self-structure ready-made and fully developed within himself. This emphasis almost tended to suggest that individuals can be helped only through some passive ritual of introspection, whether in philosophical reverie, or with the aid of a presumed mirroring agent—the therapist or counselor.

An alternative view is that an identity structure is not suddenly discovered through introspection, but is actively constructed in a developmental process of which the individual can become aware and over which he can learn to exercise some degree of control. A simple illustration may help explain the identity formation process. Let us suppose that a spy is sent into a foreign country to commit espionage. His first task is to establish an *identity*. How does he do this? He begins to develop affiliations, relationships, and commitments that establish his identity. He undertakes roles and responsibilities, gets a job, and joins groups. These are exactly the processes by which any individual develops his identity.

Helping with identity development from this point of view means not only facilitating self-exploration via the interview, but actively helping an individual to cope with environmental demands. It means active problem-solving and tryouts of alternative behaviors. Its goal is the formation of an integrated structure of values and ideals, together with a set of coping behaviors adequate to sustain a life style consistent with a well-defined identity in a real world of commitments, risks, afiliations, and responsibilities.

This way of conceptualizing the goals of developmental counseling is also useful in that it serves to integrate much that is often separated in thinking about the counseling process itself. Vocational counseling, educational counseling, marriage counseling, personal counseling—all fit together within this common framework.

NEW MODELS FOR PROFESSIONAL PRACTICE

In his efforts to facilitate the development of effective human behavior and adequate identities, the developmental counselor is able to draw upon a steadily increasing body of knowledge. More and more, psychology is moving away from its obsession with all that is abnormal, distorted, and perverse in human behavior. With this movement has come the abandonment of models of professional practice that are rooted solely in the medical tradition.

Increasingly, the modern helping professions are moving to what is sometimes called a "community mental health model." Within such a model the traditional one-to-one counseling or therapeutic interview is seen as only one among several tools or interventions available to professional practice. In educational settings a parallel version of the community mental health model has sometimes been called an "outreach" approach.

Such models assume that the professional worker will take a *pro-active* rather than a *reactive* stance, actively scanning the environments of clients or potential clients for ways to improve the quality of those settings to enhance the development of people.

The approach espoused here is very much in tune with these recent developments and in a sense seeks to push them to their fullest applications. In a very definite sense we will be moving toward the conception of a new kind of applied science and a new kind of professional person. We will be concerned about an ecology of human development; about examining the relationships and interactions between growing human beings and their social, physical, and psychological environments.

The essence of this new profession is that it is no longer willing to accept the premise that the kinds of limitations to development discussed earlier are tragic but inevitable aspects of the human condition. Many of the limitations to human freedom and human effectiveness are rooted in the very social institutions and organizations that man himself has built. Poverty, racism, authoritarianism, destructive competition, and exploitation are functions of an imperfect social environment that to a large extent man, himself, has created.

The pro-active stance which we see as the basis for a new generation of helping professions assumes that what man can invent, he can improve upon. It assumes that men and women can consistently and planfully protect and enhance the growth-sustaining, health-producing aspects of their environment. Such a view also asserts that when limitations and injustices in the environment cause human problems, then interventions should be addressed to those causes, rather than merely to urgings or exhortations to the individual victims to adjust to, or rise above, what is clearly defective in the social environment.

The Study of Environments

The study of human environments in the sense that we are concerned with them is a relatively new enterprise. For centuries we have, of course, been aware that growing human beings, like all organisms, need adequate quantities of fresh air, pure water, clear sunlight, and nourishing foods. Only recently have we become fully aware of the threats posed to our very survival by foolish and greedy manipulations of the delicate life-sustaining equilibria that control our physical world.

We are still, unfortunately, very largely unaware of many of the social and psychological forces that operate in our environments to facilitate or retard the development of human beings.

Recently, the author worked with a bright, attractive, high school senior girl in a series of developmental counseling interviews. As these sessions went on, it became clear that Linda perceived no serious home problems. She believed that her parents loved her, but she did not feel understood by them. She was popular with other young people. She achieved well in school in terms of grades and standardized tests, although she mildly disliked most of her school experiences.

As she attempted to think and talk about the future, however, it became clear that Linda was unable to commit herself to any kind of distant goal, no matter how tentative or general it might be.

Her thinking about the future was dominated by a recurring daydream that she clearly recognized as fantasy. In this daydream (which preoccupied a considerable amount of her time), Linda and a girl friend set off across the country, living in the open air, following advancing seasons, avoiding cities and civilization.

As Linda talked about the daydream, she began to express her view of the world. She saw the world in which she lived as totally absurd, incomprehensible, and uncontrollable. She expressed the firm conviction that she would die before the age of forty—that either war or pollution would destroy her. Planning, commitment, or caring about the future was futile, meaningless, and self-punishing. Only running away from the mindlessness, ugliness, and terror that she saw made sense, and Linda was far too intelligent and realistic to think that running away was possible.

She was painfully aware of and thoroughly frightened by the threats that she perceived in her physical environment. Linda was quite unaware, however, of the pollution that resided in her psychological environment. She was quite unaware that somewhere in her neat, middle-class, suburban world she was being cheated of the opportunity to become fully human, to have an identity. The sense of powerlessness that pervaded her world, the depersonalization, the diffuseness of values and challenges, the inability to experience life in an integrated way—to *feel* as well as think, to *act* as well as to reflect, to *appreciate* as well as to acquire—these vital human nutrients were missing from her environment just as surely as oxygen is missing from the cesspool waters of Lake Erie. Linda did not even have the basic cognitive structures to identify clearly the emotional starvation that existed in her affluent family and community.

Linda only knew that she could no longer plan, no longer commit energy, no longer hope and fear and love as a fully human being. Linda was a physically healthy and beautiful young creature who was in the process of being cheated of her right to develop into a person.

In one sense Linda represented the generation gap. She is a member of the post-Hiroshima generation; the first to grow up unsure that there will be a future. In another sense she is the victim of the failure of our society to create learning environments in family, school, and community that can keep pace with the shifting challenges, changing values, and frightening realities of a confused and troubled world. The developmental needs of a generation of Lindas will not be met by counseling interviews alone, but by a new generation of professionals who are sensitive enough to listen to Lindas, and skillful enough to change those environments that are constricting and immobilizing people.

AN ECOLOGICAL APPROACH

Ecology is a wide-angled, double-barreled "in" word that is commanding tremendous attention in a world engaged in slowly poisoning itself. Everywhere we are finding an awakening concern for the quality of our environment and the life experience that it sustains. Scientists, politicians, folk singers, housewives, and high school students have begun to voice their apprehensions about the dangers inherent in our military, industrial, "effluent" society. These people fear both the physically destructive and psychologically dehumanizing effects of urban ugliness and all that goes with it.

Running through all of these cries of concern and alarm is one ever-present, but often muted, theme. We must produce people and institutions capable of solving human problems in human ways, or we will rapidly forfeit our very survival as a species. Our total physical and psychological world is in ferment. The air, the water, the ideals, and the values that sustain our lives and our culture are changing at a frightening rate. We do not have a choice of *whether* to change our world. It *is* changing whether we will it to or not. Our only choice concerns our efforts to influence the directions and distances of change in an attempt to sustain and advance human values. Planning for change is merely intelligent cooperation with the inevitable.

The sense of urgency, almost of desperation, is mounting with every crisis in the streets, with every analysis of our lakes and streams, and with every confrontation on our campuses. Today, we hold the dubious distinction of being the first human beings who can walk on the moon, breathing purer air, drinking cleaner water, and enjoying greater security from violent death than is obtainable on the streets of our nation's capitol. We are no longer confident that even the Orwellian prophecy that "life will go on as it has always gone on—that is badly," is not a masterpiece of over-optimism.

A Human Environment

The central problem confronting our species today is how to produce a generation of truly *human* beings who are capable of engaging in intelligent, cooperative problem-solving behaviors across the barriers of age, sex, race, language, religion, and geography that separate people and alienate them from each other. Our problems are not technological, military, economic, or even purely social; they are human. To begin solving human problems we must begin to create those environments that give people the opportunity to become *persons*. We must create environments that can develop full human potential—potential to feel and think, to commit as well as to observe, to appreciate as well as to manipulate. Only fully human beings can solve human problems in human ways.

Ecology is a developing multi-disciplinary scientific endeavor aimed at describing, explaining, predicting, and eventually controlling the delicate and dynamic interactions between organisms and the many facets of their environments. Ecology is particularly concerned with understanding and protecting the balances that exist within environments to allow their life-sustaining and growth-producing properties to be maintained. In a human ecology, the central problems revolve around questions of the nature of the interaction between learning environments and human growth and development.

Man is distinguished from other species by his relative ability to learn and his ability to transmit that learning across individuals and generations. Man's genetically endowed, neurological structures virtually assure that he will learn new behavior. His social and linguistic attributes also insure that his behavior will be contagious—that it will spread from one individual to another and from one group to another.

Nothing in his genetic makeup or social tendencies, however, assures that man will learn to be *human* or will teach others to be *human.* He may learn to be genocidal, cannibalistic, racist, sadistic, or authoritarian. On the other hand, he may learn to be cooperative, compassionate, rational, empathic, and planful. The keys to each individual's developmental journey lie in the ecological balance that exists within his learning environment.

A Learning Environment

A learning environment is essentially a physical, social, and psychological context within which people acquire new behavior or, in other words, learn. The learning environment structures and shapes the opportunities, expectations, and perceptions of its residents and engages or disengages with their basic needs and motives.

AN ECOLOGICAL ANALYSIS
OF A LEARNING ENVIRONMENT

Counselors, teachers, and other professionals talk a great deal about human development. Often, however, they are not clear about what is meant by development, and what the precise relationship is between development and professional practices. Most of the literature of developmental psychology is primarily descriptive. It invites the student to observe more closely; it provides a framework for studying changes in behavior, but only infrequently does it lead directly to the understandings needed by counselors as they intervene to facilitate those changes in behavior that are labeled steps toward growth and maturity.

One may begin by specifying carefully what is meant by human development and what its relationship is to schools, families, and other social organizations. Human development may be defined as those change processes in the physical, mental, and emotional components of personality that are continuous and orderly and that proceed in valued directions. All change in behavior is thus not truly developmental. The mental deterioration of a schizophrenic or the escalating sociopathic behaviors of a juvenile delinquent are obvious examples of change patterns that we are unlikely to term developmental.

Educational institutions and families, for example, are social systems established by the larger society to help insure that the change processes occurring in children do in fact move in directions that are valued. Such organizations, then, stand in a uniquely significant relationship to problems of human development. Educators by the very nature of the responsibilities given them by society must be concerned with what we are beginning to call the "ecology of human development." That is, they are concerned with understanding the nature of the interaction between a developing human being and his physical, social, and emotional environment. It is in this interaction that the keys to healthy development or deterioration and alienation must lie.

Developmental Framework

Let us return now, for a moment, to the tools that are offered by developmental psychology. What kinds of frameworks are available as we seek to understand something of the ecology of students and attempt to remove the "pollutants" from the environment?

At least two kinds of developmental frameworks offer the foundations around which developmental counselors can help to design and evaluate approaches that can "clean up" the environments in school and family with which they are concerned. These frameworks allow us to take the initial steps toward defining healthy and relevant developmental processes. They offer guidelines for healthy growth and can provide direction for the evaluation of learning experiences.

Chronological Framework. The first type of framework is essentially chronological. This type is well-represented by Erik Erikson's "eight stages of man." Erikson carefully traces normal development from infancy to old age through eight well-defined life stages. At each stage he posits a central developmental task that must be accomplished if the growing person is to continue successfully to the next stage with its correspondingly more complex and difficult demands. Chapter 4 elaborates upon Erikson's concepts to formulate a developmental chronology which outlines not only a sequence of life stages and developmental tasks, but also specifies the corresponding social roles and coping behaviors that give the individual full effectiveness in his present life stage and prepare him for effective development on subsequent stages.

Chronological frameworks themselves, however, are not sufficient to solve the ecological problems with which we deal. Another kind of developmental framework is needed to supply the full picture. This framework may be called hierarchical. In a sense, of course, it, too, has chronological aspects, yet they go beyond simple chronologies to specify the directions and distance through which one can measure growth and evaluate changes in behavior.

Hierarchical Framework.   Perhaps the best known example of such an hierarchical framework is represented by Abraham Maslow's steps toward "self-actualization." Maslow's hierarchy traces the growth of an individual through a series of stages that are only loosely chronological in the sense that higher order needs cannot emerge until lower level needs are satisfied. These types of framework are elaborated on in Chapter 5.

Maslow's framework is useful because it is directional and value loaded. It can help identify ways in which developing individuals will transact with their environment and so establish the basis of their ecological balance. Here, the concept of "creative mismatch" is extremely useful. We can conceptualize growth as a function of a dynamic balance between the needs and capacities of the individual and the levels of stress and stimulation in the environment. When the latter levels are far above the capacity or "readiness" of the individual to cope, he withdraws and precious opportunities for learning and growth are lost. When the levels of stimulation in the environment are below the capacity of the individual, the rate of development is slowed because of the lack of challenge and opportunity. A stimulation level slightly higher than the chronic level is optimal. One of the primary responsibilities of school and family systems then is to create the creative mismatch or "ecological balance" between the child and his environment that will allow maximum growth to occur.

Let us combine these frameworks now to develop a concrete example. The elementary school years are, according to Erikson, the life stage in which the central developmental task is what he terms "industry vs. inferiority." This is the period in which the child wants and needs to learn how to do and make things with others. In learning to accept instruction and to win recognition by producing, he opens the way for the development of work enjoyment. The prime danger to development in this period is the formation of a sense of inadequacy and inferiority in a child who does not receive recognition for his efforts.

It is possible now to superimpose on the Erikson framework, Maslow's (6) hierarchy of needs. Maslow pointed out that in order to move toward the highest level of human growth and development—which he chooses to call "self-actualization"—the individual must first satisfy a set of lower level needs. Those needs that he classified as physiological, safety, love, and esteem needs give rise to "deficit" motivations; that is, they must be satisfied before positive motivations toward self-fulfillment or actualization are released.

In terms now of the elementary school child seeking to develop industry and to avoid inferiority, one can begin to check off the list of psychological nutrients that must exist in the environment in order to permit the kind of ecological balance or dynamic equilibrium of which we spoke. Obviously, he must be able to satisfy basic physiological and safety needs. His environment must be dependable and stable enough to provide for these. For many ghetto children or children of rural poverty even these needs may go unmet. For most children the truly problematical elements in the environment are those that deal with the needs for love and esteem.

It is at this point that the Erikson and Maslow frameworks so neatly coincide to form a complete ecological system. The basic transaction through which growth and development occur in the elementary school years is the interaction between industry or what Robert White (10) calls "competence" in the child, and the capacity of the environment to provide security and love and through them the growth of self-esteem.

An Ecological System

In the light of this dual framework then, let us extend our example to examine the ecological system represented by the elementary school classroom. This classroom represents an environment in which the growing child will spend about one-third of his waking hours for the formative periods or life stages that we call middle and later childhood. For about a thousand hours a year for more than six years this environment will determine the transactions that govern the development of the child.

Opportunity Structure.   In analyzing this ecological system, let us look at three basic subsystems. The first we may call the "opportunity structure" of the classroom. This is represented essentially by the set of tasks, or problems, or situations through which the child is able to attempt to exert mastery or control. An arithmetic problem, a puzzle, a spelling word, or a class office all represent parts of the opportunity structure. The nature of this structure largely determines the level of stimulation in the environments. That level of stimulation is measurable largely in terms of four elements: *novelty, intensity, complexity,* and *ambiguity.* As these elements increase in magnitude, they raise the level of stimulation to the point that it may be experienced as stressful by particular individuals in the environment. When such individuals experience stress they tend to reduce it by physical or psychological withdrawal from the environment. For given classroom environments to offer an ecological balance or dynamic equilibrium for twenty to thirty children differing considerably in their readiness to cope with stimulation, *the classroom environment will obviously need to offer what can be termed a broad band opportunity structure.*

Support Structure.   The second classroom subsystem observed is what can be termed the "support structure." This is essentially the set of resources available to students in the environment for coping with stress. Basically, the support structure determines the degree to which the student can manage the stress-producing elements of novelty, intensity, complexity, and ambiguity. Two kinds of resources are built into the support structure. These are the affective or relationship networks that touch the student and allow stress reduction to occur through the operation of factors of warmth, empathy, acceptance, and involvement with others. In the presence of these relationship conditions, students are better able to manage and tolerate highly stimulating situations. In addition to relationships, there are important cognitive structures that allow for improved coping with stress. These involve understanding, assessing, predicting, and labeling stress factors. Such cognitive structures particularly help to reduce ambiguity and complexity to manageable levels. *The elementary classroom then, like the family, to maintain an ecological balance must offer an affective and cognitive support structure to all members.*

Reward Structure.   The third and final classroom subsystem with which we can deal is the "reward structure." This determines the contingencies that intervene between effort expended and need satisfaction. The development of "industry" or "competence" is essentially dependent upon a belief or attitude that we can term "effort-optimism." This is essentially a set or approach to a learning experience or opportunity for growth that generates a prediction that the expenditure of effort will in fact yield important need satisfactions. The key in the elementary school in terms of the reward system is to insure the highest probability that effort expended will lead to increase in self-esteem. Any aspect of the environment that systematically interferes with that connection—be it a grading system, a teacher bias, or a random system of rewards—upsets the ecological balance inherent in the system. *The ecological principle is that the contingencies upon which rewards are distributed must be clear, consistent, and reasonable in terms of effort expended for all children in the classroom.*

SYSTEMS AS CLIENTS

The principal point in the above discussion is that if developmental counselors are to be fully prepared to facilitate the development of growing human beings, they must be aware of and ready, upon occasion, to intervene in the learning environments that so often hold the keys to future development. Essentially, this point of view means that developmental counselors must be ready to broaden their view of client to include systems as well as individuals. When counselors actively scan the environments of many of those whom they serve, it becomes clear that the real determinants of behavior—the real causes and sources of difficulty, and the real opportunities for constructive intervention on behalf of individuals—often lie in complex social organizations. Families, classrooms, peer groups, sometimes total school or community organizations, become potential clients.

Broadening the concept of client to include groups and organizations admittedly increases the complexity of the situations with which the developmental counselor must deal. It also increases the potential payoff from successful counseling.

In this section we have sketched an overview of those dimensions with which the succeeding pages will deal in greater detail. We have attempted to lay out a general philosophical and theoretical approach to professional practice. We have outlined a set of constructs and commitments, and have proposed an "ecological" model for counseling practice which goes beyond most of what is represented in traditionally oriented concepts of counseling and psychotherapy.

DEVELOPMENTAL COUNSELING AND OTHER PROCESSES

We have not attempted to differentiate developmental counseling from other processes on most of the traditional criteria. We have not been particularly interested, for example, in the usual distinctions between counseling and psychotherapy. Traditionally, most of these distinctions (2) have been based upon the presumed depth of the psychological processes involved. This type of distinction usually conceptualizes human personality in a kind of onion skin analogy, with the counselor busily peeling away the outer layers of skin, while the therapist penetrates to the inner and presumably more pungent layers of the onion core. Apparently every counselor should stop at whatever point his eyes begin to water!

These distinctions do not seem particularly useful. Counseling, psychotherapy, and consultation are processes aimed at changing human behavior and human experience. Therapists do not, of course, actually change a client's "ego strength," "personality core," or any of the other psychological constructs that have been invented to explain human behavior and human experience. If any real differences exist between counseling and psychotherapy, they must involve the kinds of outcomes that are specified for each, and the underlying assumptions that translate such outcomes into goals.

When the usual outcomes for counseling and psychotherapy are pooled, two rather dominant clusters of goals appear. These can be characterized as (a) developmental–educative–preventive goals, and (b) remediative–adjustive–therapeutic goals. It should be clear by now that what we call developmental counseling is primarily concerned with the first set.

The second set of goals, those that can be termed remediative, adjustive, or therapeutic, is generally characterized by breaking down and replacing defenses, learning to adjust to particular situations or institutions, or removing conflicts in personality organization.

When the actual processes that are familiarly called counseling and psychotherapy are examined in the light of these two clusters of outcomes, reasons for confusion in terms become apparent. Much of what has been attempted in the name of counseling has been just as remediative and adjustive in purpose as anything attempted in the name of psychotherapy. Just as most of our mental hospitals and prisons have been most successful in teaching people how to be good mental patients or good convicts rather than effective citizens of a free society, so have our schools and colleges most been concerned with teaching youngsters to be good pupils—docile, conforming, and essentially convergent in thinking. Counselors who have shared in this enterprise have prostituted themselves in attempting to adjust young people to the demands of schools and teachers. They have attempted to "cure" students of "laziness," "negativism," "aggressiveness," or "non-conformity." In many ways, such counselors' most saving grace is that they have been notably ineffective.

Assumptions of Developmental Counseling

A number of basic assumptions about the nature of counseling and clients may help to distinguish developmental counseling from much that is identified with other processes labeled either counseling or psychotherapy. These assumptions are as follows:

1. Clients are not considered to be *mentally* ill. The whole concept of "mental" illness is considered useless and inappropriate to a process focused upon changing behavior and experience. Clients are viewed as being capable of choosing goals, making decisions, and generally participating responsibly in implementing their own growth and development. When clients are *ill*—that is, are malfunctioning physiologically—they need medical treatment.
2. Developmental counseling is focused on the present and the future. The concept of development has its thrust in the future, not the past. Developmental counselors are primarily concerned with where the client is going, rather than with where he has been. In particular, developmental counselors are not concerned with compiling elaborate case histories to provide either the client or the society with a "cop-out" with which to rationalize failure and accept tragedy.
3. The client is a client, not a patient. The counselor is not an authority figure who works to create a transference relationship that creates the illusion of omniscience. He is at various times a confidant, partner, expert consultant, and teacher of his client as they move toward mutually defined and mutually acceptable goals.
4. The developmental counselor is not neutral or amoral. He has values, feelings, and commitments of his own. He discloses these in appropriate situations, but does not attempt to impose them on his client whom he recognizes as a separate person.
5. The client is seen as a unique, worthwhile person striving to develop an identity and implement it with a lifestyle that is his own. He is seen as a member of his group, a part of his culture, and is never treated as

isolated from his social environment. In many situations counseling interventions will be designed to act on the significant social systems of which the client is a member—for example his family, school, or other membership groups. In some cases such groups may be the collective client.

In the following pages, no further attempt will be made to distinguish between developmental counseling and other processes labeled psychotherapy, teaching, or whatever. A further assumption is made that the developmental counselor may be prepared through any of several disciplines or professional groups. He may, for example, be labeled formally as a guidance counselor, school psychologist, social worker, minister, teacher or principal, counseling or clinical psychologist, pediatrician or psychiatrist. He will be distinguished by his goals and methods, not by his professional pedigree.

REFERENCES

1. ALLPORT, G. W. Psychological models for guidance. *Harvard Educ. Rev.*, 1962, 32 (4), 373–391.
2. BRAMMER, L. M., & SHOSTROM, E. L. *Therapeutic psychology: fundamentals of counseling and psychotherapy.* 2nd ed. Englewood Cliffs, N.J.: Prentice-Hall, 1968.
3. BRIM, O. G., JR. Personality development as role-learning. In I. Iscoe, & H. W. Stevenson (Eds.), *Personality development in children.* Austin: University of Texas Press, 1960.
4. ISCOE, I. & SPIELBERGER, C. B. *Community psychology: perspectives in training and research.* New York: Appleton-Century-Crofts, 1970.
5. LEVINE, L., & KANTOR, R. Psychological effectiveness and imposed social position: a descriptive framework. *Personnel Guidance J.,* 1963, 42:418–425.
6. MASLOW, A. *Motivation and personality.* New York: Harper & Row, 2nd ed., 1970.
7. OTTO, H. A. The personal and family strengths research projects—some implications for the therapist. *Mental Hygiene,* 1964, 48:447–450.
8. TYLER, LEONA. *The work of the counselor.* New York: Appleton-Century-Crofts, 3rd ed., 1969.
9. WHITE, R. W. (Ed.). *The study of lives.* New York: Atherton Press, 1964.
10. WHITE, R. W. Motivation reconsidered: the concept of competence. *Psych. Rev.,* 1959, 66:297–334.

RECOMMENDED READINGS

ALBEE, G. W. The uncertain future of clinical psychology. *Amer. Psychol.,* 25:12, December, 1970, 1071–1080.
BERDIE, R. F. The 1980 counselor: applied behavioral scientist. *Personnel Guidance J.,* 1972, 50:451–456.

BLOCHER, D. H., DUSTIN, R., & DUGAN, W. E. *Guidance systems.* New York: Ronald, 1971.

CALDWELL, E. Counseling in context. *Personnel Guidance J.*, 1970, 49:271–278.

COOK, D. R. (Ed.) *Guidance for education in revolution.* Boston: Allyn & Bacon, 1971.

DINKMEYER, D., and CARLSON, J. *Consulting: facilitating human potential and change.* Columbus: Charles Merrill, 1973.

Elementary School Guidance and Counseling. December, 1972 (whole issue).

KELLY, J. G. Qualifies for the community psychologist. *Amer. Psychol.*, 26:10, October, 1971, 897–903.

LEHMAN, S. Community, and psychology and community psychology. *Amer. Psychol.*, 26:6, June, 1971, 555–560.

Personnel and Guidance Journal. February, 1974 (whole issue).

2

PHILOSOPHICAL BASES FOR COUNSELING

One of the most widely repeated statements about counseling is that it is intended to be liberating in nature (1, 16). Counseling is usually aimed at developing what Patterson (14) calls "responsible independence." Counseling is also, however, a planned, systematic intervention in the life of another human being. This intervention is aimed at changing that person's behavior. The counselor, if he accomplishes anything, inevitably influences the nature, degree, and direction of these behavioral changes.

NEED FOR A COUNSELING PHILOSOPHY

One of the basic philosophical questions that any counselor must face is that created by his dual role as an advocate of individual choice and freedom on the one hand, and as a shaper of human behavior on the other.

As powerful technologies for influencing human behavior have come into existence in our society, relatively little attention has been given to the philosophical questions that are implied by their use. Research in experimental psychology, for example, has shown that the verbal behavior of subjects in interview situations can be subtly shaped through reinforcement (4, 7). Krumboltz and Thoreson (8) have shown that these same techniques can be used to shape subsequent behavior outside the interview.

Other even more dramatic technologies involving drugs and even the manipulation of human heredity have moved from the world of science fiction squarely into the realm of reality in recent years. Market research and mass media of communication illustrate ongoing programs of "human engineering" that have evolved with little or no consideration of their ethical and social implications.

Joseph Krutch summarized this situation in an indictment that behavioral scientists of all kinds dare not ignore. He said:

> As influence, power, and authority in our society pass, as they are passing from philosophers and theologians into the hands of those who call themselves "human engineers" whether they happen to be functioning as lawmakers, publicists, teachers, psychologists, or even advertising managers, it is passing from those who were at least aware of what value judgments they were making to those who are not; passing into the hands of men who act on very inclusive and fateful judgments while believing that they are acting on self-evident principles immune from criticism. They do not know what they are making us into and refuse to permit us even to ask. Moreover, in so far as their attempt to "condition" the human beings on whom they practice their techniques are successful, they make it less and less probable that their fateful assumptions will ever be questioned. [9, p. 92.]

Unless counselors are willing to be classified with those who are unaware of the philosophical assumptions that underlie their work, they must give careful attention to the value judgments that they make.

Problem of Values and Influence

Writers as different in orientation as Patterson (13) and Williamson (19) agree on the inevitability of counselor influence on client values. For the counselor to attempt to deny responsibility for changes that occur in his clients would only be to admit his total ineffectiveness. Research by Parloff (12) and by Rosenthal (15) tends to support the position that clients' values and attitudes do change in the course of counseling, and even to suggest that in successful cases those changes are in the direction of increased similarity with the counselor's own value system.

Considerable confusion and ambivalence continues to exist regarding the effect of counselor values in the counseling process.

Hobbs maintains that:

> All approaches to psychotherapy seem to have more or less elaborated conception of the nature of man, which they, in essence, teach to the client. [5, p. 746.]

For many counselors, the result of this ambivalence and confusion has been to cause them to avoid dealing with problems or areas that are of great concern to clients. Particularly often avoided by counselors are those value areas that are controversial or emotionally loaded, such as sexual, religious, or political behavior.

The developmental counselor cannot dodge such problems. Developmental counseling is "value counseling." As Williamson says:

> . . . many of the developmental problems of the client arise out of his disturbances or conflicts among value options he has open to him for adoption as his dominant guiding motivations. [19, p. 521.]

Even when counselors do deal with sensitive value questions, many feel the uncomfortable necessity for somehow attempting to disguise or conceal their own value systems. They seem to feel that they should become neutral, transparent individuals. The obvious problem here is that neutral, transparent individuals have very little capacity for entering warm, vibrant interpersonal relationships.

As Patterson says:

> The counselor should not strive to be an amoral, ethically neutral individual. Such a goal would be impossible of achievement—all of us have values, merely by being human beings. Nor should the counselor attempt to pretend that he is amoral. It is unlikely that he could successfully give this impression to his clients, but it is also undesirable that the counselor attempt to appear to be other than he actually is. [14, p. 71.]

It appears that very little is left to the counselor except to attempt to come to grips with the value problems that confront him. This necessarily involves the construction of a personal philosophy of counseling that will enable the counselor to recognize and deal with value problems in ways that will be helpful to clients and acceptable to the counselor himself.

Mutuality and the Developmental Contract

A few observations about the nature of counseling seem useful at this point. First, it is possible for a counselor to *expose* his values in a counseling relationship without attempting to *impose* them on his client. The counselor can offer himself in the counseling relationship as a *hypothesis* rather than a *model.* Some clients may indeed move toward the counselor's value system. Others may find it only useful in sharpening their own awareness of value questions and in stimulating movement toward the formation of a value system that is uniquely theirs.

Second, counseling does inevitably involve a client relationship in which, as Meehl and McClusky (11) put it, the goals of the client become the goals of the counselor. To this extent, the counselor does become the agent of the client in furthering the latter's ends. It does not follow from this, however, that the counselor must subscribe to *any and all goals* that are sought by potential clients. Counseling occurs when there is a *mutuality of goals* achieved between counselor and client. This mutuality may be created in direct verbal structuring, or it may consist of an unspoken, but understood, agreement.

When this *developmental contract* is entered into by both client and counselor, the latter becomes the principal but not the sole agent for choosing the methodologies for carrying it through. No counselor nor any client need subscribe to developmental contracts whose ends may be considered undesirable or immoral by either. When a developmental contract is not entered into and no real mutuality of purpose exists, it is doubtful that the ensuing dialogue should really be called counseling.

BUILDING A PERSONAL PHILOSOPHY
OF COUNSELING

It is imperative for the counselor to construct a *personal* philosophy of counseling explicit enough for him to stipulate consciously the nature of the developmental contracts that he is willing to enter. He will also need a personal *theory* of counseling to enable him to choose methodologies for carrying through developmental contracts, but this will be discussed further in Chapter 3.

Building a personal philosophy of counseling is a central developmental task for the counselor. The task is one that each counselor must do largely for himself. It may be helpful, however, to examine briefly some major philosophical systems that can be used as sources for building personal philosophies. Obviously, considerable oversimplification is necessary in condensing such a topic for this kind of treatment.

Sources of Counseling Philosophy

John Brubacher (3) has proposed grouping contemporary philosophical systems into two major categories that seem to have relevance for counseling. He terms these two groups "essentialism" and "progressivism." Examining these two groups may be useful.

Essentialism. Under the "essentialism" category could be grouped the approaches usually termed rationalism, idealism, and realism.

Essentialistic philosophies proceed on the basic assumption that man is the only creature endowed with reason, and his chief function is to use this reason in order to know the world in which he lives. Truth is universal and absolute, and man's destiny is to discover truth by distinguishing between the essential and the accidental. Wrenn (20) points out three primary distinguishing characteristics of such systems: (a) the essence of reality is a system of rational principles everywhere the same, (b) the cultivation of reason is the chief aim of education everywhere, and (c) the chief repository of reason is in the works of classical thinkers (Great Books).

Idealism differs somewhat from rationalism in that it concludes that the universe is an expression of intelligence and will, that the enduring substance of the world is the nature of the mind, and that the material is explained by the mental. *Ideas* are absolute.

According to realism, ultimate reality lies in objects and situations external to the human mind in the "real" or objective world. For the realist, the universe is composed of substantial entities existing in themselves whether they are known or not.

These essentialistic systems have in common, however, a belief in the existence of fixed, unchanging absolutes of the good, the true, and the beautiful. The search for values is not essentially personal, but is universal and can be finalized when these absolutes are understood.

As Arbuckle (1) points out, belief in absolute values poses some difficulties for counselors. Can the counselor who is firmly committed to absolutistic concepts of right and wrong, truth and error, beauty and ugliness allow a client his freedom to develop values in his own unique way? Perhaps the key question for the counselor is not whether he believes in the theoretical existence of absolutes, but whether he believes that he himself has indeed finally reached full understanding of what those absolutes are. To what extent does the "essentialistic" counselor share the qualities of what Hoffer (6) would call the "True Believer?"

Progressivism. The second set of systems, which are termed "progressivistic," perhaps developed out of the steady erosion of the old certainties that formed the basis of essentialistic philosophies. As science steadily undermined notions that classical thinkers had considered self-evident, less and less confidence could be placed by many people in the existence of absolutes themselves.

Progressivistic philosophies have names such as experimentalism, pragmatism, and instrumentalism. Wrenn (20) points out that the central feature of these systems lies in their notion of the continuity between the knower and what is unknown, between object and observer. The experimental scientist has less immediate interest in a general theory of knowledge than in understanding an immediate specific phenomenon. He operates in the context of a specific problem and an immediate solution to that problem.

Progressivistic systems are not rationalistic. They do not begin with the assumption of universal truths, but with specific and particular experiences. Progressivistic thinking is not concerned with sweeping generalizations, but with empirical results. The present and the future are stressed rather than the past. The empiric method is used for problem-solving, but not in the belief that observed facts are important in themselves. The question "What is true?" is less important than "What will work?" A fact is valued for its usefulness, not its universality. Past solutions give way to more useful future ones. Truth is generated by its consequences, not its antecedents.

Values have no existence in themselves. They are individual to the observer. The experimentalist has no fixed and final values. Truth is dynamic in a world that is always changing.

Experimentalism is largely the philosophy that underlies American behavioristic psychology. It is pragmatic; that which works is good; an action is evaluated purely in terms of its consequences. No absolutes exist. There are only relative and probabilistic approximations to solutions.

Value questions are resolved not by logical speculations or reference to authority, but by public opinion polls. The Kinseys and Gallups replace the Platos and Aristotles as experts on values. The "public experience" defines what is valued or condemned.

Progressivistic philosophies are not without some difficulty for the counselor. Even though he has rid himself of the troublesome absolutes of the past, the progressivist counselor has replaced them with societal sanctions that are no less tyrannical. Is maturity and mental health to be measured in terms of adjustment and conformity? If so, conformity to whom or to what? Are groups, or, more realistically, their most vocal members, the final arbiters of what is good and true and beautiful?

Just as the scientific achievements of the nineteenth century eroded the "old certainties," so the tragic events of the twentieth century have erased confidence in the "new certainties" of science. Witnesses to the events at Auschwitz and Hiroshima can hardly be blamed for reservations about the inevitability of human progress or the moral rectitude of sick societies.

Existentialism.   Into the vacuum created by the collapse of both the old and new certainties has come the approach that is sometimes called the "Third Force" in psychology. "Existentialism" is a difficult term to pronounce with vaguely Bohemian connotations, which means little to most people.

Actually, existentialism is by no means a new philosophical system. Its roots go back into the nineteenth century. Existentialism is concerned with human longing and man's seeking for importance within himself. A. van Kamm (17) uses the word "existence" to mean standing out toward something, meaning a way of relating to the world. The root of the term comes from the Latin *ex sistere*, meaning literally to stand out or emerge.

May defines existential psychology in this way:

> *There is no such thing as truth or reality for a living human being except as he participates in it, is conscious of it, has some relationship to it.* . . . Only the truth that is genuinely experienced on all levels of being, including what is called subconscious and unconscious and never excluding the element of conscious decision and responsibility—only this truth has the power to change a human being. [10, p. 17.]

Existential psychology seems to describe an attitude and an approach to human beings rather than a formal system or group. Maslow stated it this way:

> To me it [existentialist psychology] means essentially a radical stress on the concept of identity and the experience of identity as the *sine qua non* of human nature and of any philosophy or science of human nature. [10, p. 53.]

Beck (2) describes existential philosophy as an exciting current of thought within modern philosophy. It has taken both atheistic and religious forms. The existential philosophies emphasize the view of reality that is most meaningful to man—his own existence. Leading exponents of existentialism include Jean-Paul Sartre, Gabriel Marcel, Paul Tillich, Martin Buber, and others.

Existential psychotherapy involves the application of key existentialist concepts to the treatment of emotional problems. *Daseinanalyse*, sometimes termed existential analysis, is one such approach. It involves an attempt by the therapist to experience along with his client. In a sense, it represents an approach that stresses a kind of total empathic response on the part of the therapist. The therapist attempts to reconstruct the personal meaning structure of the client.

Beck (2) has extracted a number of assumptions drawn largely from existentialism that seem to offer a useful basis for a philosophy of developmental counseling. A number of these propositions in somewhat modified form, are listed below:

1. The individual is responsible for his own actions. He has a measure of choice and must make these choices for himself.
2. Man must regard his fellow men as objects of value, as part of his concern. Since his fellow men are part of him, he must apply this concern to all of society.
3. Man exists in a world of reality. The relationship of man to his world is a threatening one, for much of what he encounters he cannot change.
4. A meaningful life must remove as much threat from reality as possible, both physical and psychological. The goal is to free man from threat so that his optimum development can be obtained.
5. Every person has his own heredity and has had experiences unique to himself. He can thus be expected to behave differently from others whose experiences are different.
6. Man behaves in terms of his own subjective view of reality, not according to some externally defined objective reality. Behavior is judgeable only in terms of personal values or external goals.
7. Man cannot be classified as "good" or "evil" by nature. These terms may apply to goals, objectives, or patterns of behavior. They have no meaning when applied to man himself.
8. Man reacts as a total organism to any situation. He cannot react intellectually or emotionally to the exclusion of the other. When man attempts to "compartmentalize" himself on such bases, he becomes anxious and less free to develop in an integrated way.

The above propositions seem to offer a possible basis for developing a philosophy of counseling. They are broadly based in terms of religious connotations. They offer a basis upon which human beings can be approached in accepting and empathic ways. They leave considerable room for a wide variety of theoretical approaches and techniques.

The formation of a philosophy of counseling is essentially a personal task that must occupy each counselor. Each of the three kinds of philosophic systems that are described so superficially here may offer rich resources to the counselor in search of a philosophical basis for his professional practice. Some central features of each system are summarized in Table 2–1.

TABLE 2–1
Principal Philosophic Systems

Group	Characteristics	Subtypes	Distinct Features
Essentialism	1. Reality based on objective, rational principles 2. Cultivation of reason 3. Emphasis on classics 4. Universal values 5. Discoverable absolutes (truth, beauty)	a. Rationalism b. Idealism c. Realism	Reason is supreme Ideas are absolute Existence of objective reality
Progressivism	1. Continuity between object and observer 2. Interest in specific phenomenon 3. Empirical results 4. Truth is dynamic 5. Values are individual	a. Experimentalism b. Pragmatism c. Instrumentalism	Underlying behavioral actions judged on consequences Truth is determined by value for action
Existentialism	1. Introspective humanism 2. Individual's intense awareness of his contingency and freedom 3. Existence of individual precedes his essence 4. Subjective view of reality 5. Religious connotations	a. Existential psychology b. Existential psychotherapy	Concept of identity Total empathic response of therapist

REFERENCES

1. ARBUCKLE, D. S. *Counseling: Philosophy, Theory and Practice.* Boston: Allyn & Bacon, 2nd. ed., 1970.
2. BECK, C. E. *Philosophical foundations of guidance.* Englewood Cliffs, N.J.: Prentice-Hall, 1963.
3. BRUBACHER, J. S. *Modern philosophies of education.* (4th ed.) New York: McGraw-Hill, 1969.
4. GREENSPOON, J. The reinforcing effect of two spoken sounds on the frequency of two responses. *Amer. J. Psychol.*, 1955, 68:409–416.
5. HOBBS, N. Sources of gain in psychotherapy. *Amer. Psychologist*, 1962, 17:741–747.
6. HOFFER, E. *The true believer.* New York: Harper & Row, 1951.
7. KRASNER, L. The therapist as a social reinforcement machine. In H. H. Strupp & L. Luborsky (Eds.), *Research in psychotherapy.* Vol. 2. Washington, D.C.: American Psychological Association, 1962.
8. KRUMBOLTZ, J., & THORESON, C. The effect of behavioral counseling in group and individual settings on information seeking behavior. *J. counsel. Psychol.*, 1964, 11 (4), 324–333.
9. KRUTCH, J. W. *The measure of man.* New York: Bobbs-Merrill, 1954.
10. MAY, R., ALLPORT, G., FEIFEL, H., MASLOW, A., & ROGERS, C. *Existential psychology.* New York: Random House, 1961.
11. MEEHL, P. E., & McCLUSKY, H. Ethical and political aspects of applied psychology. *J. abnorm. soc. Psychol.*, 1947, 42:91–98.
12. PARLOFF, M. B. Communication of values and therapeutic change. Paper read at American Psychological Association meeting, New York, August, 1957.
13. PATTERSON, C. H. The place of values in counseling and psychotherapy. *J. counsel. Psychol.*, 1958, 5 (3), 216–223.
14. PATTERSON, C. H. *Counseling and psychotherapy.* New York: Harper & Row, 1959. Part II, 31–110.
15. ROSENTHAL, D. Changes in some moral values following psychotherapy. *J. consult. Psychol.*, 1955, 19:431–436.
16. TIEDEMAN, D. V., & FIELD, F. L. Guidance: the science of purposeful action applied through education. *Harvard Educ. Rev.*, 1962, 32 (4), 483–501.
17. VAN KAMM, A. Counseling from the viewpoint of existential psychology. *Harvard educ. Rev.*, 1962, 32 (4), 403–415.
18. WHITE, R. W. *The abnormal personality.* (4th ed.) New York: Ronald, 1972.
19. WILLIAMSON, E. G. Value orientation in counseling. *Personnel Guidance J.*, 1958, 36 (1), 520–528.
20. WRENN, C. G. Philosophical and psychological bases of personnel services in education. *Fifty-eight Yearb. nat. Soc. Stud. Educ.*, 1959.

RECOMMENDED READINGS

General Philosophical Questions in Counseling

ARBUCKLE, D. S. Five philosophical issues in counseling. *J. counsel. Psychol.*, 1958, 5:211–215.

BARCLAY, J. R. *Foundations of counseling strategies.* New York: Wiley, 1971.

BECK, C. E. (Ed.). *Philosophical guidelines for counseling.* (2d. ed.) Dubuque, Iowa: Wm. C. Brown Co., 1971.

KEMP, C. G. *Intangibles in counseling.* Boston: Houghton-Mifflin, 1967.

LOWE, C. M. *Value orientations in counseling and psychotherapy.* San Francisco: Chandler Publishing Co., 1968.

MAY, R. *Psychology and the human dilemma.* Princeton, N.J.: Van Nostrand Co., 1967.

SKINNER, B. F. *Beyond freedom and dignity.* New York: Alfred A. Knopf, 1971.

Value Questions in Counseling

CURRAN, C. A. Some ethical and scientific values in the counseling psychotherapeutic process. *Personnel Guidance J.,* 1960, 39 (1), 15–20.

PATTERSON, C. H. The place of values in counseling and psychotherapy. *J. counsel. Psychol.,* 1958, 5 (3), 216–223.

PATTERSON, C. H. Control, conditioning and counseling. *Personnel Guidance J.,* 1963, 41:680–686.

ROGERS, C. R. Toward a modern approach to values. *J. abnorm. soc. Psychol.,* 1964, 68 (1), 160–168.

SAMLER, J. Change in values: a goal in counseling. *J. counsel. Psychol.,* 1960, 7 (1), 32–39.

SMITH, M. B. Mental health reconsidered: a special case of the problem of values in psychology. *Amer. Psychologist,* 1961, 16 (6), 299–306.

SZASZ, T. The uses of naming and the origin of the myth of mental illness. *Amer. Psychologist,* 1961, 16 (2), 59–65.

WALKER, D. E., PEIFFER, H. C. The goals of counseling. *J. counsel. Psychol.,* 1957, 4 (3), 111–112.

WILLIAMSON, E. G. Value orientation in counseling. *Personnel Guidance J.,* 1958, 36 (1), 520–528.

Religious Questions in Counseling

DURNALL, E. Symposium: the counselor and his religion. *Personnel Guidance J.,* 1958, 36 (5), 326–334.

MEEHL, P., *et al.* Religious factors and values in counseling: a symposium. *J. counsel. Psychol.,* 1959, 6:255–274.

MOWRER, O. H., ELLIS, A., *et al.* The role of the concept of sin in psychotherapy. *J. counsel. Psychol.,* 1960, 7 (3), 185–201.

WRENN, C. G. Psychology, religion, and the values of the counselor. *Personnel Guidance J.,* 1958, 36:331–334.

The Existential View in Counseling

DREYFUS, E. Counseling and Existentialism. *J. counsel. Psychol.,* 1962, 9 (2), 128–132.

FRANKL, V. E. *From death-camp to existentialism: a psychiatrist's path to a new therapy.* Boston: Beacon, 1959.

KNELLER, G. *Existentialism and education.* New York: Wiley, 1964.

MAY, R., *et al. Existence.* New York: Basic Books, 1959.

MAY, R., ALLPORT, G., FEIFEL, H., MASLOW, A., & ROGERS, C. R. *Existential psychology.* New York: Random House, 1961.

Rogers, C. R. The loneliness of contemporary man. *Rev. Existential Psychol. Psychiat.*, 1961, 1:94–101.

van Kamm, A. *The third force in European psychology.* Greenville, Del.: Psychosynthesis Research Foundation, 1960.

van Kamm, A. Counseling from the viewpoint of existential psychology. *Harvard Educ. Rev.*, 1962, 32 (4), 403–415.

Other Issues

Buhler, Charlotte. Humanistic psychology as an educational program. *Amer. Psychol.*, 24:8, August, 1969, 736–742.

Hitt, W. D. Two models of man. *Amer. Psychol.*, 24:7, July, 1969, 651–658.

Lefcourt, H. M. The function of the illusions of control and freedom. *Amer. Psychol.*, 28:5, May, 1973, 417–425.

Phillips, J. L., and Torbet D. Determinism, freedom and counseling psychology. *J. Counsel. Psychol.*, 1968, 15 (4), 368–371.

Robinson, D. N. Therapies: clear and present dangers. *Amer. Psychol.*, 28:2, February, 1973, 129–133.

3

SOURCES OF COUNSELING THEORY

The task of developing a personal theory or point of view upon which to base sound professional practice is far from easy. As we have seen, it begins with a sharpened awareness of self and a thorough working through of the philosophical issues and value questions that underlie the choice of professional goals and methods.

In addition to these introspective sources of theory, however, the counselor is also confronted with a vast array, or perhaps more accurately, a disarray of sometimes conflicting, often overlapping, and always competing theories of personality, behavior change, and psychological intervention. In one sense many of these theories constitute what could almost be viewed as a kind of folklore or mythology out of which a modern behavioral science is presently emerging. One of the unfortunate facts that must be faced by counselors is that our psychological theories have so far failed to generate a single, unified, and well-organized body of knowledge about human behavior upon which the professional counselor can base his practice.

Psychological theories have tended to proliferate rather than be reduced and reconciled by the accretion of empirical evidence. Adherents of particular approaches have tended to coalesce into competing camps rather than to seek out common areas of inquiry and agree upon appropriate rules of evidence through which to reduce theoretical differences. When dialogues between competing groups have occurred, they have often been characterized by less than thoughtful and dispassionate discussions that advance the state of knowledge.

In a book of this kind, it is obviously impossible to do full justice even to a few of the many theories upon which the counselor can draw. The reader is referred in the recommended readings to several recent volumes that have attempted to summarize these points of view.

Instead, an attempt is made here to construct three models of counseling practice, each based upon a specific theoretical foundation that stresses a particular approach to human personality development and behavior change. It may be useful to think of these models as approaches that emphasize a particular set of "sources of gain." In other words, each model of counseling intervention is constructed around an approach that is intended to maximize a set of psychological factors or effects that the underlying theory holds to be crucial to constructive client change and growth. We term these factors as sources of gain in our counseling efforts.

THE RELATIONSHIP MODEL

The relationship model of counseling is an approach that has developed largely out of the work of Carl Rogers (12). It was originally termed client-centered therapy, but as this approach has developed around the work of a number of psychologists it has tended to merge with some aspects of existential psychology (see Chapter 2) to form what has sometimes been called a "Third Force" in psychology (2). Perhaps the most appropriate term today to use in referring to the theoretical base underlying the relationship model is "humanistic psychology." The growing impact of this approach is indeed significant enough to consider it as a third companion to psychoanalysis and behaviorism as major forces in the development of American psychology.

Humanistic psychology has essentially developed around the merger of three major elements. The first of these elements grew out of perceptual psychology and is sometimes called perceptual field theory. Very briefly, this approach holds that all behavior is a function of the individual's perceptions at the moment of behaving. In other words, people behave according to how things seem to them. Those aspects of the environment to which an individual is reacting are called his perceptual field. This perceptual field constitutes reality to the individual and is always organized with respect to the concepts he holds of himself. The approach is *phenomenological,* that is, it construes each individual to be at the center of his own personal and largely private world of reality, rather than as operating within an objectively defined public reality.

Perceptual Psychology

As perceptions change, then, so does behavior. When people perceive differently, they behave differently. Where perceptions are vague, behavior is confused. Where perceptions are clear, behavior is purposeful and goal-directed in terms of the experienced needs of the individual.

Since behavior is a function of the perceptions of the individual, counseling interventions must be aimed at helping an individual to perceive himself and his environment more clearly. To behave effectively, a person must perceive his world as accurately and with as little distortion as possible. Perception, however, is a function of several variables. It is related to (a) the health of the person, (b) his values and goals, and (c) his concept of self.

Perception is seriously affected by threat. People tend to perceive what is *appropriate* for persons with their self-concepts to perceive. The self-concept or self-structure is the core around which all the rest of an individual's perceptions are organized. When a person's self-concepts are threatened, his field of perception is narrowed and distorted. He responds only to the threat-producing aspects of his field. Also, when threatened, he seeks to defend his existing self-organization and consequently his existing perceptual pattern.

If counseling is to result in changed perceptions, it must reduce threat and so remove the primary obstacle to clearer perceptions and more effective behaviors. The counseling relationship supplies the conditions that reduce threat.

Assumptions of Relationship Model

In an early formulation of client-centered therapy, Rogers (12) listed a number of crucial assumptions on which he based his practice. A number of these key propositions that are still basic to relationship-oriented approaches to counseling are listed below.

1. The individual exists in a continually changing world of experience of which *he is the center.* His perceptual field is not completely known to any other person. This world is his *phenomenological field,* that is, his own private world of reality. Others may come close to perceiving what another person is experiencing, but no one can completely enter the phenomenological world of another.

2. The individual reacts to his private world as he experiences it. Whatever he perceives as true is *reality* for him, and he behaves as if it were true.

3. Individuals react to their perceptual fields as organized wholes. They do not respond just in intellectual terms or in purely emotional terms, but as total human organisms.

4. Every human being has within himself one basic tendency or striving. He is constantly struggling to enhance and maintain himself. This inner growth force is fragile and weak, but when freed will unerringly direct the individual along ways of development that are desirable for him and for society. Human beings are not anti-social by nature. This forward-moving developmental tendency can only operate, however, when an individual can perceive his choices clearly. He must know the choice clearly; when he does know it, however, he always chooses to grow.

5. Behavior is the goal-directed attempt of the human being to satisfy his needs as experienced in the field as perceived. All behavior is rational and goal-directed when seen from within the perceptual field of the behaver.

6. Emotion accompanies and in general *facilitates* goal-directed behavior. The intensity of emotion is related to the degree of perceived significance of the events or the ego-involvement of the behavior. Emotions are not disruptive, but facilitate the striving of an individual to develop.

Out of these basic propositions Carl Rogers and his students developed the tremendously influential approach to counseling and psychotherapy called client-centered therapy. In more recent years another stream of influence merged into the client-centered approach. This movement, termed existential psychology, has already been referred to briefly in Chapter 2.

Existential Psychology

Existential psychology as it has contributed to the broader stream of influence that we term humanistic psychology has offered a number of concepts that are parallel to but really distinct from those that came out of the client-centered antecedents of humanistic psychology. Chief among these is the centrality of direct experiencing as the basic datum of psychology. As a philosophical position, existentialism places existence as prior to essence. That is, the most important aspect of man in the world is simply his being there. Essences, or discoverable attributes of the world, that are viewed independently of man's relation to them (such as physical laws) have little significance to him. Meaning is derived from the context of direct experiencing, not solely from some objective reality. This basic, inevitable "existing" of man is the central focus out of which real meaning can be established. Existence is a basic given. It is neither created by man, nor can he completely analyze it by his logical systems of thinking. According to existentialism, man exists first, then he begins to speculate, contemplate, and analyze concerning that existence.

This emphasis on direct experience or existence tends to blur dichotomies between observer and observed, subjects and objects, and inner and outer worlds. Man is viewed as being with and part of every object or phenomenon that he encounters. In this sense man really creates his world of experience and is an inseparable part of it. Attempts to sort out and separate man from this direct, "being-in-the-world," character of his experience simply deprive his life of meaning, alienate him from his fellows, and increase his basic loneliness and helplessness.

Out of this view of man and his essential dilemma comes an approach to counseling that places prime emphasis upon helping clients re-establish the unity and intactness of their experiencing and so enable them to find meaning in their existence. This approach stresses the inherent and inevitable freedom and responsibility of man to choose, to seek, and to find his own meaning.

In terms of counseling process, then, the purpose of counseling is to help the client experience an encounter with the counselor from which he can find greater meaning in his own existence, take responsibility for choosing his own way, and regain greater contact with his own experiencing. For the counselor the emphasis is on being authentic in this encounter, and being able to respond to the client in a deeply empathic way that will communicate an understanding of, and respect for, the client's own experiencing. At the same time, the counselor is communicating in an open and honest way his experiencing of the client and their relationship (19).

Many of the parallels between the Rogerian approach and the existential psychology movement seem apparent. A theoretical view of man's perceptual functioning and a philosophical view of his role in the world found a most compatible merger. Out of that merger came, however, a third empirical component that has provided an important impetus to humanistic psychology. This empirical component has emerged from fifteen years of research on the nature of facilitative and therapeutic relationships.

Relationship Conditions

Early in the development of the client-centered counseling movement, Carl Rogers recognized the crucial importance of the counseling relationship and went so far as to term it "the necessary and sufficient condition" for therapeutic change. The existential movement with its emphasis on the importance of the basic encounter between counselor and client and the transcending importance of the former's authenticity obviously reinforced the importance of relationship variables in the counseling process.

A program of counseling process and outcome research has emerged from these points of view that is having increasing impact on counseling, counselor education, and indeed on the entire fields of education and human relations.

Briefly, Rogers and his students (15, 18) postulated that progress in client movement or essentially counseling outcome is dependent upon the degree to which the client experiences certain basic conditions in the counseling relationship. The task of the counselor is to provide optimal levels of these growth-producing conditions which occur if:

1. The counselor or therapist is *congruent* or *genuine* in the relationship
2. The counselor experiences *unconditional positive regard* or warm acceptance for the client
3. The counselor demonstrates accurate, empathic understanding of the client's own internal experiencing or frame of reference

High levels of these three conditions experienced by the client when he is vulnerable and anxious, will, according to the theory, lead to positive client outcomes.

A very comprehensive line of counseling research done in a wide range of settings with a variety of populations has emerged from this basic theory. This research is not without methodological problems, but it has undoubtedly influenced the field tremendously. One of the major influences has been the revision of the early so-called "non-directive" view of counseling. In early formulations the counselor was viewed as taking a rather passive, neutral, and permissive stance in which his modal responses often seemed to be simply an accepting "um huh" or at most a reflection or restatement of the client's responses.

As research on facilitative conditions has grown, much more emphasis is placed upon the congruence or honesty and authenticity of the counselor. Less emphasis is placed on specific techniques and more on the communication of attitudes of prizing and respect for the client and of accurately empathic responses to his experiencing.

Truax and Carkhuff (18) have summarized much of the research on relationship variables. They present the case that a considerable part of the outcome changes found in successful counseling and psychotherapy can be accounted for in terms of the relationship conditions that were offered. This research is still proceeding and considerable refinement in instrumentation and methodology is needed before its final impact can be fully assessed. More about counseling relationship research is discussed in Chapter 9.

COUNSELING IMPLICATIONS
OF THE RELATIONSHIP MODEL

The relationship model then views the most important source of gain available to the counselor in helping his client as residing in the relationship itself. The counselor strives to communicate to the client his attitudes of caring, respect, and prizing. He attempts to communicate his understanding of the client's private world of reality with accurately empathic statements. The counselor attempts to be aware of his own inner world of experience and to share this where appropriate in an open and congruent way. He avoids responding in an artificial, phoney, or stylized manner to his client.

When the counselor is successful in offering these facilitative conditions over a period of time, the client gradually becomes able to explore his own feelings, concentrate on concrete and immediate aspects of his experience, differentiate and discriminate among his feelings toward others and himself, and become more aware of aspects of his experience that he has denied or distorted. Out of this process his self-structure becomes reorganized to include new experiences previously denied, and he increasingly tends to view himself in a more positive way, and to trust and act upon his own inner-based feelings and impulses.

The relationship model is finding greater applications outside the realm of professional counseling. It is being widely applied to general education (13), child-rearing (15), and group leadership (9). One of its most important potentials lies in the fact that relatively brief and simple training procedures offer promise in improving the relationship functioning of many people in a wide range of settings (3).

It is of course far from surprising that qualities which men and women have for centuries prized under the labels of honesty, sincerity, caring, understanding, and warmth should have positive consequences in any kind of human relationship. Perhaps the greatest impact of the formal research on relationships will be in the assistance that knowledge will have on improving the quality of teacher–student, parent–child, and supervisor–worker relationships. Training people to create their own networks of positive, growth-producing relationships in home, school, factory, and community may contribute more to total human development than any realistic amount of professional counseling services.

THE COGNITIVE MODEL

Since Breuer and Freud first evolved the "talking cure" in Vienna more than three-quarters of a century ago, one of the major sources of gain in virtually all types of counseling and psychotherapy has been its assistance to the client in developing new ideas and concepts—or in other words "insight"—about himself and his situation. One way of looking at human personality is that each individual has a story about himself, his life, and his relationships that provides a kind of central focus around which he experiences and interprets events. Much of his cognitive activity is aimed at being able to construe the world in ways that are meaningful and consistent enough to give him reasonable comfort and freedom from anxiety. This central story that serves as an anchor to provide stability in a confusing and often threatening world is largely given to the individual in childhood, primarily by his close relatives. The story tends to be elaborated and maintained throughout life because one's closest friends tend to be those who believe his story.

At times the particular story that an individual has is non-functional, that is, it yields poor predictions, leads to misinterpretations of events, or causes unduly painful and anxious responses to situations and events. One's "story" may cause him to focus on minor incidents and embellish them into major themes of rejection, aggression hostility, or insult by others. Similarly, one's story may make him inhibit appropriately assertive or protective responses to situations and relationships. Viewed in this way, personality or the collective set of stories about one's life may be a cage that imprisons and constricts development.

Perhaps the individual's story describes him as short-tempered, irresponsible, stupid, or submissive. Out of this come self-fulfilling prophecies that are translated into role expectations molding behavior into frozen patterns that resist and constrict efforts toward further growth and development.

Psychoanalysis

Several very basic theories of personality have made major contributions to the cognitive model. The earliest was of course psychoanalysis (5). Freud saw human personality as involving three major subsystems. The *id* was viewed as the original system and consisted of the total genetic or biological heritage—everything inherited and present at birth. The id represents the inner world of subjective experience and has no knowledge of objective reality. It is the energizer of personality and has as its overriding goal tension reduction, that is, returning the organism to comfortable levels of sensation.

The *superego* is the system that reflects the moral sanctions of society. In Freud's view the superego is just as irrational as the id. It operates on the principle of moral realism—behavior is either good or bad without qualifications based upon motivations or circumstances. The superego tends to reject completely those urges of the id that may run contrary to socially internalized concepts of right and wrong.

The third system, the *ego*, is the only rational element in human personality, and is inevitably caught between the demands of the id for blind, immediate, instinctual gratification and the equally irrational, absolute, moral sanctions of the superego. Freud saw the ego, however, as only an organized portion of the id that had no existence apart from it. The ego must always strive to satisfy the demands of the id, but with an avoidance of disintegrating anxiety generated by the superego.

Conflict is of course inevitable within this "troika" system. Human beings learn to deal with this inevitable conflict and consequent anxiety by learning various defenses that may modify the conflict and reduce anxiety. Most of these defenses involve changes in *thinking*. Threatening impulses, for example, may be repressed, or driven from awareness into the unconscious. Aggressive or hostile impulses may be projected into others or transformed into motives that are apparently benign and positive.

Always, however, man is seen as dealing with anxiety by cognitive distortions or repressions. The cognitive–rational system—the ego—is always forced to distort, repress, deny, or deceive. The purpose of counseling or therapy is to help the ego think more clearly and more adequately, through interpreting, slowly, carefully, and gently the true meaning of its defensive maneuvers. Only the counselor or therapist, safely removed from the inner conflict of the client and skilled in interpreting behavior can really know the full meaning of the latter's "story."

Freud's view of the human condition was, as we can see, a rather pessimistic one. Conflict and anxiety are inevitable, with the ego a fragile and dependent manager of irreconcilable demands and impulses. Other theorists who followed in the psychoanalytic tradition, however, were less pessimistic than Freud and began to focus upon the inherent strength and capacity of the ego functions. They saw man as having exquisitely organized cognitive functions that are potentially at least capable of solving his personal and societal problems.

Ego Psychology

One of the first and most significant of the people to revise classical psychoanalytic theory was *Alfred Adler* (1). Adler searched for the roots of personality development and personality conflict in social rather than psychological processes. He assumed that man was basically a social being and that his primary motivations were based upon his social interactions. Adler viewed the primary human motivation to be a striving for superiority or perfection. He believed that this striving was manifested in every human life, but that it took many different forms and patterns in individual lives. The way in which the basic striving for superiority is translated into behavior is in what Adler called an individual's *style of life*. Style of life is a global construct used to understand and explain human behavior. Everyone has his own unique style of life.

Adler was basically positive and optimistic about human beings and the human situation. He saw man as generally a socially involved and socially responsive being with the potential for cooperative, problem-solving capacities and relationships. Man's behavior was viewed as rational and understandable within the framework of his own unique style of life.

One person may strive for perfection and superiority through athletic prowess, another through sexual attraction, another through academic achievement. All of these struggles can potentially be channeled into both personally satisfying and socially productive means. When man's behavior is either self-defeating or socially destructive it is because of imperfect self-understanding or social institutions, rather than because of dark and destructive impulses within himself.

Karen Horney (7) developed another of the psychosocial approaches to personality than stemmed from psychoanalysis. Horney sought to understand behavior within the construct of *socially induced* anxiety. Her model viewed the developing child as experiencing feelings of isolation and helplessness in an essentially hostile and chaotic world. The child is small and relatively helpless in a world of competitive, dominating adults who are always able to defeat, overpower, or shame him.

In coping with the feelings elicited by this unequal struggle, the child may develop any one of several strategies. He may move *toward people* and be submissive, dependent, and parasitic in order to win love, support, and approval. He may, on the other hand, move *away from people* to become independent, isolated, and self-centered. Finally, he may move *against people* and become hostile, aggressive, and domineering.

None of these strategies is necessarily undesirable or "neurotic" unless it is used rigidly and inappropriately in self-defeating, destructive, or irrational ways. The difference between neurotic and effective behavior is a difference in the control and flexibility with which it can be applied in specific situations. When one is aware of a variety of possible strategies and can analyze situations accurately—or in other words is insightful—he can behave effectively. The ineffective person is blindly driven by anxiety, is relatively unaware of his present behavior, has few alternatives available, and resorts to an excessive and inappropriate use of a given strategy in a compulsive and insensitive way.

Erich Fromm is another of the neo-analytic theorists who focused upon social interaction as the fundamental ingredient in personality development. He based his approach upon a study of man's socially based needs. These needs stem from men's and women's existence as social creatures and include the need for *relatedness*, the need for *creativeness*, the need for *belongingness*, the need for *identity*, and the need for a *consistent way to view the world*. The latter is very similar to what we called earlier one's basic "story" (6).

When people are unable to meet these basic needs in society, they become alienated and hostile. If they are not permitted to love or relate in positive ways they will learn to hate. The key to helping is in understanding the ways in which people meet their inner needs within the restraints and opportunities provided by their society. The means of assisting a given individual to grow lie in helping him to be aware of his own needs and find positive and constructive ways to meet them.

Harry Stack Sullivan (17) was another personality theorist who carried the psychosocial view still further. He viewed personality to *be* basically the total set of interpersonal strategies by which an individual interacts with others. Personality development is the process of learning to satisfy needs and reduce tensions within one's network of significant interpersonal relationships.

COUNSELING IMPLICATIONS OF THE COGNITIVE MODEL

Basically, the cognitive model of counseling rests on the view that people's greatest resource in growing and developing effectively lie in their abilities to *think* rationally and analytically about themselves and their world. These rational, problem-solving functions that Freud termed ego functions are the basic human resources. The basic psychological model is that awareness or insight leads to control of behavior and so to growth and development.

The counselor is in a very real sense a teacher who helps his client to think more sensitively, through greater awareness of self, and more clearly, through more accurate perceptions of reality. The counselor helps the client to interpret internal and external events, reconstruct his past experiences in a more coherent and realistic way, and utilize his new-found insight to plan and problem-solve.

He tends to lead a joint search, with his client, for alternative ways to construe events, for greater awareness of subtle feelings, for more integrated themes within his view of self and the world.

The counselor maintains a warm and concerned relationship with his client, not for its own sake, but to provide the relatively safe environment within which the client may search out meanings and insights that may be frightening and disturbing. The counselor seeks to help his client "get things together," working through both the emotional and cognitive aspects of his roles and relationships. There is more emphasis on rational and cognitive factors than on sheer emotional expression. The primary goal is not merely to solve immediate practical problems, but rather to understand the nature of basic motives and conflicts so that psychological growth and effective functioning can be enhanced. When real insights occur they are expected to generalize across many situations and times.

One of the primary techniques employed is the controlled use of ambiguity. Since some of the client's basic motives and important feelings may be outside of his immediate awareness, the counselor uses ambiguous leads or may even ask the client to "free associate," that is, simply to relate anything that comes into his mind. Usually counselors —as opposed to classical psychoanalysts—use less extreme degrees of ambiguity.

A high degree of ambiguity in either the counselor's leads or in the nature of the relationship may elicit meaningful material but is also often threatening to the client. Moderate levels of ambiguity, such as open-ended leads or encouragement to talk freely about feelings or deep concerns, facilitates the communication of material which may be highly important even though the client has not yet become aware of its significance. Great emphasis is placed upon empathic, active listening by the counselor as he strives to understand and relate bits of information about the client and help him reconstruct a more adequate picture of himself in the world.

Applications of Cognitive Theories

Much vocational–educational counseling is cognitive in nature. Often, however, it is based upon trait and factor theories of personality rather than psychoanalytic or neo-analytic positions. The trait and factor approach to human personality takes the position that an individual can be described by assessing a finite set of personality traits, interests patterns, and abilities or aptitudes.

Learning to plan intelligently for one's educational and vocational development necessarily involves an understanding of one's own patterns of traits, interests, and abilities in relationship to those demanded by the requirements or expectations set by employers or educational institutions.

The process of counseling involves assessing and interpreting information about the client's aspirations, opportunities, and resources so that he can plan intelligently. Much of the information may be obtained from psychological tests as well as from direct interview material.

Another very important cognitively loaded counseling approach is that developed by *Albert Ellis* (4). Rational–emotive Therapy, as Ellis terms his treatment, is an approach to human behavior that emphasizes the concept that emotional responses are largely controlled by and flow from cognitive or ideational processes. In other words, Ellis believes that unhappiness or painful emotional responses are not produced directly by environmental circumstances, but rather by the way in which the individual *thinks about* those circumstances.

In this view, feelings such as anger, frustration, sorrow, or self-pity are triggered literally by the sentences people say to themselves about their circumstances. Most human misery is caused by "insane sentences" or logical fallacies in people's thinking.

For example, a young man rejected by a girl friend may say the following sentences. "She doesn't like me . . . I am worthless, unattractive, a terrible person, my life is miserable." Such *catastrophisizing* triggers appropriately corresponding emotional responses and the basic *non-sequitur.* "She doesn't like me—therefore my life is miserable" is converted into a self-fulfilling statement.

Treatment in rational–emotive therapy consists largely of teaching clients to think clearly and rationally and to act upon these rational premises rather than upon their former confused and illogical thought processes. In a sense, rational–emotive therapy is an almost ultimate extension of the cognitive view of counseling.

THE BEHAVIORAL MODEL

Most of the approaches to counseling that have been discussed in the earlier parts of this chapter stemmed largely from the clinical experiences of professionals directly engaged in helping clients. Often, the theory that was developed was somewhat of an after the fact explanation for something that had been found to be practically helpful in the consulting room.

The behavioral model of counseling is to a large extent the direct opposite of the theories described above. It stems heavily from years of work by experimental rather than applied psychologists. Beginning in the 1920's, scientific psychology in this country was tremendously influenced by a method or point of view that came to be called *behaviorism*. Very briefly, behaviorism was the view that psychology was a science that dealt almost exclusively in *observables*—that is, data based upon what was overt and directly observable or in other words, behavior. As this view prevailed, the particular unit that behavioral psychologists were most concerned with studying was the stimulus–response connection or "SR bond." In other words, psychologists studied the observable responses or movements of an organism that were directly connected to a specific stimulus event in its environment.

Within this view psychological theories that invented elaborate construct systems to explain what went on *inside* the organism (such as the Freudian constructs of id, ego, and superego) were viewed with disdain as empty fictions at worst, and as unnecessary baggage at best.

Out of the laboratories of behavioral psychologists over the past forty or so years has come a tremendous quantity of research done with both human and infrahuman subjects. One of the primary leaders of this movement is *B. F. Skinner*. Skinner and his associates, as a result of many years of painstaking research, have developed a system and language for studying behavior called the *experimental analysis of behavior* (16).

Skinnerian Approaches

Skinner and his system are still the subject of much controversy. His impact upon psychology and many other fields of human thought is undeniable, and he undoubtedly will rank with Freud as one of the great contributors to the way men think about themselves in the world.

Very briefly, Skinnerian learning or operant conditioning is an approach to psychology that uses the units of stimulus and response to study observable behavior under carefully controlled conditions. The approach does not use elaborate constructs to explain or infer what happens inside the organism. It focuses instead primarily upon the stimulus conditions that occur in the presence of the organism and the responses or movements that the organism emits upon the presentation of these stimuli.

Reinforcement.   From this approach it has been empirically established that certain stimuli following a particular response will significantly increase the probability of occurrence of that response. These stimuli are called reinforcers. Reinforcers are generally drive-reducing or pleasure-producing stimuli such as food, water, or sexual stimulation. They may also be *negative reinforcers*, those that remove an essentially unpleasant stimulus such as excessive heat or light. They may include social interactions such as praise or encouragement or recognition. Once a particular response has been paired with a reinforcing stimulus it is termed a "conditioned response" and may be experimentally predicted or controlled by manipulation of the reinforcing stimulus.

At this point we should probably note that we have not explained anything that is very new, original, or earthshaking about human behavior. It is probable that in the ten thousand years or so of man's linguistic history, few individuals have not understood intuitively that much of human behavior is controlled by rewards and punishments. The "law of effect" is a pretty obvious statement of phenomena.

Behavioral psychology has succeeded, however, in developing a relatively simple yet powerful methodology and language by which to study what are intuitively recognized as the very powerful effects of reward and punishment. Skinner has particularly focused attention upon the power of positive reinforcement to control behavior, and has pointed out the ineffectiveness and destructive consequences of the use of aversive stimulation or punishment in controlling behavior in much of our inhuman, human history.

Schedules of Reinforcement.   Research has also shown that the frequency and duration—or "resistance to extinction"—of responses are heavily determined by the schedule of presentation of the reinforcing stimulus. For example, when the reinforcer is presented on an aperiodic or random schedule, the organism continues to respond at a high level for a relatively long period of time after the last presentation of the reinforcer. This kind of schedule then produces a pattern of behavior that is resistant to extinction. Extinction is the term describing the eventual breakdown of the link between stimulus and response when the conditioned response is repeatedly produced by the organism without reinforcement.

No careful observer who has ever visited the slot machine section of a Las Vegas casino could seriously doubt that such random schedules of reinforcement do control *some* human behavior *some* of the time.

Extensive experimentation with animal subjects has produced a considerable body of knowledge about the effects of operant conditioning procedures. It is not at all surprising then that recent years have seen a tremendous surge of interest in the use of reinforcement techniques with human beings in a wide range of practical situations.

A large and in many ways very persuasive body of literature has been built up reporting the use of behavioral techniques in counseling and therapy (10). The language and methodology of the experimental analysis of behavior has several compelling advantages as well as some disadvantages. Perhaps the most important advantage is that "behavior modification" techniques virtually force the counselor or teacher to specify very precisely what changes in behavior they are committed to help produce.

Counseling Implications of the Behavioral Model

The behavioral counselor must define carefully the specific class of behaviors that are goal-oriented for him and his client. He cannot deal only in rather vague and ambiguous goals such as self-actualization or ego strength or improved functioning. He must define observable classes of responses to which reinforcement and "shaping" procedures can be applied.

The counselor is forced to think very carefully about his goals before intervening, a process that would seem to be healthy for a counselor of any persuasion. Defining goals and objectives behaviorally, may, however, be difficult and even limiting in some situations.

A second major advantage of the behavioral model is that it requires a careful examination of the client's environment to identify and locate stimuli that will in fact be reinforcing. Much of the art that is involved in the behavioral model is concerned with the creative search for effective reinforcers to use with a particular client.

It is in this context that many of the prevailing myths about behavior modification and behavior modifiers can best be laid to rest. Somehow the fact that many of the behavioral counseling techniques have come from the learning laboratory has conjured up images of the behavior modifier as a cold, distant, uncaring technician in a white coat who manipulates people with no more warmth than he might show in removing a white rat from a Skinner Box.

Such an image and the feelings it connotes are, of course, pure hokum. The behavioral counselor *is* quite concerned with relating to the client in warm, empathic, and caring ways. It is through such a relationship, of course, that the counselor would be likely to become a social reinforcer for the client. Perhaps, even more importantly, it is only through such a relationship that the counselor would be able to get to know his client well enough to identify appropriate reinforcers and those relationships that could be used to schedule and deliver reinforcements.

Similarly, many people have an image of the behavioral counselor as a kind of subtle, Machiavellian manipulator who manages to control people without their awareness or knowledge. Again, on the contrary, the behavior modifier who did not utilize the awareness and cooperation of his clients whenever and wherever possible would simply be inefficient.

The experimental literature is divided about the *necessity* of subject awareness and cooperation for conditioning to occur. Indeed, it is exceedingly difficult experimentally ever to be sure that a subject is aware or unaware of the reinforcing stimulus or target behavior or reinforcement contingency. There is ample evidence to indicate that such awareness and will to cooperate enhances learning.

In many behavioral counseling situations the client himself can administer the reinforcer, as, for example, the college boy who rewards himself for completing an assignment by scheduling a date with his girl friend, or the dieter who rewards her abstinence from bread and potatoes by buying a new and more becoming wardrobe. For the most part, behavioral counseling consists of helping a client to specify carefully a set of behaviors that are goal-oriented for him and assisting him to pair these new behaviors with a set of rewards that he has helped to choose under conditions that will enhance the efficiency and effectiveness of his new learning.

Classical Conditioning

A second major aspect of the behavioral model stems from the classical conditioning paradigm first demonstrated by Pavlov. Skinner's analysis of behavior deals primarily with responses called operants. Generally, these are responses that act upon the environment in some direct way. Communication patterns, both verbal and non-verbal, are operants in the sense that they elicit a reaction from those who receive the communication.

Pavlov was concerned with responses that are of a different character. Much behavior is respondent—that is, it is triggered directly by stimuli in the environment. Emotional responses are of this kind. A pedestrian narrowly missed by a speeding truck experiences a strong fear response. His breathing, pulse rate, perspiration, stomach contractions, etc., are rapidly affected. Pavlov and his followers found that many of these "smooth muscle" responses are controlled by learning. The famous bell-salivation experiment with dogs is the classical example. Food is presented, the dog salivates. Food and a bell tone are presented and the dog again salivates. The bell tone is presented alone, the dog salivates. A new learned pairing of stimulus and response has been achieved.

Desensitization

A major counseling treatment derived indirectly from classical learning approaches is *Joseph Wolpe's* desensitization technique (20). This approach has been found very effective in treating anxiety and phobic reactions. It involves the use of deep relaxation and vicarious learning. Briefly, a subject who, for example, experiences undue anxiety in an academic testing situation is helped to relax completely. He is then presented with a hierarchy of various anxiety-producing images ranging from his feelings when a test is first announced for the following week, through his reactions the night before the test, to his anxiety at the moment he reads the first question.

As he is able to proceed further and further through the hierarchy without experiencing anxiety tension that interrupts his relaxed state, he is being desensitized to the anxiety-producing stimuli. Eventually he will be able to re-enter the testing situation directly without the crippling anxiety experienced before. He is said to be "desensitized."

Both operant and classical learning approaches offer valuable sources of gain to the developmental counselor. These behavioral approaches can be utilized and incorporated into the practice of the developmental counselor without compromising his commitment to values of human freedom and dignity. They can be utilized with the full awareness and consent of clients. They do not detract from the establishment of warm, empathic, caring relationships, but in fact are probably fully effective only in conjunction with such relationships. The language of behavioral counseling is often not a particularly comfortable or easy one for counselors who are by pre-disposition very "people-oriented." The potential sources of gain available in these approaches make learning the new language and translating it into philosophically acceptable forms most worthwhile. Krumboltz and Thoreson (8) have applied operant principles to many counseling situations and have coined the term "behavioral humanism" to describe such a translation. The marriage in concepts and values represented in such a term has much to commend it.

SUMMARY OF COUNSELING MODELS

Three major models of counseling each based upon a distinct set of sources of gain have been described. Relationship, cognitive, and behavioral models have all demonstrated relevance to developmental counseling. We have pointed out that while each approach "loads" its counseling treatment upon a particular source of gain, they are not necessarily mutually exclusive or incompatible in terms of either techniques or philosophical commitments.

In Chapter 16 we describe a systematic eclectic model that combines the sources of gain from each model into a powerful and practical approach.

REFERENCES

1. ADLER, A. *The practice and theory of individual psychology.* Paterson, N.J.: Littlefield, Adams, 1963.
2. BRUCE, P. Three forces in psychology and their ethical and educational implications. *The Educational Forum,* 1966, 30 (3), 227–285.
3. CARKHUFF, R. *Helping and human relations: a primer for lay and professional helpers.* New York: Holt, Rinehart, Winston, 1969. 2 volumes.
4. ELLIS, ALBERT (Ed.). *Sound of reason: verbation cases in rational–emotive therapy.* Palo Alto: Science and Behavior Books, 1971.
5. FREUD, S. *General introduction to psychonanalysis: the authorized English translation of Sigmund Freud.* New York: Simon and Schuster, 1969. Rev. ed.
6. FROMM, E. *Crisis of psychoanalysis.* New York: Holt, Rinehart, Winston, 1970.
7. HORNEY, KAREN. *Neurosis and human growth: the struggle toward self-realization.* New York: Norton, 1950.
8. KRUMBOLTZ, J. D., & THORESON, C. E. (Eds.). *Behavioral counseling cases and techniques.* New York: Holt, Rinehart, 1969.

9. MOUSTAKAS, C. *Individuality and encounter: a brief journey into loneliness and sensitivity groups.* Cambridge, Mass.: Howard Doyle, 1968.

10. NEURINGER, C., & MICHAEL, J. L. *Behavior modification in clinical psychology.* New York: Appleton-Century-Crofts, 1970.

11. ROGERS, C. R. *Carl Rogers on encounter groups.* New York: Harper & Row, 1970.

12. ROGERS, C. R. *Client centered therapy.* Boston: Houghton-Mifflin, 1951.

13. ROGERS, C. R. *Freedom to learn.* Columbus, Ohio: Charles Merrill, 1971.

14. ROGERS, C. R. *On becoming a person.* Boston: Houghton-Mifflin, 1961.

15. ROGERS, C. R. *The therapeutic relationship and its impacts: a study of psychotherapy with schizophrenics.* Madison: University of Wisconsin Press, 1967.

16. SKINNER, B. F. Operant behavior, *Amer. Psychol.* 1963, 18:503–515.

17. SULLIVAN, H. S. *The interpersonal theory of psychiatry.* New York: Norton, 1963.

18. TRUAX, C., & CARKHUFF, R. *Toward effective counseling and psychotherapy.* Chicago: Aldine, 1967.

19. VAN KAAM, A. *Existential foundations of psychology.* Garden City, N.Y.: Doubleday, 1969.

20. WOLPE, J. *Practice of behavior therapy.* Elmsford, N.Y.: Pergamon, 1969.

RECOMMENDED READINGS

BERENSON, B. G., & CARKHUFF, R. R. (Eds.). *Sources of gain in counseling and psychotherapy.* New York: Holt, Rinehart, 1967.

CUNNINGHAM, L. M., & PETERS, H. J. *Counseling theories.* Columbus, Ohio: Charles Merrill, 1973.

FORD, D., & URBAN, H. *Systems of psychotherapy: a comparative study.* New York: Wiley, 1963.

HALL, C. S., & LINDZEY, G. *Theories of personality.* New York: Wiley, 1957.

PATTERSON, C. H. *Theories of counseling and psychotherapy.* 2d. ed. New York: Harper & Row, 1973.

STEFFLRE, B., & GRANT, W. H. *Theories of counseling.* 2d. ed. New York: McGraw-Hill, 1972.

4

THE DEVELOPMENT
OF HUMAN
EFFECTIVENESS

The developmental counselor is concerned with understanding the complex processes through which effective human behaviors are acquired and modified. The counselor is concerned with understanding the nature of these processes so that he may intervene to facilitate their smooth and orderly operation. From this standpoint, the counselor is interested in the *etiology of human effectiveness*, that is, the study of the causes of effective behavior and development. This interest is similar to the interest of the psychiatrist in understanding the etiology of mental illness. Unfortunately, much of the attention that has been given to the problem of personality development has centered upon the latter rather than the former set of causes.

Perhaps the most useful way to look at the role of the facilitator of development is with the model provided by Heisler (13). She conceptualizes the development of mental health or effective behavior as the product of the interaction of two basic human tendencies. These are the need for *homeostasis,* or, in other words, a comfortable level of equilibrium between inner needs and outer forces, and the need for *differentiation*, that is, the need of the organism to grow in self-actualizing ways.

Heisler conceptualizes effective development as a kind of cyclical process of differentiation, followed by homeostatic equilibrium. Healthy development requires a kind of dynamic balance between these two forces so that a basal personality organization is gradually developed resilient enough to support the ongoing process of differentiation without disrupting the homeostatic balance of the organism at intolerable levels, as we noted in Chapter 1.

Development requires an effective balance between differentiation and homeostasis. When the developing child does not have the security that insures tolerable homeostatic levels, all of his energy goes into maintaining such levels. This is a *growth-arresting* kind of equilibrium. If, on the other hand, there is not enough stimulation in his environment for all differentiating processes to occur, the situation is equally growth-arresting, although the comfort level of the child may be higher.

The developmental counselor must be sensitive to the operation of this process in order to intervene or cause the intervention that can restore this dynamic, *growth-producing* balance. Such intervention is most likely to be needed at points in the developmental process at which *cultural or physiological discontinuities* occur and the dynamic balance is violently disturbed. Aspects of intervention are discussed in Chapters 9, 10, 11, and 12.

ASSUMPTIONS ABOUT DEVELOPMENT

Before the discussion of particular phases of development is undertaken, certain basic assumptions and definitions need to be stated. The approach taken here is that development is a lifelong set of psychological, social, and physiological processes that encompass the entire pattern of human existence from birth to death. From this standpoint, developmental processes involve interactions between the developing organism and his environment. The *physiological* processes that define the organism in a physical sense and the *environmental* forces, including culture, that act upon him are mediated by a set of *psychological* processes. These processes involve the ways in which the individual perceives himself and his environment, the set of meanings that he organizes around these perceptions, and the behaviors that he acquires in coping with his needs and his environment.

Development thus is seen to combine growth, maturation, and learning. It is seen to be influenced by environmental factors, within whose context developmental processes must be understood. All developmental processes are considered interrelated.

The development of effective behavior is not an area in which any great wealth of knowledge is available. At the present state of that knowledge, however, it is possible to outline in sketchy and tentative terms at least some of the parameters involved in effective development. In this particular approach to human development, heavy emphasis is placed upon constructs suggested by Erik Erikson (7). His "Eight Stages of Man" seems to offer one of the most useful approaches to the conceptualization of developmental tasks available. Other approaches are obviously badly needed to broaden understanding of developmental processes.

One of the first issues to be encountered in any attempt to outline human developmental processes is whether development is smooth and continuous or whether it indeed occurs in recognizably discrete stages. The most probable answer to this question involves a middle-of-the-road position. Some of the physiological processes that are developmental catalysts, such as the onset of puberty, are relatively discrete events. Others are, of course, very gradual and continuous in nature. As Muuss (19) points out, however, in Western culture, at least, society reinforces stages of development by organizing social institutions around such stages. For example, grade levels in school, types of schools, legal definitions of adult status such as legal ages for driving, drinking, voting, and marriage all reinforce the discreteness of developmental stages. In less highly organized cultures, the discreteness of developmental stages might be less pronounced.

Many attempts have been made to analyze development in terms of particularly significant stages (3, 5, 7, 23). In this analysis, five major stages are conceptualized. They are: (*a*) *Organization* (birth to about age fourteen), (*b*) *Exploration* (fifteen to about thirty), (*c*) *Realization* (thirty to about fifty), (*d*) *Stabilization* (fifty to about sixty-five), and (*e*) *Examination* (after sixty-five). The age limits that are descriptive of these stages are, of course, highly general approximations that may be expected to vary considerably from one individual to another.

The usefulness of a life-stages approach lies chiefly in the general concept that cultural forces and maturational changes acting at particular times in the lives of human beings will result in particular kinds of problems, crises, and behavior patterns. The interaction between the culture and the developing individual can best be understood in terms of these life stages.

Development is then seen as a patterned, orderly, lifelong process that leads to effective behavior; that is, behavior that permits long-term control of environment where possible, and control of the individual's affective responses to those aspects of the environment that he cannot control. The process of development includes gaining understanding, assigning meanings, and organizing behavior. Development is orderly, but each individual develops in his own unique way (2).

The development of effective behavior will be viewed within the framework of three major constructs discussed in Chapter 1. These are: (*a*) Social Roles, (*b*) Coping Behaviors, and (*c*) Developmental Tasks. Each needs to be defined.

Social Roles

Perhaps the most economical definition of *role* is that given by Allport (1). He says that *role* is a structured means of participation in social life. More simply, it is what society expects of an individual occupying a position in a group. Allport goes on, however, to elaborate four significant aspects of role that are differential determinants of how an individual reacts to given role situations. These aspects are:

> *Role-Expectations*—these are the cultural prescriptions that are generally assigned to the role by society
>
> *Role-Conceptions*—these involve the way in which the participating individual actually perceives or interprets the expectations
>
> *Role-Acceptance*—this entails the willingness of the individual to involve himself in the role
>
> *Role-Performance*—this involves the actual behavior of the individual in the role situation

Taken together, these four meanings define the significance of role in personality development. They form one of the key factors in the ensuing outline of effectiveness development.

Developmental Tasks

Havighurst defines developmental tasks in the following way.

> A developmental task is a task which arises at or about a certain period in the life of the individual, successful achievement of which leads to his happiness

and to success with later tasks, while failure leads to unhappiness in the individual, disapproval by the society, and difficulty with later tasks. [10, p. 2.]

The important part of this concept is, of course, the idea that each task is ideally mastered at a particular stage of development, and that such mastery is necessary for the continuation of optimal development.

Coping Behaviors

Coping behaviors are defined by Kroeber as

> . . . behaviors that are particularly relevant to an active, effective person dealing with demands, often conflicting, of a biological, psychological or social nature. [16, p. 179.]

Coping behaviors then are the source of human effectiveness. Each individual acquires both a set of coping behaviors and a general style of coping that he learns to use.

ORGANIZATION STAGE

Organization is the life stage that is dominated by the phenomenon of physiological unfolding of the organism. The developmental crises of this period are dictated primarily by the organism's struggle to meet its emerging physical and emotional needs within a society that defines the ways in which these needs can be met. The stage can be broken down into four substages: infancy, early childhood, later childhood, and early adolescence.

Infancy (birth to three years)

The human infant at birth is in one sense a bundle of potentialities. He is, as Allport (1) suggested, a *psychological thing* rather than a personality. In spite of this amorphous and plastic tendency, however, in the first three years of life, the infant emerges into separateness and individualization in a way that lays down the foundations for his entire subsequent development.

Social Roles in Infancy. The term "social role" when applied to infant status may at first appear inappropriate or even absurd. In our child-centered culture, however, the infant is at once an important and closely managed social being. That a set of role expectations do exist for the infant may be seen in the fact that mothers habitually talk of even week-old infants in terms such as "He is a good baby." As the baby grows, these adult expectations are rapidly expanded. The infant is expected to be responsive to affection, compliant to adult wishes, and to alternately be cute and quiescent. As the infant grows during the first three years of life, unceasing expectations are made for conformity in habits of elimination, eating, and interpersonal behavior.

The way in which the infant is able to handle the increasingly complex role expectations for him determines in part at least the nature of the social interaction through which he will acquire attitudes and concepts about himself and his relationship to significant others. If social role expectations for him are unreasonable, arbitrary, or capricious, he will have difficulty in coping effectively enough with them to achieve some sense of security and mastery in his environment. At the same time, if social role expectations are not clearly articulated in infancy, he will have difficulty in moving on into much more complex forms of social interaction that are involved in his subsequent stages of development.

Developmental Tasks of Infancy.   The central developmental task of infancy is, as Erikson (7) says, the development of the ability to trust. Erikson discusses the phenomenon of trust in this way.

> The first demonstration of social trust in the baby is the ease of his feeding, the depth of his sleep, the relaxation of his bowels. . . . In his gradually increasing waking hours he finds that more and more adventures of the senses arouse a feeling of familiarity, of having coincided with a feeling of inner goodness. . . . The infant's first social accomplishment, then, is his willingness to let the mother out of sight without undue anxiety or rage, because she has become an inner certainty as well as an outer predictability. Such consistency, continuity, and sameness of experience provides a rudimentary sense of ego identity . . . [7, p. 247.]

The sense of trust develops out of the primary relationship between mother and child and then is generalized toward significant others. Mothers enable infants to develop a sense of trust by sensitive, consistent reactions to the child's needs, and by communicating a deep sense of confidence in their own adequacy as mothers to protect and nurture the child. Other significant persons in the child's life similarly help him to trust by demonstrating sensitivity, consistency, and self-confidence. The ability to trust is not dependent on the level of need satisfaction alone. Infants and children are able to handle increasingly significant levels of frustration and satisfaction deferral when such situations are handled in consistent ways and are accompanied by the kind of confident parental attitude that communicates that the frustration is meaningful and growth-producing rather than capricious or punitive.

Other important developmental tasks of infancy are:

1. Learning to eat solid foods and feed self
2. Learning to manipulate objects
3. Learning to walk
4. Learning to explore immediate environment
5. Learning to communicate
6. Learning to control elimination

Coping Behaviors of Infancy. The significant coping behaviors associated with infancy stem rather directly from the developmental tasks listed above. The development of a sense of trust enables the infant to begin to *defer immediate gratifications* and to start to behave as a *separate, but secure,* individual.

Eating a variety of nourishing, available foods is obviously a simple but necessary nutritive condition for further development. Learning to control elimination and behaving in conformity to socially approved habits for elimination gives the infant considerable control over the nature of his interpersonal relationships. He learns to please others and to keep himself in a physical condition of cleanliness in which others will approach him in positive ways.

Manipulative and exploratory behaviors are extremely important for the infant. Research in sensory deprivation and environmental constriction with both humans and infrahumans suggests that the infant must receive an increasing amount of sensory stimulation of all kinds if cognitive development is to proceed normally (4, 9, 12, 14, 17, 18). If the infant is overprotected, overfearful, or physically unable to manipulate, explore, and interact with his environment, he is not likely to develop optimally. He may actually suffer from what might be called "perceptual starvation."

Learning to walk and learning to communicate are obvious forms of behavior that tremendously broaden the infant's world and enhance the possibilities for further development. Learning to communicate involves both talking—that is, learning to articulate words—and also handling verbal symbols in ways that make possible the formation of countless new meanings and inferences. Communication also means being able to respond in a variety of ways that communicate attitudes and emotions. These emotional responses are a necessary part of being able to *move toward others*, to establish patterns of affiliation and relatedness with others. The central coping behaviors of this period are *approaching, receiving*, and *accepting* behaviors.

Early Childhood (ages three to six)

As the infant emerges into early childhood, his world becomes rapidly more complex. The relatively simple role expectations that defined his position before are rapidly differentiated and expanded. New roles that are thrust upon him include those of *sibling* and *playmate*. Both involve expectations for cooperativeness and mutuality that are new. Also in this period, role expectations begin to be differentiated into *sex-appropriate* behaviors. The child learns that little boys, for example, are no longer expected to cry, and that little girls are not usually supposed to be brash or adventurous. Such early learnings may have very damaging long-term consequences for the child. New expectations of *sharing, cooperating, handling aggression, dealing with anxiety, responding to authority, expressing feelings*, etc., must be internalized, and effective coping behaviors acquired.

Developmental Tasks of Early Childhood. The central developmental task of this stage, according to Erikson (7), is the development of a sense of *autonomy*. Autonomy is the basis for the sense of separateness and responsibility that is essential in the development of responsible independence. The child must learn to make choices, assume responsibility for them, and accept the consequences that they imply. These consequences must not be so disintegrating, however, that he will shrink from them or be forced to repress or deny them. This is the stage in which parents can foster development by maintaining a sensitive balance between firm, consistent outer controls for the child and the need for development of inner-based controls that must be exercised to be developed. They must accept the child's need to make choices, to throw off arbitrary external controls, while still supplying the firmness that will protect the child against the disintegrating consequences that his lack of inner-based impulse-control may invite.

Other important developmental tasks of early childhood are:

1. Developing a sense of self—including a self-image
2. Developing a sense of extension of self—that is, belonging and mutuality with others
3. Learning appropriate roles and identification

4. Learning to manage aggression and frustration in minimally disintegrating ways
5. Learning to follow verbal instructions
6. Learning to focus attention and concentration
7. Learning to become reasonably independent in self-care (washing, dressing, toilet functions, etc.)
8. Developing realistic concepts of the physical and social world (time, space, distance, relationships, authority, etc.)

Coping Behaviors of Early Childhood.   Coping behaviors for this stage may be listed under the following headings:

1. *Cooperative behaviors.* The child must learn cooperative behaviors of listening, sharing, joining, communicating, and defending. By using these kinds of behaviors appropriately, he can extend himself into new situations and achieve formerly unattainable goals.

2. *Control behaviors.* These behaviors involve the control of behavior over increasing time spans. They include concentration, attention, silence, restraint of movement, etc.

3. *Substitution behaviors.* The child must learn to cope with the demands of his environment and his own inner needs by learning to substitute verbal symbols for actions, acceptable expressions of feelings for unacceptable expressions, and acceptable ways of dealing with frustration for unacceptable ones.

Later Childhood (ages six to twelve)

In this stage of development, the child's social world becomes rapidly more complex. Entry into school, for example, brings the new social role of *student*. Increased capabilities lead to new role expectations of *helper, big brother* or *sister*. These new social roles require the mastery of new developmental tasks, and failure to master developmental tasks at this stage involves drastic consequences to future development.

Developmental Tasks of Later Childhood.   The key developmental tasks at this stage are Erikson's (7) concepts of *initiative* and *industry*.

By *initiative* and *industry*, Erikson means the qualities of planning and attacking tasks. Involved are undertaking projects for the sake of being active and on the move. Initiative requires the confidence and surplus energy to bounce back from defeats and forget failures quickly. It is the quality of responding to challenges with *resilience, resourcefulness*, and *enthusiasm*.

Parents and teachers can contribute to the development of initiative and industry by helping the child to regulate his ambitions and channel his zest for accomplishment into growth-producing projects. The danger at this stage is the development of inferiority. The child is very conscious of rivalry and competition. He is constantly comparing himself and his performances with those of others. Parents and teachers can work to prevent destructive competition and to help the child channel his energies into areas that promise reasonable opportunities for personally earned success and mastery experiences. He needs to feel acceptance and worth in the eyes of others for being *himself*, and worth and acceptance within himself from his performances.

Out of such experiences, the child can gradually develop a sense of personal responsibility and pride. He can gain more realistic ways of judging his own and others' performances, and can gain confidence and satisfaction from helping others.

Other important developmental tasks at this stage are:

1. Learning to read and calculate
2. Learning to value himself and feel valued by others
3. Learning to defer immediate gratifications for the reaching of greater anticipated rewards
4. Learning to control emotional reactions with greater flexibility
5. Learning to deal with abstract concepts such as truth, beauty, and justice (ending infantile moral realism)
6. Learning to give of himself to others
7. Learning to formulate values and make value judgments

Coping Behaviors of Later Childhood.   Coping behaviors at this stage may be grouped into several categories:

1. *Mastery behaviors.* Mastery behaviors are those that give the child, through his own efforts, a feeling of control and mastery over his environment. They involve the reaching of formerly unattainable goals and the achievement of performances that compare favorably with others.

2. *Value-relevant behaviors.* These are behaviors that are based upon internal judgments of good and bad, right and wrong, rather than on externally imposed authority or fear of punishment. This value-relevant behavior goes beyond what Piaget (20) calls "moral realism" to take into account intentions and circumstances as factors in moral judgments.

3. *Work-relevant behaviors.* These behaviors involve organizing time

and energy for doing school work and chores. *Deferring immediate gratifications* for the sake of larger goals (for example, putting work ahead of play in appropriate circumstances), *setting realistic standards* for performances and products, and *taking pride in achievements* and in *self as a worker* are important coping behaviors.

Early Adolescence (ages twelve to fourteen)

Early adolescence is well known as one of the most critical and painful stages of human development. The resurgence of drastic physiological changes of many types produces a profound *disequilibrium* in the life of the early adolescent. At the same time, he is confronted with a frightening new cluster of social role expectations that are often ambiguous and ambivalent in themselves.

Social Roles in Early Adolescence. Two major changes in role expectations occur during early adolescence that are of major importance. These are *peer roles* and *heterosexual roles*. These two new sets of roles form the basis for what Coleman (6) calls the "Adolescent Society." In early adolescence, the peer expectations begin to shape the youngster's behavior to ever-increasing degrees. These expectations begin to carry more weight than the family and school sanctions that were formerly the primary shapers of behavior. When the peer and family–school expectations conflict, the adolescent is put in a position of acute choice anxiety. Competing and conflicting expectations for behavior may make it difficult or impossible for him to conform to both peer and parental expectations. The situation is further complicated by the emergence of heterosexual relationships with which the adolescent has had little experience, but which are activated by powerful new biological needs. Within this confusing new psychosocial matrix, the adolescent has to establish a new identity.

Developmental Tasks of Early Adolescence. The primary developmental task for the entire adolescent period involves what Erikson (7) calls the conflict between identity and role confusion. The integration of new roles, the casting off of old dependencies, and the establishment of new values are all part of what is called the period of "identity crises." The most critical phase of this process in early adolescence is the development of a sexual identity. The adolescent must answer the question of "Who am I?" first within the context of masculinity–femininity and the roles and relationships that accompany sexual identifications in our culture. To a great extent, identity development involves a continuity between *past* experiences of self and others with the prospect of *future* experiences in harmony with that past. In adolescence, the emerging changes of puberty make inevitable a *discontinuity* that leads to *identity diffusion.*

The adolescent seeks increased clarification of identity through his peer groups and through new heterosexual relationships. Within the relative intimacy of such relationships, he is able to get some increased definition of his own identity by projecting and reflecting it upon others. The sense of *belonging with* and *belonging to*, which is part of these adolescent relationships, are clarifiers of personal identity. The adolescent girl or boy can identify as "Johnny's steady girl," "Joan's best friend," "one of the crowd at school," etc. Such relationships thus reduce the anxiety of identity diffusion. The relative impermanence of these relationships together with the general instability of the future as perceived by the adolescent makes them only temporary *identity anchors*, however.

The adolescent can be helped in his struggle to rebuild his lost identity through the creation of a period of *psychosocial moratorium* (7) in which the inevitable conflict between school and family expectations and peer demands are accepted rather than punished. This is a period in which the youngster is given as much freedom as possible to experiment and to make mistakes that are not irreversible. Such freedom cannot be complete, of course, but parents and schools can do much to smooth the path of adolescent development by recognizing the rebellions, the moods, the fads, and the crushes as the symptoms of growth that they are, rather than the dire predictors of disaster that they sometimes appear to be in the eyes of overanxious adults.

Other Developmental Tasks of Early Adolescence. The early adolescent needs to achieve *control of impulses*, particularly in the sexual area. He needs to achieve a set of *positive attitudes toward work.* These include *setting realistic standards of achievement, learning to defer gratifications for increasing periods of time, and learning to identify himself as a responsible and productive worker.* He needs to learn how to *study effectively, organize his time, and plan his activities* in accordance with a *personally relevant value hierarchy.*

Coping Behaviors of Early Adolescence. The most important coping behaviors of early adolescence can be classified under the following headings.

1. *Social behaviors.* These are the general social skills that are necessary for getting along in group interactions. Meeting people, being able to engage in conversation, being able to get along in groups and at parties, giving help and being able to accept help from friends are all important social behaviors.

2. *Sex-appropriate behaviors.* These behaviors are the ones that implement sex-role concepts. They involve the behaviors that communicate masculinity and femininity.

For many boys, these center about physical prowess, driving a car, being aggressive, and other essentially narrowly adaptive measures of masculinity. Obsessive concern with implementing masculinity in rigid and stereotyped ways may interfere with the acquisition of many kinds of more valuable coping behaviors in intellectual and social areas. For girls, the same kind of obsessive compulsive attention to the sexually attracting elements of femininity may detract from other coping behaviors. The acquisition of a wide range of flexible and adaptable sex-appropriate behaviors is very important.

3. *Achievement-oriented behaviors.* These behaviors are essentially those necessary for effective work. They include *concentration, organization, planning, gratification deferral, self-criticism, intellectual curiosity, logical problem-solving, and critical thinking.*

EXPLORATION STAGE

The *Exploration* stage begins in mid-adolescence and moves the individual through later adolescence and early adulthood. The Exploration stage is characterized by a reaching out for new values, ideals, motivations, and purposes. Just as in the Organization stage where the emerging organism was preoccupied with the growth changes unfolding within him, in the Exploration stage, the individual is intent upon reaching out into the environment to find the elements to which he can relate his new-found sense of physical maturity. The key coping behaviors in this broad stage are *reciprocal* behaviors as contrasted with the *dependency* behaviors of childhood. In the Exploration stage, the young person reaches out to establish new reciprocal relationships in friendship, courtship and dating, educational achievement, and career development. He has to learn to give and receive in a variety of situations based upon *mutuality* and *cooperation.* Failure to learn effective *reciprocal behaviors* will make the development of these relationships difficult or impossible.

Later Adolescence (ages fifteen to nineteen)

The period of later adolescence is concerned with a continued working through of the problems encountered in early adolescence.

Social Roles of Later Adolescence.   New social roles are encountered in almost bewildering profusion. The social world of the adolescent mushrooms in size and complexity as he enters high school and college years. The new dimension of sexuality complicates all kinds of interpersonal relationships. New roles of worker, leader, follower, supervisor, subordinate, and colleague begin to appear as the adolescent begins to participate in activities organized on adult models rather than on childhood models. Many of these new role expectations conflict and produce demands for coping behaviors of greater complexity than ever before.

Developmental Tasks of Later Adolescence.   The central developmental task of later adolescence is still concerned with identity formation. In early adolescence, the prime threat of identity diffusion stemmed from the sexual changes of puberty. Identification with sexual roles was the developmental imperative.

In later adolescence, once sexual identity is at least partially acquired, the nature of the identity crisis shifts to the establishment of *identity as a worker.* In later adolescence, the youngster is faced with a process of development in which many key decisions, some of which are irreversible, are thrust upon him. Decisions about education and career are relatively inescapable. The vocational development process of which these choices represent crises is one, as Super (23) says, of implementing a self-concept in the world of work. The process of choosing a career involves much more than finding a way to make a living. It determines in a very large part the whole style of life of an individual. Career choice involves choice of friends and associates, loyalties and affiliations, locations of home and family, etc. In large part, the development of personal identity at this stage is synonymous with career development.

Society can assist youth by providing effective vocational guidance services and experiences. Vocationally oriented, developmental counseling plays a vital role at this stage of development. The total educational process, however, must combine to meet the vocational needs of youth. The adolescent should have exposure to large amounts of realistic information about the world of work. Much of this information goes beyond the usual wages, hours, working conditions, and training information contained in typical occupational libraries. Developing realistic stereotypes of people in various career fields and realistic and well-elaborated concepts of self and ideal self are very important (8).

Other developmental tasks of later adolescence are:

1. Achieving personal friendships on the basis of individualized relationships rather than group memberships
2. Achieving emotional autonomy in learning to make decisions, choose values, and take responsibilities independently of home and family
3. Learning to produce in work situations under adult performance standards

Coping Behaviors of Later Adolescence.   The central coping behaviors of later adolescence can be categorized under the term "reciprocal behaviors." These are essentially the interpersonal behaviors necessary to function within close, equalitarian relationships. Much of the adolescent's past interpersonal relationships have been within essentially authoritarian relationships or within rather loosely structured peer groups where the emphasis was upon blind conformity rather than individualized responsibility. In later adolescence, two social developments place great stress upon reciprocal behaviors. The demands of fraternal living in college or in early working years require the acquisition of reciprocal behaviors. The experiences of dating and courtship similarly require such behaviors at deeper emotional levels.

Reciprocal behaviors include *trusting, sharing, fulfilling promises, keeping confidences,* responding positively to *supervision and criticism, meeting others' needs* as well as one's own, and *accepting responsibility* in joint projects.

Other important categories of coping behavior at this stage are *leadership behaviors, work-relevant behaviors,* and *value-choice behaviors.*

Young Adulthood (ages twenty to thirty)

Early adulthood is the crucial period in which the adequacy of earlier developmental patterns is put to test. In terms of social roles, the two major testing areas are marriage and work. For the first time in his life, the young person finds out that he is "playing for keeps." Relatively few of the crises encountered earlier were so final and irreversible as those that are now met on an almost daily basis. For the first time, as Havighurst (10) says, the individual's success and prestige depend not on age, but on skill, strength, wisdom, and social connections.

Social Roles of Young Adulthood. The primary new role is, of course, marriage. This role combines for the first time many other roles and relationships that could formerly be separated into relatively simple and discrete compartments. The wife or husband is at one time a roommate, a co-worker, a lover, a companion, and a confidant.

Even when the young adult has learned to cope with these situations effectively in separate roles, the conflict and ambivalence that their consolidation within the marriage relationship produces brings difficult problems. The individual is forced to meet sexual, interpersonal, and economic needs within one highly emotionalized relationship.

The second major social role area is the career role. Career role is somewhat different from the roles presented by part-time, temporary, or entry jobs that the young adult has experienced earlier. In these situations, the stakes were relatively small and the contacts of brief duration. In the career roles that the young adult enters, the expectations and relationships are lifelong, and the stakes involved in meeting these expectations and functioning within these relationships are crucial to both the individual and the family.

The third major role of this period is, of course, parenthood. Here again the role is very different from those that have been experienced formerly. The emotional and material demands are great, and the responsibilities for shaping another human life are the greatest that the individual has ever undertaken. Failure or perceived failure in this role can lead to a lifetime of guilt and self-recrimination.

Developmental Tasks of Young Adulthood. The central developmental tasks of young adulthood are *intimacy* and *commitment*. *Intimacy*, as Erikson (7) describes it, involves the capacity to commit oneself to concrete affiliations and partnerships and to develop the ethical strength to abide by such commitments even though they call for major sacrifices and compromises. Without such capacities, the chance of maintaining a successful marriage relationship is slight.

Commitment, which is necessarily a part of intimacy, is generalized beyond close interpersonal situations to include commitment to ideals and causes and to organizations and enterprises. The successful implementation of career roles usually requires this kind of commitment. Commitment again involves the capacity to invest considerable portions of one's time, energy, and self-esteem in causes, organizations, or institutions. Without such commitments, career development possibilities are very limited.

The third developmental task of young adulthood is what Erikson terms *"generativity."* This is the developmental stage necessary for successful parenting. Generativity includes productivity and creativity, but goes beyond this to encompass the concern to nurture and guide the next generation, usually primarily through one's own offspring. It is within this task of generativity that the genuine capacity to give unilaterally rather than reciprocally is developed.

Coping Behaviors of Early Adulthood.   Coping behaviors at this stage include:

1. *Sexual behaviors.* Successful sexual behavior at this stage includes what Erikson describes as:

1. Mutuality of orgasm;
2. With a loved partner;
3. Of the other sex;
4. With whom one is able and willing to share a mutual trust;
5. And with whom one is able and willing to regulate the cycle of work, procreation, and recreation;
6. So as to secure to the offspring a satisfactory development. [7, p. 266.]

2. *Risk-taking behaviors.* These behaviors involve the willingness to take appropriate, reasonable, and calculated physical, economic, and psychological risks in order to reach desirable personal, family, and career goals.

3. *Value-consistent behaviors.* These behaviors are unifying and integrating behaviors that cut across role situations to supply the sense of meaning and purpose to life. They are motivated by value judgments and ways of implementing values across many areas of living. The most crucial of these behaviors are the *giving and helping* behaviors that are essential to marriage and parenthood. As they are generalized further and further beyond immediate family situations, the individual is able to make greater and greater contributions and to move into the next stage of *Realization.*

REALIZATION STAGE (ages thirty to fifty)

Realization represents the culmination stage of effective human development. Physical maturation is complete, and psychological growth through exploration has hopefully laid down a set of personality structures and behavior patterns that will support a very high level of functioning. Realization, then, represents a state of human functioning that goes far beyond the concept of "adjustment" or getting along. It presumes a level of functioning in which the organism is able to gain control of large segments of environment that are most meaningful to him, and has learned to relate himself to those factors in his life that are resistant to such control.

Any description of traits and behaviors that constitute a high level of functioning or maturity involves the use of philosophical values. Several typologies built on such descriptions are discussed in Chapter 5. At this point, Realization will be described in only the simple terms of definitions such as Jahoda's (15). She describes an effective person as one who actively masters his environment, demonstrates a considerable unity of personality, and is able to perceive himself and his world realistically. Such a person is independent and able to function effectively without making undue demands on others. This definition seems useful so far as it goes. Shoben (22) goes beyond the self-sufficiency criterion to propose that the mature person is one who extends his functioning beyond self-control and personal responsibility into the area of social responsibility and commitment to some set of external values.

The Realization stage can be described in terms of a set of social roles of a somewhat unusual order. These social roles are considerably more generalized and diffuse in expectations than earlier and simpler roles. The key to Realization in these social roles lies in the role aspects of role conception and role acceptance. Since the social roles of the Realization stage are general and diffuse, considerable ambiguity is involved in their interpretation. Similarly, the degree to which an individual internalizes or accepts these roles is less a product of overt social pressures than of his own inner needs.

The Realizing individual does not assume roles that are contrary to his own value system. He does not conform blindly to others' expectations. If he accepts a role, however, he will commit himself fully to fulfilling the responsibilities involved as he perceives and accepts them. The Realizing person is flexible enough to assume a variety of roles that are acceptable to him without being driven in an "other-directed" sense to conform for the sake of social approval.

Social Roles in the Realization Stage.   The following are the various social roles in the Realization stage.

1. *Leadership roles.* These are roles in which individuals are able to make outstanding contributions to the success of group projects or the achievement of group goals.

2. *Helping roles.* These are roles in which an individual is able to make a significant contribution to the growth and development of another individual.

3. *Creative roles.* These are roles in which individuals have opportunities to make new and original contributions to human welfare. These may be in any of many fields of endeavor and are not necessarily confined to arts or sciences.

4. *Accomplishment roles.* These are roles in which an individual has an opportunity to achieve a very high level of performance or unique accomplishment in some personally worthwhile activity, whether or not it is of a particularly original or creative nature.

Realization then from the social role standpoint consists largely of conceptualizing and accepting role opportunities in ways that allow the individual to make important contributions within the framework of his life situation. The circumstances of the individual's life situation influence, but do not completely determine, his ability to conceptualize and accept new opportunities. Most individuals in our society have opportunities to play Realization roles.

Developmental Tasks of Realization.   The central developmental task of this period is the development of unity and integration. This is a kind of harmony between the individual's life style and the values of his culture. This harmony gives meaning to life and overcomes the existential despair that arises from the inevitability of death. It is the serenity and confidence that such integrity gives that, when communicated to infants, gives them the ability to trust. As Erikson (7) says, children will not fear life if their elders have integrity enough not to fear death.

Other developmental tasks essential at this stage are:

1. *Development of inner directedness.* Riesman (21) suggests that people may be tradition-directed, inner-directed, or other-directed. The Realizing person is to a large extent inner-directed; that is, through role interpretation, he exercises positive control over direction and degree of conforming or non-conforming behavior that he uses.

2. *Development of appropriate attitudes of interdependency.* Levine

(18) points out that high levels of personal and social development are characterized not by separation from others, but by mutually constructive participation with them.

3. *Development of constructive ways of handling cognitive dissonance.* Cognitive dissonance may be defined as the difference between what one perceives and what he would like to perceive. Without some dissonance between perceived self and ideal self, for example, there would be little motivation to change and grow. On the other hand, if dissonance is intolerable, self-deceptive mechanisms may be invoked. As Levine says:

> The individual who is functioning effectively will have available to him behavioral patterns which will assist in the resolution of dissonances. The patterns represent efforts at mastery rather than defense; they are directed toward active solutions of problems . . .[18, p. 367.]

4. *Development of flexible yet effective emotional controls.* The effective person is able to exert considerable control over the level and kind of emotional responses that he produces. As Levine points out:

> The person functioning effectively not only can experience a wide range of emotional responses, but also is aware of himself and his feelings, and consequently is able to know what others mean when they make subtle distinctions between emotional states. Awareness of his own broad range of emotions contributes to a zest for living, and an avoidance of "sameness" and shallowness of his feelings. The person's accessibility to his own feelings depends on the degree to which they engender threat and have to be walled off. For the person functioning at a high level of effectiveness, little energy is committed to blocking off, denying or avoiding emotions. [18, p. 378.]

5. *Development of creative thought processes.* Creative thinking involves the ability to see subtle relationships, to exercise independent judgments, and to find unusual solutions to problems. In other words, it is the ability to think in *divergent* ways.

6. *Development of effective problem-solving techniques.* Effective problem-solving requires the ability to perceive problems in their entirety, the ability to maintain *tentativeness of outlook* while examining alternative solutions, and the ability to analyze probable outcomes of alternative solutions.

Coping Behaviors in Realization. Perhaps the best analysis of the characteristics of coping behaviors in mature adults is that given by Kroeber (16). Kroeber discriminates between coping behaviors and defense behaviors under the following behavior categories.

1. *Discrimination*. This is the ability to separate feelings and ideas into meaningful units. The coping behavior is *objectivity*, that is, separating ideas and feelings into meaningful categories so that objective evaluations can be made.

2. *Detachment*. This is the ability to let the mind roam freely, to speculate, analyze, and create without restrictive inhibitions. The coping behavior is *intellectuality*, that is, the ability to think clearly and logically even in emotionally loaded situations.

3. *Means–end symbolization*. This is the ability to analyze cause-and-effect relationships and to anticipate outcomes and consider alternatives. The coping behavior is *logical analysis*, or thoughtful, careful, systematic analysis of causal factors, personal and otherwise, in situations. Logical analysis is seen as opposed to the *defensive* behavior of *rationalization*, or looking for *acceptable causes or explanations*.

4. *Selective awareness*. This is the ability to focus attention. The coping behavior is *concentration*—the ability to focus attention even on unpleasant and disturbing content. It is opposed to *denial*, which is the refusal to deal with threatening thoughts.

5. *Sensitivity*. This is the ability to recognize and understand another's feelings even when partially or subtly expressed. The coping behavior is *empathy*, the ability to assume another's frame of reference. It is opposed to *projection*, or attributing one's own denied feelings on others.

6. *Delayed response*. This is the ability to hold up on decisions or responses. The coping behavior is *tolerance of ambiguity*, or the ability to handle cognitively or affectively complex or ambivalent situations. It is the ability to make qualified judgments, to think in *both–and* rather than *either–or* terms in complicated situations or where sufficient evidence is unavailable.

7. *Time reversal*. This is the ability to recall or recapture experiences, feelings, or ideas from the past. The coping behavior is *playfulness*, the ability to use the richness and flexibility of past experiences to enjoy and profit from immediate situations.

8. *Impulse diversion*. This is the ability to modify the aim or object of an impulse. The coping behavior is *sublimation*, or the finding of alternative channels and socially acceptable means for satisfying inner needs. It is opposed to the defense behavior of *displacement*, which attempts to repress unacceptable impulses, but which results in their being displaced in *unconscious* ways to other situations.

9. *Impulse transformation.* This is the ability to use the energy from inner needs and impulses in appropriate ways through disguising it through symbolization as an opposite. The coping behavior is *substitution,* or using energy from primitive impulses in a secure manner so that socialized opposites are evident.

10. *Impulse restraint.* This is the ability to control impulses by inhibiting their expression. The coping behavior is *suppression,* that is, holding an impulse in abeyance until it can be expressed at the proper time and place in an appropriate way. This is opposed to the defense of *repression,* or the total inhibition of the feeling or idea.

STABILIZATION STAGE (ages fifty to sixty-five)

The *Stabilization stage* is that stage of development in which an already high level of functioning is continued and refined. This stage is not just a maintaining of the status quo or a digging in to hold previous gains. Rather the term "stabilization" connotes the presence of a vibrant, dynamic, ongoing equilibrium in which controlled growth continues to enhance the behavior of the individual. The age limit of sixty-five is rather arbitrarily set for this stage, largely because it is a cultural norm for retirement from active pursuits. There is no evidence that for many people the Stabilization stage cannot continue well into the seventies or even beyond.

Social Roles of the Stabilization Stage. The social roles of the Stabilization period remain relatively similar to the Realization stage. The Stabilization roles may offer relatively more protection or insulation from *feedback.* More deference and submissiveness may be given rather than earned during this period. There is a danger of failing to be stimulated by conflicting and competing ideas and attitudes during this period.

Developmental Tasks of the Stabilization Stage. Several unique developmental tasks can be seen for this stage. They can be discussed under the following headings:

1. *Development of awareness of the inevitability of change.* This task is particularly relevant to the Stabilization stage because skills, beliefs, and attitudes that have had proven value for past functioning may tend to form a rigid residual of a non-utilitarian nature as environmental conditions change.

2. *Developing and maintaining the attitudes of tentativeness as opposed to dogmatism.* This is essentially keeping a belief system that is rich and meaningful but that is still *open.*

3. *Developing and maintaining an attitude of broad intellectual curiosity.* In the Stabilization stage, there is some danger of narrowing and closing out interests. The effective Stabilizer is able to broaden and extend interests rather than narrow them.

4. *Developing attitudes of realistic idealism.* This is an important factor in avoiding the involutional tendencies toward depressive reaction and disillusionment. It combines the understanding of experience with mature belief in the future.

5. *Development of a time perspective in observing and evaluating problems that goes beyond the limits of one's own life span.* At this stage, the Stabilizer must be able to make plans, adopt values, and perceive relationships that transcend his own life expectancy. Failure to accomplish this leads to a progressively debilitating attitude of the fruitlessness and meaninglessness of one's remaining life.

Coping Behaviors of the Stabilization Stage.   Coping behaviors for this stage include:

1. *Change-oriented behaviors.* These include *adaptability, flexibility,* and *open-mindedness.*

2. *Value-relevant behaviors of a self-transcending nature.* At this stage, striving for striving's sake tends to give way to a motivational system based on self-transcending values.

3. *Sensitivity behaviors.* These are behaviors that help an individual be aware of and able to modify his subsequent behaviors on the basis of "feedback" regarding the reactions that others have to him.

EXAMINATION STAGE (ages sixty-five plus)

Examination as a final life stage is characterized by reflection, active disengagement from events, and playing roles of observer and mentor rather than participant and actor. The danger in this stage is *isolation* and *detachment,* which will deprive life of its sense of meaning and reality.

Social Roles of the Examination Stage.   The new social roles of being a retired person, a non-producer, and no longer having authority and responsibility roles are major changes in social interactions. They can produce devastating consequences in self-perception.

TABLE 4–1

Principal Developmental Tasks and
Coping Behaviors by Life Stages

Life Stages	Social Roles	Developmental Tasks	Coping Behaviors
Examination (65+ years)	Retirement roles Non-worker roles Non-authority roles	Learning to cope with death, cope with retirement, affiliate with peers, cope with reduced physical vigor, cope with changed living conditions, use leisure time, care for the aging body	Affiliative behaviors Productive leisure time behaviors Personal enhancement behaviors
Stabilization (50– 65 years)	Leadership, helping, managing, creative accomplishments, authority, prestige roles	Ego-Integrity: Learning to be aware of change, have attitude of tentativeness, develop broad intellectual curiosity, develop realistic idealism, develop time perspective	Change-oriented behaviors Value-relevant behaviors Sensitivity behaviors
Realization (30– 50 years)	Leadership, helping, creative, accomplishment roles	Ego-Integrity: Learning to be inner-directed, be interdependent, handle cognitive dissonance, or be flexible and effective emotionally, develop creative thought processes, develop effective problem-solving techniques	Objectivity, intellectuality, logical analysis, concentration, empathy, tolerance of ambiguity, playfulness, sublimation, substitution, suppression behaviors
Exploration Young Adulthood (20–30 years)	Marriage roles Career roles	Intimacy and Commitment; Generativity: Learning to commit self to goals, career, partner; be adequate parent; give unilaterally	Sexual behaviors Risk-taking behaviors Value-consistent behaviors
Later Adolescence (15–19 years)	Peer roles Heterosexual roles	Identity as a Worker: Learning to move from group to individual relationship, achieve emotional autonomy, produce in work situations	Reciprocal behaviors Cooperating behaviors Mutuality behaviors

TABLE 4–1 (Continued)

Life Stages	Social Roles	Developmental Tasks	Coping Behaviors
Organization Early Adolescence (12–14 years)	Peer roles Heterosexual roles	Identity Development: Learning to be masculine or feminine, belong in various relationships, control impulses, be positive toward work, study, organize time, develop relevant value hierarchy	Social behaviors Sex-appropriate behaviors Achievement-oriented behaviors
Later Childhood (6–12 years)	Student, helper, big brother, or big sister roles	Initiative-Industry: Learning to read and calculate, value self and be valued, delay gratification, control emotional reactions, deal with abstract concepts, give self to others, formulate values	Environmental mastering behaviors Value-relevant behaviors Work-relevant behaviors
Early Childhood (3–6 years)	Sibling, playmate, sex-appropriate roles	Autonomy; Sense of Separateness: Developing sense of self, sense of mutuality, realistic concepts of world. Learning to be a boy or girl, manage aggression and frustration, follow verbal instructions, pay attention, become independent	Cooperative behaviors Control behaviors Substitution behaviors
Infancy (birth–3 years)	Love-object roles; receiving and pleasing	Trust: Learning to eat solid food and feed self, control elimination, manipulate objects, walk, explore immediate environment, communicate	Approaching behaviors Receiving behaviors Accepting behaviors

Developmental Tasks of the Examination Stage. Havighurst talks of this period in the following terms. He says it is:

> . . . a period of learning, rather than a period when learning is past. It is a period of facing new and unresolved problems rather than a period of floating gently on the surface of familiar solutions to familiar problems. [11, p. 442.]

Developmental tasks for this period, according to Havighurst (11), include:

1. Learning to cope with death of spouse and friends
2. Learning to cope with retirement and reduced income
3. Learning to affiliate within an age group of elders
4. Learning to cope with reduced physical vigor
5. Learning to cope with changed living arrangements
6. Learning to develop new social roles that will bring recognition and respect
7. Learning to use new leisure time in constructive, satisfying ways
8. Learning to care for an aging body

Coping Behaviors of the Examination Stage. The coping behaviors of this stage include:

1. *Affiliative behaviors.* These include making new friends and maintaining old friendships and affiliations in spite of changed status.

2. *Productive leisure time behaviors.* These activities may be hobbies, volunteer work, or even recreation, but they are seen as personally and socially worthwhile by the individual. They may involve increased interest in church, civic, and community events.

3. *Personal enhancement behaviors.* These include physical grooming, learning new skills, and social accomplishments.

The developmental scheme presented in this chapter is summarized in Table 4–1.

REFERENCES

1. ALLPORT, G. *Pattern and growth in personality.* New York: Holt, Rinehart, 1963.
2. BERNARD, H. W. *Human development in western culture.* Boston: Allyn & Bacon, 2d ed., 1968.
3. BRAMMER, L. M., & SHOSTROM, E. L. *Therapeutic psychology: fundamentals of counseling and psychotherapy.* Englewood Cliffs, N.J.: Prentice-Hall, 2d ed., 1968.
4. BRUNER, J. S. The course of cognitive growth. *Amer. Psychologist,* 1964, 19:1–15.

5. BUEHLER, CHARLOTTE. *Der menschliche lebenslauf als psychologisches problem.* Leipzig: Hirzel, 1933.
6. COLEMAN, J. S. *The adolescent society.* New York: Free Press of Glencoe, 1962.
7. ERIKSON, E. H. *Childhood and society.* New York: Norton, 1950.
8. GONYEA, G. G. Job perceptions in relation to vocational preference. *J. counsel. Psychol.,* 1963, 10:20–27.
9. HARLOW, H. F., & HARLOW, MARGARET K. Social deprivation in monkeys. *Sci. Amer.,* 1962, reprint no. 473.
10. HAVIGHURST, R. J. *Developmental tasks and education.* New York: David McKay, 3d ed., 1972.
11. HAVIGHURST, R. J. Social and psychological needs of aging. In L. Gorlow & W. Katkovsky (Eds.), *Readings in the psychology of adjustment.* New York: McGraw-Hill, 1959.
12. HEBB, D. O. *The organization of behavior.* New York: Wiley, 1949.
13. HEISLER, VERA. Toward a process model of psychological health. *J. counsel. Psychol.,* 1961, 11 (1), 59–62.
14. HERON, W. The pathology of boredom. *Sci. Amer.,* 1957, reprint no. 430.
15. JAHODA, MARIE. Toward a social psychology of mental health. In M. J. E. Senn (Ed.), *Symposium on the healthy personality.* New York: Josiah Macy Jr. Foundation, 1950.
16. Kroeber, T. C. The coping functions of the ego mechanisms. In R. White (Ed.), *A study of lives.* New York: Atherton, 1964.
17. LEVINE, L. S. Stimulation in infancy. *Sci. Amer.,* 1960, reprint no. 436.
18. LEVINE, L. S. *Personal and social development: the psychology of effective behavior.* New York: Holt, Rinehart, 1963.
19. MUUSS, R. E. *Theories of adolescence.* New York: Random House, 2d ed., 1968.
20. PIAGET, J. *The moral judgment of the child.* New York: Collier Books, 1962.
21. RIESMAN, D. *The lonely crowd.* New York: Doubleday, 2d ed., 1969.
22. SHOBEN, E. J. Toward a concept of the normal personality. *Amer. Psychologist,* 1957, 12:183–190.
23. SUPER, D. E. *The psychology of careers.* New York: Harper & Row, 1957.

RECOMMENDED READINGS

Some General Approaches to Development

ALLPORT, G. *Pattern and growth in personality.* New York: Holt, Rinehart & Winston, 1963.
BERNARD, H. W. *Human development in western culture.* Boston: Allyn & Bacon, 3d ed., 1970.
BERNARD, H. W. & HUCKINS, W. C. (Eds.), *Readings in human development.* Boston: Allyn & Bacon, 1967.
Daedalus J. Amer. Acad. Arts Sci. "Twelve to Sixteen: Early Adolescence." Fall, 1971.
FLACKS, R. *Youth and social change.* Chicago: Markham, 1971.
GRINDERS, R. E. (Ed.), *Studies in adolescence.* London: Macmillan, 1969.
WINDER, A. E., & ANGUS, D. L. (Eds.), *Adolescence: contemporary studies.* New York: American Book Co., 1968.
WINTER, G. D., & NUSS, E. M. (Eds.), *The young adult.* Glenview, Ill.: Scott Foresman, 1969.

Career Development

BOROW, H., & WRENN, C. G. (Eds.), *Career guidance for a new age*. Boston: Houghton Mifflin, 1973.

OSIPOW, S. *Theories of vocational development*. 2d ed. New York: Appleton-Century-Crofts, 1973.

ZYTOWSKI, D. *Vocational behavior*. New York: Holt, Rinehart & Winston, 1968.

5

MODELS
OF HUMAN
EFFECTIVENESS

The problem of typology in the study of human effectiveness presents considerable difficulty. Any description of traits associated with optimum human development hinges partly at least upon some kind of philosophically derived value system. It is impossible to approach this problem outside the framework of some set of values concerning what is good and true and beautiful in human existence.

When models of effectiveness are based upon actual case studies or descriptions of behavior, they may be a bit more realistic than an "armchair" compendium of what human beings ought to be like. Even here, however, value questions are inescapable. What kinds of criteria can be used to identify people operating at high levels of effectiveness? Should such criteria involve socially determined symbols of success such as wealth or power? Are there characteristics of effectiveness that are independent of cultural values?

Even developing a set of constructs or concepts that can be used to describe high-level human functioning presents problems. Are constructs developed primarily to describe pathological behavior useful in explaining human effectiveness? What, if any, are the polar opposites of constructs like anxiety, defensiveness, self-deception, and so forth? An example of the relatively impoverished state of conceptualization represented in psychological thinking on this problem is Karl Menninger's (9) use of the phrase "weller than well." We simply lack terms and concepts that are descriptive of high-level aspects of human behavior.

In searching out human lives on which to model our conceptions, are the best sources historical personages such as soldiers or politicians? Do we use the biographical materials that have filtered through the hero-worshipping lenses of the culture's history, or do we use contemporary judgments of human lives, and if so whose judgments?

Problems such as these are inherent in each of the several models of human effectiveness described in this chapter. Despite the difficulties involved, developmental counselors do need some kind of relevant basis upon which to conceptualize the upper levels of human functioning. For the most part, the models discussed here were based upon the clinical experience of authors or upon very limited research rather than from large-scale studies.

The models obviously represent to some extent the underlying philosophical and theoretical biases of the model builders. They are offered as a framework around which the counselor can build his own model of the effective human personality.

MASLOW'S SELF-ACTUALIZING PERSON

Abraham Maslow (6) was one of the first American psychologists to become interested in the problem of high-level human functioning. Maslow approached his study of positive functioning with the assumption that man does indeed have an essential nature or set of genetically based tendencies. He viewed these tendencies as giving rise to needs that are on their face *good or neutral, rather than bad.*

Maslow further conceptualized human development as the process through which these basic human tendencies are actualized and full human potentialities fulfilled. He thus saw human personality as basically growing from within, rather than being shaped from without. Psychopathology, on the other hand, is seen largely as the result of frustrating or twisting man's essential nature from without.

Within the value system generated by this approach to human nature, then, anything that contributes to the development of man's inner nature is *good*, while anything that disturbs, blocks, or denies that nature is *bad* or *abnormal*. Maslow described this further when he said:

> This inner nature [of man] is not strong and overpowering and unmistakable like the instincts of animals. It is weak and delicate and subtle and easily overcome by habit, cultural pressure and wrong attitudes toward it. Even though weak, it rarely disappears in the normal person, perhaps not even in the sick person. Even though denied, it persists underground . . . [8, p. 4.]

Maslow (7) postulated the conditions for optimum development or actualization within a theory of "hierarchy of needs." Briefly, Maslow classified human needs into a series of increasingly "higher-level" motivations, each of which emerges as soon as the next lower-level needs have been satisfied. This hierarchy is given below:

1. Physiological needs
2. Safety needs
3. Love needs
4. Esteem needs
5. Self-actualization needs

Since the higher-order needs will emerge only when lower-order needs have been reasonably well satisfied, Maslow points out that the best way to obscure the higher motivations of man is to keep him chronically hungry, insecure, or unloved. Viewing men in such primitive need states will give a warped picture of true human potentialities.

On the other hand, if an individual's developmental history is such that his lower needs are chronically satisfied, his motivations will focus upon the higher-level need of self-actualization, and his inner potentialities will be realized.

Maslow has attempted to study the nature of this self-actualization level of human functioning through the study of biographical materials of a group of contemporary and historical persons who were commonly judged to operate at this high level. From this study, Maslow lists fifteen characteristics of the self-actualized person (6). They are:

1. *Realistic orientation.* Self-actualizers are efficient perceivers of reality and are relatively unthreatened and unfrightened by the unknown. They do not show an overpowering need for certainty, safety, definiteness, and order.

2. *Acceptance of self, others, and the world.* Self-actualizers tend to accept themselves, their fellow human beings, and the natural world without shame, disgust, or hostility.

3. *Spontaneity.* Self-actualizers tend to possess a zest and enthusiasm for living. They are able to capture "peak experiences" of living, and to savor those without being weighed down by conventional cares and responsibilities.

4. *Problem-centeredness, not self-centeredness.* Self-actualizers tend to focus on real problems and solutions. They work effectively and persistently at problem situations. They are not preoccupied with self-pity or inescapable circumstances.

5. *Detachment.* They have an air of detachment and a need for privacy. They have a quality of self-sufficiency, and their interpersonal relationships are not characterized by possessiveness, dependency, and intrusiveness.

6. *Autonomy and independence.* They are not overconforming or other-directed. They are not unduly affected by fads or crazes of the moment. They are relatively unaffected by either flattery or criticism.

7. *Appreciation.* They have a wholesome, fresh appreciation for people and things. They are not rigid or stereotyped in their responses.

8. *Spontaneity of experience.* Most self-actualizers have experienced some sort of deep mystical or "oceanic" experience.

9. *Identification with mankind.* They have a basic feeling of caring and belonging to humanity. They experience genuine sympathy, compassion, and affection for their fellow man.

10. *Deepness of interpersonal relationships.* They share intimate relationships with a few specially loved people. They are selective in the establishment of such close relationships, but also handle more superficial relationships smoothly and effectively.

11. *Democratic values and attitudes.* They show religious, racial, and ethnic acceptance rather than intolerance.

12. *Differentiation of ends and means.* They are able to distinguish between ends and means and pursue ethical ends with firmness and certainty.

13. *Philosophical humor.* They possess a spontaneous, philosophical sense of humor. Their humor is not hostile or degrading to others.

14. *Creativeness.* They are creative, original, and divergent in thinking.

15. *Resistant to conformity.* They are resistant to blind conformity to the culture. They exercise individuality and thoughtful responses to cultural patterns.

The characteristics cited above are obviously not mutually exclusive or even unrelated. They were obtained from an examination of

subjectively selected personal histories. Nevertheless, these characteristics form a useful basis for conceptualizing the product of high levels
of human development.

ALLPORT'S MATURE PERSONALITY

Gordon Allport (1), in attempting to describe the nature of
psychological maturity, listed six major characteristics. Allport's list is
not unrelated to the descriptions given by Maslow, but differs enough
to warrant separate examination. Allport's list is as follows:

1. *Extension of self.* The mature person is able to extend his concept
of self through feelings of caring and belonging to other individuals,
causes, and institutions and even to mankind itself. Through this
process of self-extension, the welfare of others becomes as important
as the welfare of self. Out of this extension comes the commitment to
participate actively in significant human causes and affairs. The
mature person is able *to participate, to identify,* and *to strive* for
purposes larger than himself.

2. *Warm relating of self to others.* The mature person is capable of
intimacy and love. His interpersonal relationships are characterized by
empathy and *compassion,* rather than possessiveness and hostility. The
mature person is able to *give love,* while the immature person wants to
be loved. The mature person gives love rather than exchanges it.

3. *Emotional security.* For the mature personality, emotional
security arises out of acceptance of self. This security allows him to
tolerate frustration and avoid overreaction to disturbing, but relatively
inconsequential, situations. This security is reflected in self-control and
the ability to defer gratifications or adjust to the inevitable. With
emotional security, the mature person can maintain a realistic outlook
and control the flow of emotional impulses.

4. *Realistic perceptions, skills, and assignments.* The mature person
is able to function efficiently in the areas of perception and cognition.
He is capable of accurate and realistic intellectual behavior. He also
has a repertory of effective problem-solving skills and techniques. He
is able to focus his energies in the accomplishment of appropriate
tasks. He is independent and self-sufficient.

5. *Self-objectification, insight, and humor.* The mature personality
has realistic self-insight. He understands himself. He has a corresponding sense of humor. He is able to laugh at himself. These characteris-

tics are a result of his ability to put himself in perspective without distortion. He can put his own characteristics in an objective perspective and laugh at those elements that are absurd or incongruous.

6. *A unifying philosophy of life.* The mature personality has worked out some type of unifying approach to life that gives consistency and meaning to his behavior. He has developed out of this approach a personally relevant value system and a conscience or guide to behavior that helps him to implement his values. This unifying approach to life may or may not take the form of what is usually called a religious orientation.

Allport thus described the mature personality as a reaching out, socially concerned type of person. He is active, effective, and value-oriented.

ROGERS' FULLY FUNCTIONING PERSON

Carl Rogers (10) has approached the construct of effective human personality out of his own theoretical orientation and clinical experience. He conceptualizes particularly the "fully functioning person" as the fully successful patient in client-centered therapy.

Rogers lists three major characteristics of this hypothetical personality:

1. This person would be open to his experiences; that is, he is not defensive or resistant to those aspects of his environment that might produce change. All the aspects of his environment are available to him in the form of accurate, realistic perceptions. There are no built-in barriers that shut out the possibility of fully experiencing his environment.

2. This person will live in an existential way; that is, he experiences life in terms of an ongoing, *becoming* process. He lives in a fluid stream of experience rather than in a rigid or stereotyped way. There is an absence of tight organization or imposed structure.

3. This person trusts himself. He is willing to do that which "feels right," and finds his feelings a trustworthy guide to behavior. He has the feeling of direction and consistency that flows out of him rather than feeding in from his environment.

Rogers summarizes these three trends in the following way:

> He is more able to experience all of his feelings and is less afraid of any of his feelings; he is his own sifter of evidence from all sources; he is completely

engaged in the process of being and becoming himself, and thus discovers that he is soundly and realistically social; he lives completely in this moment but learns that this is the soundest living for all time. He is a fully functioning organism, and because of the awareness of himself which flows freely in and through his experiences, he is becoming a fully functioning person. [10, p. 192.]

SHOBEN'S NORMAL PERSONALITY

Shoben (11) approaches the question of normality by pointing out that the concept may be defined in a statistical way in which the sheer statistical frequency of occurrence of the behavior is the index of normality, or in a culturally relative way in terms of the manner in which an individual's presumed characteristics or behavior relate to the values of some reference group.

Shoben believes, however, that four kinds of characteristics can be defined independently of either group or statistical norms and that these characteristics are descriptive of normal development in any group or culture. These are:

1. *Willingness to accept the consequences of behavior.* This is the personal responsibility or self-control dimension.

2. *Capacity for interpersonal relationships.* This is the ability of man to function as a social animal.

3. *Obligation to society.* This characteristic involves the ability to identify as a group member and to subscribe to the goals and purposes of the group.

4. *Commitment to ideals and standards.* This represents the ability of the individual to commit himself to some set of values that go beyond himself.

BARRON'S SOUND PERSONALITY

Frank Barron (2) used the concept of "soundness" to study the effective personality. Barron selected a population of university graduate students and had faculty members rate them on a nine-point scale for "all around soundness as a person." This soundness was essentially defined as maturity and effectiveness in interpersonal relationships. Eighty of the rated students were studied by psychologists over a two-day period of intensive testing and interviewing.

The results of this study discriminated between the students rated as sound and less sound on the basis of the following four characteristics:

1. *Effective organization of work.* The highly rated subjects tended to be more *adaptable* and *resourceful* and to have greater *energy* and *resistance to stress.*

2. *Accurate perceptions.* The highly rated group scored higher on tests of perceptual accuracy. They also seemed to have greater *insight and understanding about themselves.*

3. *Ethical integrity.* The higher rated group was described as more *dependable* and to have strong, internalized, moral *principles.*

4. *Adjustment to self and others.* The "sound" group was considered less *defensive, distrustful, and egotistical.* They described themselves as happier.

HEATH'S REASONABLE ADVENTURER

Roy Heath (5) has investigated the problem of typologies in normal personality in one of the more systematic studies available in the literature. Heath followed thirty-six Princeton freshmen through college graduation and ten years beyond. He used regular individual interviews as the primary basis for data collection.

Heath found that the majority of his subjects could be classified into three distinct types on the basis of their interview behavior. Heath assigned letters to these three types.

The *X* type was essentially a *non-committer* who instinctively avoids tangling commitments. He is a *security-seeker* who is motivated by caution and restraint. The *X* type often feels that he could be very successful if he really committed himself but is always afraid to take the risk.

The *Y* type is the *hustler.* He is *active* and *purposeful, aggressive* and *competitive.* He is relatively *insensitive* to others and constantly finds it necessary to reassure himself through new successes. He is a *driven* type of personality. He is *competent but unoriginal.* He is relatively out of contact with his own feelings.

The *Z* type is an *impulsive* and relatively *disorganized* person. He is *spontaneous and likable,* but is often frustrated by his own lack of direction and purpose.

Heath found that a few of his subjects fitted none of these categories. They seemed to function on a different level from the others. Heath called these men the "Reasonable Adventurers." Their characteristics included:

1. Contact between inner and outer selves
2. Initiative coupled with reflection
3. Curiosity coupled with critical thinking
4. Close interpersonal relationships but independence of judgment
5. Tolerance of ambiguity
6. Sense of humor

Heath's evidence, however, suggested that the Reasonable Adventurers were not one discrete subtype, *but that some had developed out of each of the other subgroups.* In other words, X, Y, and Z types were *all potentially capable of becoming Reasonable Adventurers,* given the right kind of developmental climate. Thus, his Reasonable Adventurer is not merely a paragon of philosophically conceptualized virtues, but a striving human being who achieves a high level of functioning through his own unique pattern of individual development.

THE EFFECTIVE PERSONALITY

An attempt to synthesize some of the ideas presented in the six models discussed above seems to be in order. Most of these descriptions of optimum human functioning utilized essentially "armchaired," philosophically derived judgments about human behavior. From one standpoint, they could be conceived as more nearly representing idealized paragons of virtue than flesh-and-blood human beings. In thinking through the concept of the "Effective Personality" as opposed to some of the more highly idealized conceptualizations, five sets of characteristics seem particularly relevant. These clusters of behaviors may be categorized as follows.

1. *Consistency.* The effective person is reasonably consistent in his behavior both within social roles through time and across social roles. This element of consistency is based upon a well-integrated sense of personal identity that gives direction and unity to behavior.

2. *Commitment.* The effective person is able to commit himself to goals and purposes. He is able to take reasonable, calculated risks of psychological, economic, and physical kinds in order to move toward desired goals. He is able, on occasion, to commit himself to *self-transcending* values that give meaning and purpose to his life and so protect him from "existential despair" or obsessive fear of death.

3. *Control.* The effective person is able to control his emotional impulses and responses. He is able to accept the unalterable and

inevitable without emotional responses that are inappropriate in nature or intensity. He is particularly able to cope with *frustration, ambiguity,* and *hostility* without such emotional responses.

4. *Competence.* The effective person has available a wide range of coping behaviors. He is an effective problem-solver. He has a repertory of effective interpersonal understandings for dealing with his environment in both vocational and avocational roles. He is able to *master* environment within the limits of the possibilities available to him.

5. *Creativity.* The effective person is capable of thinking in original and divergent ways. He does not stifle ideas and impulses that are unconventional or novel. Perceptually, he is sensitive to relationships and distinctions that are hidden from many people because they may be incongruent with fixed expectations. His thought processes are fluent and he is deeply in touch with his own feelings.

Perhaps each of these five characteristics could be best explained by reference to an actual life.

Consistency is essentially the quality that gives unity to an individual's life style. Chesterton (4), a biographer of Leo Tolstoy, for example, pointed to this quality in the life of the great Russian novelist. He described Tolstoy as a person whose attitude toward life was so entirely his own that his attitude would be safely predicted on almost any topic. This is of course an extreme case in point.

Another illustration from the life of Albert Einstein shows the same kind of unity. A recent character sketch of Einstein by a personal acquaintance describes him in this way:

> He was the only person I knew who had come to terms with himself and the world around him. He knew what he wanted and he wanted only this: to understand within his limits as a human being the nature of the universe and the logic and simplicity of its functioning.
>
> To do his work he needed only a pencil and a pad of paper. Material things meant nothing to him. I never knew him to carry money because he never had any use for it.
>
> He was devoid of the human feelings that can cause trouble and misery. In the twenty-three years of our friendship, I never saw him show vanity, bitterness, anger, resentment or personal ambition. [3, p. 46.]

The characteristic of reducing life to a relatively few basic terms and of living consistently with these seems to be one important aspect of human effectiveness.

Commitment, too, is an essential aspect of effectiveness. Allport (1) cites the life of polar explorer Roald Amundson as an outstanding example of deep, lifelong commitment. Amundson had experienced one overwhelming motivation from the age of fifteen to the end of his life. His great goal of reaching the South Pole was finally accomplished, and he reached the pinnacle of success. Even after this, however, he persisted in overcoming great difficulties to fly over the North Pole, and finally lost his life in a rescue expedition.

His life seems to illustrate the element of very deep and enduring commitment to goals. Such commitment allows the individual to persist despite great physical and psychological risks and discomforts. Interestingly, it does not seem to be greatly affected by extremes of either success or failure.

Control is a third central factor in human effectiveness. A striking example of this factor at work is recorded in the circumstances that followed the assassination of President Kennedy. Mrs. Kennedy, although obviously overwhelmed by personal grief, was compelled to play the leading role in the solemn drama that is represented in the funeral of a great world leader.

Her role in this drama called for tremendous self-control in submerging personal feelings to conform to the needs of a grieving nation and world. She was able to react in this moment of personal tragedy with great dignity and sensitivity.

It is important to distinguish between the kind of control illustrated here and the pseudo-control seen in many disturbed individuals. The control involved in human effectiveness is not a turning away from feelings and emotions or a repression of their true depth. It is rather the result of an inner strength and conviction that one is adequate to meet even the most tragic circumstances of life.

Competence is the fourth element in human effectiveness. White (15) points out that competence, or at least the search for it, is characteristic of human development from early childhood. An example of outstanding human competence evident at even a relatively early age is seen in the character sketch discussed below.

In 1898, Steevens, a British journalist, met the then twenty-three-year-old Winston Churchill. Steevens was so impressed by this casual meeting that he wrote a sketch of Churchill that predicted the latter's world renown and described him in these words:

> In years he is a boy; in temperament he is also a boy; but in intention, in deliberate plan, purpose, adaptation of means to ends, he is already a man. . . . Mr. Churchill is a man with ambitions fixed, with the steps toward their attainment clearly defined, with a precocious, almost uncanny judgment as to the efficacy of the means to the end. [12, p. 63.]

Competence then is ability in defining and solving problems in making decisions and choices, and in pushing out to master situations within the outer limits of one's possibilities.

The final element of effectiveness is *creativity*. Creativity is necessarily harder to describe than the other factors listed. Perhaps Louis Sullivan, the great American architect, described the creative impulse most clearly when he said:

> There exists in us the . . . power to make something . . . the . . . desire to image ourselves forth. But intellect has long held repressive sway. . . . We have been "practical" so long that what we have imaged is relatively . . . untrue to man's oneness. Modern man is a traitor to himself in suppressing one-half of himself . . . [14, p. 167.]

Edward Albee, the American playwright, in an interview regarding his own creative process described it in these terms:

> How does it happen? I usually discover that I have started thinking about an idea which I know is going to be a play. This process may take anywhere from six months to two and a half years, and during that period I don't think about the play very much except that I realize from time to time that I *have* been thinking about it, and when the characters who are going to be in the play begin to take shape, I improvise with them.
>
> I try to let the unconscious do as much work as possible, since I find that's the more efficient part of my mind. [13, p. 63.]

Much that is involved in creativity thus seems to be an intactness of personality, an ability to be in touch with feelings and impulses—letting the unconscious do part of the work in Albee's terms.

Human effectiveness as seen here, then, is a product of a number of factors. It may be helpful for the counselor to conceptualize these in terms of the constructs provided here or to group them in ways that have more meaning for him.

The important fact is that the counselor devoted to facilitating human effectiveness will have some kind of typology available for conceptualizing its end points.

REFERENCES

1. ALLPORT, G. W. *Pattern and growth in personality.* New York: Holt, Rinehart and Winston, 1963.
2. BARRON, F. Personal soundness in university graduate students. *Publications in Personality Assessment and Research.* No. 1. Berkeley: University of California Press, 1954.

3. BUCKLEY, T., with BLANK, J. Einstein: an intimate memoir. *Harper's*, September, 1964, 43–48.
4. CHESTERTON, G. K., *et al. Leo Tolstoy.* London: Hodder & Stoughton, 1903.
5. HEATH, S. R. *The reasonable adventurer.* Pittsburgh: University of Pittsburgh Press, 1964.
6. MASLOW, A. H. *Motivation and personality.* New York: Harper & Row, 2nd ed., 1970.
7. MASLOW, A. H. A theory of human motivation. In L. Gorlow & W. Katkowsky (Eds.), *Readings in the psychology of adjustment.* New York: McGraw-Hill, 1959.
8. MASLOW, A. H. *Toward a psychology of being.* Princeton, N.J.: Van Nostrand, 2nd ed., 1968.
9. MENNINGER, K. *The vital balance.* New York: Basic Books, 1964.
10. ROGERS, C. R. Toward becoming a fully functioning person. In A. W. Combs (Ed.), *Perceiving, behaving, becoming.* Washington, D.C.: Yearbook Association for Supervision and Curriculum Development, 1962.
11. SHOBEN, C. J. Toward a concept of the normal personality. *Amer. Psychologist,* 1957, 12:183–190.
12. STEEVENS, G. W. When Churchill was twenty-three. Reprinted in *Atlantic,* March, 1965, 63–64.
13. STEWART, R. S. John Gielgud and Edward Albee talk about the theater. *Atlantic,* April, 1965, 61–68.
14. SULLIVAN, L. *Kindergarten chats and other writings.* New York: Wittenborn, Schultz, 1947.
15. WHITE, R. Competence and the psychosexual stages of development. *Nebraska Symposium on Motivation.* Lincoln: University of Nebraska Press, 1960.

RECOMMENDED READINGS

ALLPORT, G. W. *Becoming: basic considerations for a psychology of personality.* New Haven: Yale University Press, 1955.
BLOCK, J. Ego identity, role, variability and adjustment. *J. consult. Psychol.,* 1961, 25 (5), 392–397.
COMBS, A. W. A perceptual view of the adequate personality. In A. W. Combs (Ed.), *Perceiving, behaving, becoming.* Washington, D.C.: Yearbook Association for Supervision and Curriculum Development, 1962.
DUNKLEBERGER, C., & TYLER, LEONA. Interest stability and personality traits. *J. counsel. Psychol.,* 1961, 8 (1), 70–74.
HEATH, S. R. The reasonable adventurer and others. *J. counsel. Psychol.,* 1959, 6 (1), 3–14.
MASLOW, A. H. Some basic propositions of a growth and self actualization psychology. In A. W. Combs (Ed.), *Perceiving, behaving, becoming.* Washington, D.C.: Yearbook Association for Supervision and Curriculum Development, 1962.
ROGERS, C. R. *On becoming a person.* Boston: Houghton Mifflin, 1961.
SEEMAN, J. Toward a concept of personality integration. *Amer. Psychologist,* 1959, 14 (10), 633–637.
WRENN, R. H., & RUIZ, R. A. *Normal personality: issues and insights.* Belmont, Calif.: Wadsworth Publishing Co., 1970

6

THE COUNSELOR
AS A BEHAVIORAL
SCIENTIST

The developmental counselor is by necessity a behavioral scientist in the broadest sense of the term. The behavioral sciences are those disciplines that center around behavior as a primary source of data. They include sociology, psychology, anthropology, economics, and political science as well as other newer disciplines. They share in common the goal of understanding human behavior in all its contexts. Man is a social animal who develops within the context of a society through which he derives his humanity. Human development is impossible to understand or to facilitate without consideration of the social forces with which the developing human being interacts.

The individual and social forces that interact to produce human behavior are varied and complex. They do not confine themselves to convenient limits arbitrarily established within a single discipline. The developmental counselor is interested in *problems,* not in *disciplines.* He must be prepared to seek the knowledge needed to solve problems wherever and however that knowledge is organized. In this sense, he seeks an *interdisciplinary* approach to the problem of human development.

The fact that most such problems do cut across disciplines is rather obvious. The problem of juvenile delinquency, for example, is one that interests anthropology, psychology, psychiatry, education, sociology, political science, and jurisprudence. The problems of human learning, socialization, or acculturation are of concern to education, psychology, anthropology, and sociology. The impact of social change on human behavior and development is a concern of sociology, anthropology, social psychology, education, economics, history, and political science.

For the developmental counselor to attempt to isolate himself within the boundaries of any of these disciplines to the exclusion of relevant knowledge organized within another is obviously self-defeating.

The counselor is a behavioral scientist for still another reason, however. Perhaps the most important contribution that the behavioral sciences can confer upon the developmental counselor is not a body of facts, but a set of *attitudes*. The most important single distinguishing characteristic of the behavioral scientist is his willingness to look at all forms of human behavior, human institutions, and human interaction as *phenomena* that can be studied and understood. Most human beings are incapable of bringing this kind of attitude to many human problems. To them, behavior is too often frightening, shocking, threatening, or irrational. It is consequently incomprehensible and unacceptable. The behavioral scientist is one who is able to view human behavior, including his own, as relevant, potentially understandable, and inevitably interesting.

One note of caution should be sounded as the counselor looks at the behavioral sciences. Much of the research in the behavioral sciences is highly specific and highly tentative. The counselor looks not so much for solutions to problems, but for approaches, methods, and perspectives that will enable him to ask more fruitful questions in more appropriate ways as he goes about the task of defining and investigating his own problems.

A number of behavioral science disciplines have organized knowledge of social and behavioral processes that influences development. The developmental counselor needs an understanding in depth of the relevant contributions of these disciplines. Obviously, such a level of understanding cannot be obtained within the context of a book such as this. Instead, this chapter deals with a few relevant topics within several such disciplines that may serve as examples of possible contributions. The bibliography at the end of this chapter is intended to provide a vehicle by which the reader may enter the literature of these disciplines to deepen his own understanding of their contributions.

SOCIOLOGY AND COUNSELING

Sociology is one of the social sciences whose aim is to discover the basic structure of human society, to identify the factors that influence group interaction, and to learn the conditions that control social life (3). Sociology, like other behavioral sciences, is only at the very outer edges of its quest for knowledge.

A great many areas of sociology are of relevance to developmental counseling. This section will discuss briefly six such topics that may serve as samples of the knowledge that can be gleaned from this discipline. These include the study of *social organization, socialization, primary groups, reference groups, social stratification,* and *population and ecology.*

Social Organization

One of the basic premises of sociology is that people's behavior is largely determined by their social interactions, that is, their relationships as individuals and as group members. Social organization refers to stable or patterned relationships between individuals and groups (3). One of the inevitable outcomes of social organization is *social control.* As patterns of social organization such as family, community, profession, and other formalized groups or institutions put people in contact, they tend to become interdependent; that is, the behavior of one person tends to exert increasingly significant effects upon the life of another.

As this interdependency grows, methods are correspondingly developed that will tend to protect the interests of interdependent individuals or groups. These methods may take the form of systematic and overt controls such as legal obligations; they may be relatively loosely structured expectations for behavior expressed in mores and customs; or they may be quite subtle forms of control exerted through conditioning of attitudes, interests, and values.

The developmental counselor needs to be very much aware of the patterns of social organization within which the growing human being interacts. He needs to understand how the patterns and purposes of units exercising social control over the individual merge or conflict in their impact upon him. For example, the counselor needs to understand how social control processes at work in the family, the school, the peer group, and the neighborhood reinforce or conflict with each other, and how the individual copes with their influences.

Merton (19) examines the question of the impact of social structure on the individual and the methods of adaptations through which the individual copes with social control phenomena. Merton proposes that there are five general means by which the individual can cope. These are:

1. *Conformity.* This is the most common means of coping in a stable society. It represents both conformity to the goals of society and the institutionalized means that the society recognizes as appropriate for reaching these goals. Conformity is a strategy that the individual may use with varying effect. It may be useful and adaptive or may become rigid and stultifying in terms of the individual's development.

2. *Innovation.* Innovation usually consists of incorporating societal values, but using divergent methods for reaching them. These may include methodologies on which the society frowns in a moralistic sense, or may simply be those that are original and divergent in concept. The innovator may be a high risk-taker who operates on the basis that the end justifies the means.

3. *Ritualism.* This strategy involves the scaling down of lofty cultural goals to the point where the individual's aspirations can be satisfied. The counselor who is engaged in "downgrading" student aspirations may be involved in a kind of ritualistic phenomenon. The individual still functions within institutionalized norms but accepts lower-level satisfactions. An example is the boy who gives up being a physician to enter medical technology. In terms of his philosophic approach to life, the ritualist is a low risk-taker who plays it safe.

4. *Retreatism.* The retreatist is the person who internalizes social goals and methodologies but who finds the path to those goals irrevocably blocked. The retreatist abandons the struggle although not the goals. He may tend to daydream about that "one lucky break" needed for success. He risks little and competes little.

5. *Rebellion.* Rebellion is the form of adaptation in which both the goals and methods of the social organization are rejected. The rebel seeks to destroy the old and build a new social structure. The true rebel rejects the whole existing social schema. He is active and a high risk-taker. He may have great capacity for organizing and leading

opposition to the social organization. The delinquent gang leader or the political extremist may use this strategy.

Merton hypothesizes that the nature of social structure makes pressures for deviant behavior or "anomie" inevitable among elements who cannot resolve goal-blocking frustration through conformity. The counselor needs to be sensitive to the strategies people use in coping with social control.

Socialization

The process by which social control is exerted upon new members of social organizations is called socialization. From the standpoint of social groups, socialization is the process through which the values and purposes of the group are transmitted to the individual, and he is fitted into the pattern of social organization (6). Socialization occurs through social relationships and is a function of social interaction.

From the standpoint of the developing individual, socialization has a somewhat ambivalent connotation. As Elkins (6) points out, socialization does not typically deal with the uniqueness of individuals. Socialization tends to focus less on individualization than on those aspects of development that concern the adaptations and adjustment *to* the culture or society. Socialization processes typically act on the individual primarily to further the goals of the group rather than to further the development of the individual.

In another sense, however, as Broom and Selznick (3) point out, socialization humanizes the individual organism and makes possible the potentialities for personal growth and development. The same socialization processes that represent the forces of social control and conformity are also the forces that give rise to those social products that we refer to as *a self; a sense of personal identity;* and a set of *individual ideals, values, and aspirations.* The person who is totally unsocialized is also *directionless* and *valueless.* Examples of such people are individuals who are called "psychopaths." Among other characteristics, these individuals show flattened emotional reactions of either positive or negative feelings. They are incapable of following through on long-term goals or aspirations. They have difficulty establishing any kind of permanent interpersonal relationships (17).

Socialization thus regulates behavior, but also sets the context within which individuality, self-awareness, and identity can develop. A society becomes at once a vehicle for enhancing individuals' development and a prison for encapsulating it. It is because of this two-edged nature of socialization processes that an understanding of sociology is so important to the developmental counselor.

The developmental counselor must have a thorough understanding of the nature of social control and socialization processes operating in the lives of clients. One of the most important of these understandings is that socialization is by no means a unitary process exerted in a simple way in the life of a human being. Socialization processes represent a whole series of different and differing social forces operating from various groups and institutions to which the individual relates.

In a pluralistic society such as ours, many types of socialization processes are at work. Socialization processes exerted upon a child may stem from family, school, church, neighborhood, ethnic group, peer group, and so forth. When these socialization processes represent conflicting and irreconcilable objectives and values, it is difficult for the child to experience any real sense of personal identity.

In a society characterized by what Merton and Barber (20) call "sociological ambivalence," the socialization process that attempts to impart to the individual a set of incompatible attitudes, values, and aspirations may be essentially neurosis-producing on its impact. Much of the phenomenon that Erikson (7) terms "identity diffusion" may be explained by this factor in our pluralistic and ambivalent society. The child who is simultaneously taught to love and to hate, to compete and to cooperate, to give and to seize is introjecting a set of attitudes that bears the seeds of inevitable conflict.

When others view the child's behavior within the context of a single social organization such as the school, they may view his behavior as unsocialized. Instead, he may be reacting to other conflicting socialization processes from family, social class, or peer groups.

The role of the developmental counselor in socialization is a difficult and delicate one. In a sense, as a member of one of the social organizations exerting social control in the life of a developing individual, the counselor is a part of one of the socialization processes acting on him.

The developmental counselor is a unique component in the socialization process in many ways, however. His *primary* commitment is to *individual* growth and development rather than to the facilitation of *institutional ends for their own sake.* The developmental counselor is particularly concerned with facilitation of those socialization

processes that contribute to the development of identity, self-awareness, value formation, and aspiration levels. These socialization factors
can never be separated completely from those that lead to conformity,
mediocrity, and other-directedness. The developmental counselor is
not interested in facilitating conformity for conformity's sake. He is
instead interested in helping the individual become aware of all the
socialization processes that are at work in his life and to learn to gauge
the probable effects of these processes upon his future growth and
development.

Too often, approaches to the effects of socialization have represented the most naïve kind of either–or thinking. Approaches to
personality development based on psychoanalytic principles have
often tended to stress the anxiety-producing and debilitating effects of
socialization. Psychologists such as Mowrer (22) on the other hand
have rejected these hypotheses and have conceptualized the disturbed
personality as the undersocialized individual.

A more sophisticated approach than either of these would seem to
be one that views socialization processes as extremely complex forces
that have the capacity to exert powerful influences on the lives of
developing individuals in many and diverse directions. The developmental counselor is not concerned with helping the individual to
adjust to or to resist those forces, but rather to learn to harness them in
ways that will bring about optimal personal development in terms of a
personal value system derived in the humanizing context of an open
and pluralistic society.

Primary Groups

Primary groups are those groups in which an individual experiences
deeply personal, face-to-face contacts and relationships. These include
the family, play groups, neighborhood groups, classroom groups, or
church groups. Many of the early socialization experiences of the child
occur in such primary groups. These groups are extremely important
in laying down the bases for future development. Developmental tasks
are met within the context of these groups and under rules laid down
by them.

Primary groups play particularly important functions in development in two ways. First, primary groups supply the affiliations and
relationships within which the child builds his concepts of self and
others. Here, if at all, he experiences feelings of security, belonging,

worthwhileness, and acceptance. If primary groups do not furnish affection, nurturance, and support, the child will not build needed security and self-esteem, and will not be able to develop from a homeostatic base.

Primary groups also play a key role in transmitting social control. Since the primary group possesses the capacity for extending or withholding affection, approval, and support to the child, it exercises great control over his behavior. The ways in which this control is exercised constitute important determinants of development.

The developmental counselor needs to understand the nature and organization of the primary groups of which the client is a member. The counselor needs to understand the methods by which control is exercised within these groups and the ends toward which the control is directed.

Understanding the nature of a client's primary group experiences is important for the counselor also because these experiences will largely shape the client's expectations of the primary group experience represented by the counseling relationship itself. Clients who have experienced rejecting or authoritarian relationships in other primary groups may well approach the counseling relationship with similar expectations. Those who have experienced supportive and dependent relationships in such groups may expect similar relationships in counseling.

Reference Groups

Reference groups constitute another important aspect of the group life of an individual. Reference groups are those groups to which an individual relates himself or aspires to relate himself (26). These groups may not necessarily be membership groups or primary groups. Reference groups may be large groups and may have considerable social distance from any membership group to which the individual actually belongs. They may, for example, be represented by political parties, religious groups, socioeconomic classes, racial or ethnic groups, occupational or professional groups, or other quite remote groups. The importance of reference groups is that they are a major source of an individual's attitudes, values, and aspirations. They also furnish many of the role models around which the individual will organize his own behavior. As Sherif and Sherif express it, the values or norms of reference groups constitute the major anchorages in relation to which the experience of self-identity is organized (26).

The experience of being or wanting to be a Republican, a Unitarian, a Rotarian, an army officer, a physician, an airlines pilot, or a socialite may be powerful determinants of values, attitudes, and standards of behavior. When individuals are caught in situations where major gaps intervene between the standards and values of *membership groups*, particularly *primary groups* and important reference groups, they are likely to experience *identity diffusion* with resulting anxiety.

Much adolescent behavior becomes understandable when one understands the reference groups to which the adolescent relates himself and the values that these groups are perceived to espouse (26). The delinquent, for example, may be acting in a way that is considered normal and proper within the reference groups of the gang. The gang values are essentially deviant from the standpoint of the society. The individual delinquent's behavior may not necessarily be deviant in terms of the reference group.

The developmental counselor needs to understand how the individual's reference groups are functioning as sources of models and values. He further needs to understand the relationships between the reference groups and the membership groups to which an individual belongs. The task of the developmental counselor is often to help a client to understand the nature of influences operating in his development from various groups, and to resolve or choose between competing influences in terms of their consequences for his future development.

Social Stratification

Social stratification is a confusing but significant factor in understanding development in American society. Traditional American values tend to de-emphasize the importance of social position. The ideal of "from log cabin to White House" or some set of variants of it are cherished myths in modern American folklore. Social differences and distinctions are very real and important factors in our society, however. Their complexity is such that it is difficult to study their precise effects.

Attempts at classification of people according to social strata in our society give somewhat differing results, depending upon the particular method used. When so-called objective methods of classification are used such as *income, cost of home,* and *area of residence,* one picture emerges. Such methods give the picture of wide ranges of differences with a considerable number of fairly discrete groupings possible.

When people are asked to rate their own status or that of others, the picture is one of relatively greater homogeneity and fewer discrete groupings (3).

The important fact for the developmental counselor to understand is that social stratification in many forms is a reality in American society. Social stratification factors are important determinants of developmental processes. The style of life of any individual is drastically influenced by his social-class membership (21). Two rather contrasting points of view regarding the effects of social stratification on development can be seen in a pair of studies that are "must" reading for the developmental counselor.

Hollingshead, in his classic study (11), stresses the inherent inequalities of opportunity that result from social stratification. He points out that the child receives the great majority of his formative experiences during preschool years in the home and neighborhood. During this period, the essential aspects of the class culture to which the family belongs are transmitted. Upper- and middle-class youngsters during this period learn politeness, good manners, acceptable speech, and other behaviors acceptable in the dominant middle-class society. They learn to avoid physical aggression, to select friends carefully, and to avoid children unlike themselves.

Lower-class children, on the other hand, learn that their families are stigmatized in many ways and that they are looked down upon because of family status. They learn physical aggression, profanity, and resistance to institutionalized social controls. The opportunities for self-realization and social mobility for these youngsters are obviously severely limited. Hollingshead highlights the contrast between the stark realities of social-class conditioning and the values implied by the American Dream.

Havighurst, in another classic sociological study, paints a somewhat brighter picture. He says:

> Social class can be seen in either of two ways. It may be regarded as the villain causing conflict and disharmony in society. On the other hand, it may be seen as an inevitable part of social structure. Social classes may be seen as working harmoniously together to get the business of society accomplished and to give some order and stability to social life. [10, p. ix.]

Regardless of which of these views the counselor takes, he must recognize the realities of social stratification and their impact upon developing individuals. Since most counselors are themselves native to the middle class, they particularly need to understand the language and thought patterns as well as the values and attitudes of those who are socially different (24). These differences are many, but three such differences between middle-class and lower-class patterns may serve as particularly striking examples that middle-class-reared counselors are unlikely to understand readily.

1. *The belief in fate* (8). Generations of relatively low-psychological effectiveness—that is, inability to control significant segments of environment—produce this kind of resigned and fatalistic approach to life among many lower-class individuals. The belief that one can take charge of his own life and control important aspects of his environment is only reinforced by some success at doing it. The individual who has neither experienced nor observed effective human behavior is not likely to have great faith in its possibilities. Such an individual instead is likely to respond in the same way as the primitive person who is continually at the mercy of uncontrolled natural phenomena. Such cultures typically show a passive and fatalistic view of existence.

Such an outlook is almost totally incompatible with the goals of planfulness, awareness, and responsible independence that are part of counseling. Until the developmental counselor can recognize, deal with, and eventually change this pattern of passivity, he is unlikely to be effective with lower-class individuals of this type.

2. *Dichotomized stereotypes of masculinity–femininity* (8). One significant pattern of lower-class American life is the sharp polarization of behavior in terms of masculinity–femininity. In lower-class homes and neighborhoods, masculine and feminine social roles tend to be widely separated. Even in recreational activities, relatively little mixing of the sexes is likely to occur. The result of this polarization is the formation of identity structures based upon exaggerated stereotypes of masculinity–femininity. The lower-class boy, for example, is likely to see activities such as scholarship, development of easy social skills, and working at white collar jobs as essentially threatening to his masculinity. Particularly during adolescence when he is preoccupied with proving masculinity, such attitudes may be self-limiting and self-defeating. In an economy and society where the separation of the sexes in terms of both social roles and division of labor is rapidly breaking down, such attitudes are even more costly than ever before.

3. *The need for immediate gratifications.* One of the most common requirements for living in middle-class society is the ability to defer need gratifications. Middle-class children are typically taught to gratify

social, psychological, and biological needs only at socially prescribed times and places and in socially approved ways. Resulting from this kind of socialization process is the development of considerable ability to defer gratifications in planful ways. To the lower-class person who has not experienced this kind of systematic socialization process and whose general level of need satisfaction has been largely marginal, this kind of pattern may not exist. Since much of what middle-class society has defined as success in terms of work, education, and social achievement can only be obtained by rigidly disciplined deferral of all kinds of immediate gratifications, the individual who has not learned to postpone immediate satisfaction for the sake of anticipated rewards is severely limited.

The counselor who is unable to understand and accept individuals whose social-class backgrounds have produced differing patterns of behavior and perception is unlikely to be effective in working with them. The developmental counselor cannot afford to remain culturally encapsulated within the cocoon of his own middle-class origin.

Population and Ecology

Two important phases of sociological research involve the study of population and population changes. Included in this phase of sociology is physical ecology, or the study of spatial shifts and densities of population. Human ecology involving the physical and geographical distribution of population is an important factor in development. Two movements in population are of particular importance in our society. The movement from rural living to urbanization is an extremely important factor. The very rapid decline of economic opportunities in rural areas and small towns has precipitated rapid shifts in population. With these shifts have come violent upheavals in the way of life of those human beings involved. The rural southern black transplanted to Chicago or Detroit, the Puerto Rican farmer moving into New York, or the son of the Appalachian coal miner moving into Atlanta, Memphis, or Pittsburgh all face tremendously difficult adjustments to profoundly different ways of life. The developmental counselor who works with such transplanted populations needs to be acutely aware of the factors of cultural alienation and identity diffusion that accompany such shifts.

Another less-dramatic but equally significant shift in population that is occurring in American society is the move from city to suburb. This trend has produced with it a whole galaxy of social problems. Viewed from a purely ecological standpoint, the move to the suburbs can be seen as the competition of organisms for available resources of space, fresh air, and sunlight. The economically successful in this struggle leave the smoky, congested inner city for the more desirable living space of the suburb. Sociologically, this movement leaves a residue of unsolved social problems within the city.

For the developmental counselor, the primary meaning of this movement is in terms of its impact upon development. For the suburbanite, the movement means development within a highly homogeneous environment where socioeconomic differences are largely eliminated, where a highly unified social organization has the opportunity to exert powerful social controls over almost every phase of the developing individual's life. In this kind of environment, the growth of conformity is just as choking as that of the crabgrass. Schools, churches, neighborhoods, and families all unite in shaping values, attitudes, and aspirations in essentially similar directions. Socialization processes in this kind of environment may be stifling to individuality, spontaneity, and creativity.

Another aspect of suburbia is its relatively matriarchal power structure. The suburban home is likely to be dominated by the ever-present mother, while the commuting father has relatively little contact with his children. Fathers are relatively unavailable as either role models or authority figures.

The developmental counselor in such a setting needs to understand the social dynamics of suburbia and their impact upon developing individuals. Seeley *et al.* (25) have made a sociological study of suburbia that should be of interest to all counselors.

ANTHROPOLOGY AND COUNSELING

Anthropology is a coordinating science that cuts through and across many of the problems studied by other behavioral science disciplines, particularly sociology and psychology. Anthropology itself has a number of important divisions. To many people, anthropology connotes an image drawn largely from two of its most romantic divisions: archaeology and physical anthropology. Although anthropology is concerned with excavating remains of ancient civilizations and with examining the prehistorical antecedents of mankind, anthropologists are also vitally concerned with the problems that confront modern man in highly organized as well as primitive societies.

Kluckhohn in defining modern anthropology makes the following statement:

> Anthropology is the study of the similarities and differences, both biological and behavioral, among the peoples of the world from the dawn of human history to the present day. Anthropology excavates and analyzes the remains of past civilizations (archaeology); describes the evolution and present biological characteristics of our species (physical anthropology); traces the development and spread of customs and technologies over the face of the earth, showing how these forms, arts, faiths and tools satisfy the psychological needs of individuals and keep societies together (cultural anthropology); defines the varieties of human speech and the relationships among the tongues of men (linguistics). [12, p. 319.]

The area of anthropology that has the greatest special significance to the developmental counselor is cultural anthropology. Cultural anthropology as the name implies is centrally concerned with the concept of human culture.

It is anthropology's central commitment to the concept of culture that gives it a coordinating or unifying role within the behavioral sciences. Anthropology looks at man from the broadest possible viewpoint from within the total context of all the human inventions and adaptations that govern his individual behavior.

It is precisely this breadth of approach that makes anthropology so important to the developmental counselor. The most important contribution of anthropology in this regard is the opportunity to observe human behavior across cultures and from outside the usual limitations of cultural inhibitions.

The developmental counselor needs to be able to put on the cross-cultural glasses of the anthropologist in viewing human development. He needs to be able to view developmental processes from outside the values, biases, and inhibitions that are built into these culturally determined developmental processes themselves.

The anthropologist who learns to study cultures systematically and objectively learns to free himself from many of the culturally determined illusions that permeate a particular society. The anthropologist is able to point out, for example, that much of the behavior that, when viewed from within a culture, seems a right, proper, and inevitable part of the nature of man is actually culturally determined and may vary widely in other cultural situations. Perhaps the greatest single contribution of anthropology is the wealth of evidence that it has furnished about the plasticity of human behavior and the importance of cultural factors as behavioral determinants. Such anthropological evidence has done much to help break down the narrowly parochial and smugly self-righteous attitudes that always seem to insulate particular cultures from reality and self-awareness.

The developmental counselor is particularly interested in the results of cross-cultural methods of observation when applied to American society. Two examples of this approach are used here to illustrate the worth of anthropological insights.

Cultural Values

The problem of values is a central one for the developmental counselor. Values form the nucleus around which an individual organizes his own identity. Values are of course largely learned from within the context of the particular culture. Anthropologists are therefore particularly interested in examining value systems within cultures.

Cora Du Bois (5) describes "The Dominant Profile of American Culture" in a special issue of the *American Anthropologist* devoted to examining the United States as anthropologists see it. This entire issue is of great interest to counselors.

In examining American culture, Dr. Du Bois outlines the value premises that are central to the dominant middle-class culture of the United States. She lists three such central propositions or premises on which American values are based. These are:

1. The universe is mechanistically conceived and man is its master.
2. Men are essentially equal.
3. Men are perfectible.

These basic premises about the nature of man and his world then give rise to what Du Bois calls a set of focal values, that is, values around which other more specific values tend to cluster. Three of these focal values are listed:

1. *Materialism.* Material well-being is an important focal value in American culture. This value stems from the premise that man can control and master his environment; that he can create conditions for his own material comfort and well-being. Such a value is central to the operation of our industrial and economic system.

2. *Conformity.* Conforming to modal ways of behaving is a focal value drawn from the premise of equality. Class and cultural

differences exist, but tend to be de-emphasized and devalued. Assimilation in the "melting pot" is the valued norm. Conformity has replaced liberty as a focal value.

3. *Effort-optimism.* This is the focal value of achievement, self-improvement, and hard work. Man is perfectible and therefore *should* perfect himself. The world is controllable and hard work and effort will pay off. Youthfulness, energy, and enthusiasm are valued. Aspirations should be high, and high achievement a prime virtue.

For the developmental counselor, some objective way of looking at cultural values and value formation is important. The counselor should be able to conceptualize how cultural values impinge upon the individual and his development. He should be able to understand how the value structure of an individual is influenced by his culture and how conflicts between individual and cultural values influence development. Such conflicts occur when the individual or his particular subcultural group resist the values of the dominant culture.

Cultural Discontinuity

Another anthropological concept of considerable importance to developmental counseling is that of *discontinuity* (2). Discontinuity as a factor in development has been discussed in earlier chapters. Discontinuity within a culture is essentially represented by factors that result in sharp differences in expectations for behavior in various levels of development.

Kneller (14) maintains that discontinuity is a factor built into most modern industrial societies. In many different ways, these societies sharply differentiate between behavior appropriate to adults and that appropriate to children. Developing individuals in these societies face major discontinuities as these differentiated expectations impinge upon them at various stages of development.

In other less highly organized societies, these kinds of cultural discontinuities do not exist at the same levels. In some primitive societies, the process of acculturation runs more smoothly from childhood to adulthood without the imposition of such pronounced demarcations.

Kneller (14) lists four major dimensions of development in which discontinuity factors are especially pervasive in American society. These include:

1. *Family vs. the higher society.* One of the major elements of

discontinuity in our society is represented in the relative isolation of the family. From the standpoint of the developing child, the family is in a sense an enclosure that separates him from the rest of the society. With the decline of kinship in American culture, the American family is virtually restricted to a dominant, ever-present mother, a semiabsentee father, and the children. In this family unit, the mother is the pervasive adult figure who alone furnishes the authority figure and role model.

In contrast, many primitive societies make less distinction between the family and other social groups. The family is often a large, amorphous social group that merges almost imperceptibly into the larger society. Aunts, uncles, cousins, grandparents, godparents, and others are intimately involved in child-rearing processes. No sharp separation from a childhood restricted to the family to an adulthood characterized by broad social interaction is imposed on the child.

In American life, several sharp discontinuities along this dimension may lead to difficulties that require the intervention of the developmental counselor. The first such discontinuity is, of course, the entry into school. A second is entry into secondary school and the shift in allegiance from family to peer group that occurs at approximately the same time. Another major discontinuity occurs at graduation from high school.

2. *Dependence vs. independence.* In modern American society, childhood and adulthood are sharply differentiated on the basis of social and economic independence and responsibility. Children play a negligible role in the economic production of a modern industrialized society. They remain relative economic liabilities almost totally dependent upon the family well into physical maturity. Social independence and responsibility is similarly restricted, often being tied to economic independence. The consequences of this kind of discontinuity is that children, adolescents, and even young adults have somewhat restricted opportunities to try out vocational roles and to develop feelings of self-worth and confidence based upon relative self-sufficiency.

In many primitive societies, such discontinuities are less pervasive. The family is an economic unit as well as a social entity. Children learn early to work alongside parents in a wide variety of situations. Economic self-sufficiency comes in a gradual transition that is completed at about the same time that sexual maturity brings with it the desire to marry and establish a family.

Much of the need for developmental counseling in the vocational–educational area comes from the discontinuities imposed by a complex, highly industrialized society. Vocational tryouts or even role models are difficult to find. The suddenly imposed demand for economic self-sufficiency after high school or college is threatening to many adolescents and young adults.

3. *Submissiveness–dominance.* Another dimension of development in which discontinuity is an important factor in American culture is that of dominance and submission. In our society, children are expected to be submissive and adults aggressive and dominant. The adolescent or young adult who had long been conditioned in school and family to submission to adults is often ill-prepared to exercise authority in responsible ways. When adult restraints are suddenly removed, the individual may overreact in blind rebellion against imposed adult standards or may be anxious and uncertain in the authority vacuum left by change in status.

In many primitive societies, this kind of discontinuity is less prevalent. Small children are supervised by older siblings or cousins. In turn, as the child matures, he will exert authority over younger children. Consequently, he experiences roles that involve dominance as well as submission.

The developmental counselor will encounter situations in which discontinuities in the dominance-submission dimension produce conflicts and may threaten to arrest developmental processes.

4. *Impulse control vs. impulse gratification.* In American society, children are typically expected to deny or control impulse gratification, particularly those that involve behavior of a sexual or aggressive nature. Impulse denial in the sexual area, for example, is expected through the age spans at which physiologically determined sex drives are strongest and when socially learned controls are weakest.

In many other societies, impulse gratifications are permitted to occur as the underlying physiological needs on which they are based emerge.

Many of the developmental problems in the sexual area that occur in our society result from a kind of unspoken adult conspiracy to view children, adolescents, and young adults as asexual beings until the society finds it convenient to recognize their sexuality.

Such developing human beings are constantly bombarded with the sexual stimuli produced in an adult society that is preoccupied with sex. Because of the adult society's deep ambivalence about its own sexuality, social controls are confused, diffuse, and largely ineffective.

Developmental counselors need to be able to get outside the cultural conspiracy that surrounds sexuality and to help developing human beings deal with impulses that cannot be denied but must be controlled.

A quotation from anthropologist Margaret Mead seems to sum up the problem of discontinuity in our society:

> In small societies children learn by imitating their parents, relatives and neighbors. In our huge society we use our mass entertainments to instruct our children on how they should express their emotions and what values they should have. . . . We are showing our youngsters exactly the opposite of what we want them to imitate. We are showing them men who brutally attack others when angry. We show people who murder because of hatred and expediency. We show that love is expressed only by hungering for another's body. And we show them little else. [18, p. 12.]

Anthropology is one of the broadest of the behavioral sciences. It is also one of the least ordered and precise. It offers a wide range of important understanding about the nature of environmental forces. Such understanding must be coupled with an understanding of the individual to give a total picture of human development.

SOCIAL PSYCHOLOGY AND COUNSELING

Social psychology is a discipline that is very difficult to separate from either sociology or anthropology. Allport has defined social psychology most simply as "an attempt to understand and explain how the thought, feeling and behavior of individuals are influenced by the actual, imagined or implied presence of other human beings" (1, p. 3).

Social psychology is thus in a sense an integrating discipline that connects the traditional preoccupation of psychology with individual behavior with the broader group-oriented viewpoints of sociology and anthropology. Social psychology has also supplied a relatively rigorous research methodology for the empirical testing of hypotheses drawn from other disciplines. Two general approaches to personality development that have been drawn largely from social psychological approaches are represented by Gardner Murphy (23) in his biosocial approach, and Kluckhohn, et al. (13) in their study.

Research in modern social psychology cuts across many different problems. Two specific areas are selected here to furnish an example of the relevance of the field to developmental counseling.

Social Influences on Perception

Bruner (4) points out that contemporary social psychology has been greatly concerned with perceptual processes in human beings. Psychology has long been aware of the fact that considerable individual differences in perception of similar stimuli occur. Hundreds of examples could be cited to show that different people perceive differing aspects of a stimulus situation. The old story about the three blind men examining the elephant shows that this phenomenon is well recognized even in folklore.

Social psychology, however, has attempted to tie these differences in perception to social situations and social group membership. Why, for example, in social situations do some people react to the color of a man's skin rather than to the texture of it, or to the color of his hat?

Social psychologists have intensively investigated perceptual phenomena from a social point of view. They have used stimulus situations in which ambiguity and limited time factors were used to exaggerate the effects of selective perception and cognition.

Bruner summarizes the results of this research as follows:

> Perceptual readiness, the ease with which items are recognized under less than optimal viewing conditions, seems to reflect not only the needs and modes of striving of an organism but also to reflect the requirement that surprise be minimized—that perceptual readiness be predictive in the sense of being tuned to what is present in the environment as well as what is needed for the pursuit of our enterprises. [4, p. 90.]

An often cited example of the perceptual phenomena noted by Bruner are the studies on perception of coin sizes by children of differing socioeconomic levels. These studies have suggested that poor children tend to magnify the size of coins to a greater degree than relatively more economically privileged youngsters.

Bruner in reviewing the literature on social psychological studies of perception reaches the following conclusion:

> . . . once society has patterned a man's interests and trained him to expect what is likely in that society, it has gained a great measure of control not only on his thought processes, but also on the very material on which thought works—the experience data of perception. [4, p. 94.]

For the counselor to understand the way in which an individual copes with his environment, he must understand what that environment is to him. In one sense, entering a counseling relationship with a client involves attempting to understand his past experiences, social group memberships, and needs thoroughly enough so that communication can occur within a reasonably similar perceptual pattern.

Social Psychological Influences on Motivation

The psychology of human motivation is one of the most crucial areas of interest to the developmental counselor. McClelland (15, 16) has studied problems of human motivation and has developed the construct of need achievement to explain the behavior of persons who exhibit high motivation for socially valued achievements. McClelland and his associates view need achievement, or as they notate it n Ach, as a socially learned tendency toward behavior. The construct of n Ach has been usually measured by the use of projective techniques such as the Thematic Apperception Test in which the subject's story about an ambiguous picture is analyzed. On the basis of these kinds of data, McClelland (15) lists three basic characteristics of people with high n Ach. These are:

1. High n achievers like situations in which they take personal responsibility for finding solutions to problems.
2. High n achievement people tend to set moderate achievement goals and to take calculated risks. They are motivated to get satisfaction from positive accomplishment rather than by avoiding failure.
3. High n achievement people want concrete feedbacks on the results of their efforts. They want to be able to measure results and to evaluate their performances.

In our culture, behavior tendencies such as those conceptualized in n Ach are obviously very important to both individual development and social well-being. The individual who is extremely low in achievement motivation is unlikely to develop educationally and may well be unable to function in a society that places great premium on individual effort and responsibility.

McClelland (16) examines three aspects of development that are seemingly related to n Ach out of the context of both experimental and cross-cultural research.

Researchers studying motivation in the United States find that low n Ach in boys is significantly related to membership in broken homes or where fathers are generally absent. When cross-cultural studies were done, the findings generally showed that n Ach among boys was low in cultures where the family is organized in a mother–child pattern with the influence of the father absent or relatively slight. This evidence is further supported by the experience in lower-class homes where the mother is the central figure and no consistent father model is available.

Research has also shown that n Ach is related to social variables outside the family. For example, n Ach has been found to be higher in middle-class children than in lower-class children in American society. Cross-cultural studies have shown that the patterning of n Ach levels varies among social classes from one society to another.

The developmental counselor needs to be sensitive to the effects of family and social-class influences upon the motivational growth of youngsters.

In some situations where cultural influences are obviously restricting the development of minimum levels of achievement motivation, the counselor may have to find strategies for intervening to facilitate motivational development. Some counselors, for example, are now working with populations that are the third generation of families supported entirely by public welfare. Others are working with children reared in homes where no role model of a father who is the economic and social head of the household exists. If these youngsters are ever to develop as self-respecting and self-reliant members of society, strategies must be evolved for facilitating motivational development.

PREFERENTIAL BEHAVIOR AND COUNSELING

A number of relatively new behavioral science disciplines or subdisciplines can be grouped under what Handy and Kurtz (9) call studies of "preferential behavior." Under this label are included game theory, decision-making theory, and value inquiry. Each of these approaches has special relevance to the developmental counselor. Counseling is directly concerned with conceptualizing alternatives, making decisions, estimating the consequences of courses of action, and establishing preferences among alternatives and consequences in terms of some set of values.

Game Theory

Game theory is an attempt to develop mathematical descriptions of human behavior in situations of cooperation and competition where all participants are well informed and competent and seeking common goals according to a set of rules. The name "game theory" is obvious since the conditions described above most commonly occur in situations such as bridge or chess or other games.

Game theory attempts to study human behavior in highly goal-directed kinds of activity. One such way of approaching behavior is that an individual or group is striving to maximize some quantity, as for example the accumulation of money or property in a game like Monopoly.

One of the properties of the game theory approach that is at once an advantage and a limitation is that it is primarily concerned with how man would act *rationally* when confronted with situations in which he knew clearly both his own goals and the goals of cooperating or competing participants.

Practically, of course, in counseling situations, clients are not always clear and rational in their approaches to their own or others' goals and behaviors. Yet in one sense, the counselor is engaged in the process of helping the client to make choices and to behave rationally and in goal-directed ways under conditions that could optimally approach those conceptualized in game theory.

For example, the client who is making a vocational or educational choice is essentially selecting a pattern of behavior that is intended to maximize a certain value or set of values. He is interested at least in knowing the course of behavior that will be most likely to eventuate in maximum satisfaction or goal fulfillment.

An example of the use of game theory in the solution of human problems is the "minimax" principle. Under this principle, a player in a game situation chooses a strategy that will minimize maximum loss or risk and of course conversely maximize gain compared to other alternative strategies. In a sense, the student attempting to choose a college by using expectancy information about probable success or failure in various colleges faces a somewhat similar situation. He has ranked the alternative colleges in terms of desirability or "gain." He wants to maximize this gain, but at the same time wishes to minimize "loss" or risk of failure. He must choose an alternative compatible with both elements.

Decision-making Theory

Closely allied to game theory is another approach termed "decision-making theory." Decision theory is aimed at studying human behavior in situations where choices are to be made among a number of known alternatives. One useful theoretical framework for studying decision-making behavior is in terms of the relative desirability of possible outcome and the degree to which each outcome is considered probable.

Decision theory includes the establishment of mathematical models, the description of processes by which decisions are actually arrived at, and the evaluation of consequences that are attached to particular decisions.

Value Inquiry

Value inquiry is another term describing a behavioral discipline devoted to studying preferences among alternative choices and the criteria involved for establishing preferences. The subject matter is very similar to decision theory and game theory with the major distinction being the focus that is put on the criteria used for selecting preferences. Workers in the area of value inquiry use polling techniques to assess attitudes and opinions, and personality inventories and experimental situations designed to elicit value behavior. Individuals, small groups, and entire societies and cultures are studied. The consistency and rationality of value behaviors are studied.

Results in value inquiry are limited by semantic problems regarding definitions of values and by the lack of sophisticated techniques for measurement.

Many aspects of the study of preferential behavior are relevant to the counselor. To a large extent, however, these approaches are limited to conceptualizations about how a "completely rational" man fully aware of his goals and the consequences of alternative courses of action to them would be expected to behave. Counselors realize that clients generally meet none of these conditions to a high degree. They are typically not completely rational. Who is? They are seldom fully aware of their own goals and values, at least initially. They and their counselors are far from omniscient about the consequences of alternative courses of action.

The counseling process does, however, have a central concern for decision making, value formation, and selection of alternative courses of action. Any systematic attempt to study these aspects of human behavior is potentially worthwhile to the developmental counselor. The counselor is inevitably viewed by clients as an expert in processes involving choice and decision. He needs to be aware of theoretical and research contributions in these areas.

ECONOMICS AND COUNSELING *

Economics is a behavioral science that has obvious relevance for counselors. Since one of the primary goals of a counselor is to help a client develop economic self-sufficiency and adequacy, the counselor needs to understand something of the economic system within which his clients will live.

One vital area of understanding for counselors is the field of labor economics. There is an extensive literature on trade-unions, union practices, labor mobility, employment, and unemployment of which most counselors are almost totally unaware. Counselors need to understand the effects of apprenticeship practices, union and closed shop regulations, hiring practices, and technological changes on the economic opportunity structure available to clients. They further need to be able to interpret to labor and business people in the community the implications of these practices for the development of young people.

POLITICAL SCIENCE AND COUNSELING †

Political science is the study of power and power relationships. It is too often considered to be only the description and analysis of formal governmental institutions. The counselor needs to understand very thoroughly the power structure within the institution and community within which he operates. He needs to be sophisticated enough to recognize and understand the hidden power structure in the community as distinguished from the formal power structure represented by office holders. The counselor must understand how the various power structures impinge upon clients, and how the power structure can be utilized to bring about constructive changes in the community.

An attempt has been made in this chapter to deal with a handful of relevant concepts to which substantial contributions have been made

* For further discussion see Chapter 7.
† For further discussion see Chapter 12.

in behavioral science disciplines not usually thought of as central to counselor education. To acquire any degree of competence as a behavioral scientist, the development counselor will have to explore well beyond the boundaries that are usually put around counselor education.

REFERENCES

1. ALLPORT, G. In G. Lindzey and E. Aronson, (Eds.), *Handbook of Social Psychology.* Vol. 1. Reading, Mass.: Addison-Wesley, 2d ed., 1968.
2. BENEDICT, RUTH. Continuities and discontinuities in cultural conditioning. In W. Vinacke, W. Wilson, G. Meredith (Eds.), *Dimensions of social psychology.* Chicago: Scott, Foresman, 1964.
3. BROOM, R., & SELZNICK, P. *Sociology.* Evanston, Ill.: Row, Peterson, 4th ed., 1968.
4. BRUNER, J. S. Social psychology and perception. In E. Maccaby, T. Newcomb, & R. Hartley (Eds.), *Readings in social psychology* (3d ed.), New York: Holt, Rinehart, 1958.
5. DU BOIS, CORA. The dominant profile of American culture. *Amer. Anthropologist,* 1955, 57 (6), 1232–1240.
6. ELKINS, F. *The child and society.* New York: Random House, 1960.
7. ERIKSON, E. H. Youth: fidelity and diversity. *Daedalus J. Amer. Acad. Arts Sci.,* 1962, 91 (1), 5–27.
8. GANS, H. *The urban villagers: group and class in the life of Italian-Americans.* New York: Free Press, 1962.
9. HANDY, R., & KURTZ, P. *A current appraisal of the behavioral sciences.* Behavioral Research Council Bulletin, Great Barrington, Mass., 1963.
10. HAVIGHURST, R. J., BOWMAN, P. H., LIDDLE, G. P., MATTHEWS, C. V., & PIERCE, J. V. *Growing up in river city.* New York: Wiley, 1962.
11. HOLLINGSHEAD, A. B. *Elmtown's youth.* New York: Wiley, 1949.
12. KLUCKHOHN, C. Anthropology. In J. Newman (Ed.), *What is science?* New York: Simon & Schuster, 1955.
13. KLUCKHOHN, C., MURRAY, H., & SCHNEIDER, D. *Personality in nature, society and culture.* New York: Knopf, 1959.
14. KNELLER, G. *Educational anthropology.* New York: Wiley, 1965.
15. McCLELLAND, D. C. *The achieving society.* Princeton, N.J.: Van Nostrand, 1961.
16. McCLELLAND, D. C., *et al. The achievement motive.* New York: Appleton-Century-Crofts, 1953.
17. McCORD, W., & McCORD, JOAN. *The psychopath.* Princeton, N.J.: Van Nostrand, 1964.
18. MEAD, MARGARET. *The educative environment.* The News Letter Bureau of Educational Research and Service. Ohio State University, May, 1961, 26 (8), 2. Quoted in G. Kneller. *Educational anthropology.* New York: Wiley, 1965.
19. MERTON, R. K. *Social theory and social structure.* (Rev. ed.), New York: Free Press, 1968.
20. MERTON, R. K., & BARBER, ELINOR. Sociological ambivalence. In E. A. Teryakian (Ed.), *Sociological theory values, and sociocultural change: essays in honor of Pitirim A. Sorokin.* New York: Free Press, 1963.
21. MILLER, S. M., & RIESSMAN, F. The working class subculture: a new view. *Social Problems,* 1961, 9:86–97.

22. MOWRER, O. H. *The crisis in psychiatry and religion.* Princeton, N.J.: Van Nostrand, 1961.
23. MURPHY, G. *Personality.* New York: Harper & Row, 1966.
24. PETTIGREW, T. F. *A Profile of the Negro American.* Princeton, N.J.: Van Nostrand, 1964.
25. SEELEY, J. R., SIM, R. A., & LOOSLEY, ELIZABETH W. *Crestwood heights.* New York: Basic Books, 1956.
26. SHERIF, M., & SHERIF, CAROLYN W. *Reference groups: exploration into conformity and deviation in adolescents.* New York: Harper & Row, 1964.

RECOMMENDED READINGS

CHILDE, V. G. *Piecing together the past.* New York: Praeger, 1969.
DAHL, R. A. *Polyarchy: participation and opposition.* New Haven, Conn.: Yale University Press, 1971.
DUFF, R. S., & HOLLINGSHEAD, A. B. *Sickness and society.* New York: Harper and Row, 1968.
EISENSTADT, S. N. (Ed.). *Political sociology.* New York: Basic Books, 1971.
EISENSTADT, S. N. (Ed.). *Readings in social evolution and development.* (Readings in Sociology Series). Elmsford, N.Y.: Pergamon Press, 1970.
FIRTH, R. (Ed.). *Themes in economic anthropology.* (A.S.A. Monographs Series No. 6). New York: Barnes and Noble, 1967.
GOULDNER, A. W. *Coming crisis in western sociology.* New York: Basic Books, 1970.
HANDY, R. *Value theory and the behavioral sciences.* Springfield, Ill.: Charles C. Thomas, 1969.
HSU, F. K. (Ed.). *Kinship and culture.* (University Library of Geography). Chicago: Aldine Publishing, 1971.
HSU, F. *Psychological anthropology.* 2nd ed. Cambridge, Mass.: Schenkman Publishing, 1971.
KATZ, I., & GURIN, P. (Eds.). *Race and the social sciences.* New York: Basic Books, 1969.
LASSWELL, H. D. *Pre-view of policy sciences.* New York: Elsevier Publishing, 1971.
LAZARSFELD, P. F. *Language of social research.* New York: Free Press, 1971.
LAZARSFELD, P. F., *et al.* (Eds.). *Uses of sociology.* New York: Basic Books, 1967.
LAZARSFELD, P. F., & HENRY, N. W. (Eds.). *Readings in mathematical social science.* Cambridge, Mass.: M.I.T. Press, 1968.
LEWIS, O. *Anthropological essays.* New York: Random House, 1970.
LIPSET, S. M. *Politics and the social science.* Fair Lawn, N.J.: Oxford University Press, 1969.
LOOMIS, C. P., & LOOMIS, Z. A. *Modern social theories: selected American writers.* 2nd ed. New York: Van Nostrand, 1965.
MEAD, M. *Anthropologist at work: writings of Ruth Benedict.* Chicago: Aldine, 1966.
MEAD, M. *Culture and commitment.* Garden City, N.Y.: Natural History Press, 1970.
MILLER, C. *On group theoretic decision problems and their classification.* (Annals of Mathematics Studies, Vol. 68). Princeton, N.J.: Princeton University Press, 1971.
MILLER, S. M., & RIESSMAN, F. *Social class and social policy.* New York: Basic Books, 1968.
PARSONS, T. *Politics and social structure.* New York: Free Press, 1969.
ROGOW, A. A. (Ed.). *Politics, personality, and social science in the twentieth century: essays in honor of Harold D. Lasswell.* Chicago: University of Chicago Press, 1969.

SCHWEBEL, M. *Who can be educated.* New York: Grove, 1968.

SHERIF, M. *Social interaction: processes and products.* Chicago: Aldine Publishing, 1967.

SMITH, M. BREWSTER. *Social psychology and human values.* Chicago: Aldine Publishing, 1969.

SPINDLER, G. D. *Being an anthropologist: fieldwork in eleven cultures.* New York: Holt, Rinehart, 1970.

7

COUNSELING
AND SOCIAL
CHANGE

The developmental counselor is inevitably oriented toward the future. The nature of that future is vague and unclear even to contemplate. The one certainty that exists beyond question is the certainty of change. As the developmental counselor works with growing human beings who are struggling to relate themselves to an uncertain future, few values are not open to question, few axioms are not problematical, and few principles are not merely predictions. As Wrenn says:

> It is obvious that our society faces a complex of new situations and intensified change. Some of the changes ahead are as exciting as a novel of the future. Some are most uncomfortable to contemplate. [10, p. 11.]

The nature of these changes is impossible to forecast with any degree of certainty. Most of the attempts at prediction necessarily come up with a series of "if and/or but" statements that can be subsumed under only one generalization: change will take place.

For the counselor "in a changing world," it is important to be able to grasp the sweep and magnitude of changes and the intensity with which they will impinge upon the lives of men.

CHANGES IN THE ECONOMY

From the standpoint of world history, the most important contemporary event is the second stage of the Industrial Revolution: automation. Automation actually represents only the natural development of the use of machines for economic production that began two hundred years ago. The uses of technological developments that began by using machines and fuels to replace human skills and animal muscles have progressed to the point that machines in many forms are able to replace human beings in many kinds of operations including cognitive and decision-making areas.

The most significant and long-term meaning of this continuation of the Industrial Revolution is simply that the production of material goods is no longer a significant human problem in industrialized societies. The production of unlimited quantities of almost any type of manufactured product is well within the technological capabilities of modern industrial systems. Scarcity of material goods is no longer a necessary reality in a modern industrial society. Moreover, economic scarcity can be overcome with such ease that human life no longer needs to be organized within the framework of an economic model. Man can supply all his material needs with a very minimal commitment of his own time and energy. Much more of his time and energy will have to be devoted to learning how to consume goods than in arranging for the production of them.

Man will particularly have to give his attention to problems of pollution and exhaustion of non-renewable resources on his planet. He will have to face the basic fact that his awesome power to produce is a double-edged sword that can ultimately destroy him.

Much of man's affluence may prove illusory when he faces an accounting with his abuse and waste of precious natural resources and life-sustaining systems.

While technological changes have enormous potential for the enhancement of human development on a truly utopian scale, they also bring with them inevitable degrees of disequilibrium and distress.

A number of these problems need to be considered. First, these potentials for production exist only in societies that are highly industrialized (9). So-called underdeveloped countries will be no closer to meeting even the minimal subsistence needs of their exploding populations because of these developments unless completely new concepts of international trade and exchange are rapidly innovated. A non-industrial society is almost completely helpless to compete for available raw materials, or to accumulate the enormous capital investments necessary for an automated economy. A world already sharply divided in terms of "have" and "have not" will be even more divided than ever before. Any degree of international stability will be difficult to obtain in a world in which material utopia exists beside unparalleled conditions of mass distress.

Even within industrialized societies, severe dislocations in economic and vocational life seem inevitable in the immediate future. The beginning phase of the Industrial Revolution displaced two forms of human labor in large quantities. The highly skilled artisan and the laborer who contributed only sheer muscle were largely displaced by machines. In turn, however, many new jobs were created in the semi-skilled and managerial areas.

For the first time in human history, great numbers of minimally skilled human beings became economically productive at a high level. Also, for the first time in history, a managerial class developed that built its power and prosperity around its ability to organize and manage human beings in essentially economic rather than military activities.

Automation, as the latest phase of the Industrial Revolution, is in the process of destroying the economic foundations upon which both of these groups are based. Automated production processes are very rapidly displacing the semiskilled machine operator and even the skilled machinist. The army of blue collar jobs that had represented the broad base of employment in the first half of the twentieth century is the continued trend shrinking perceptibly. The 1970 census showed the continued trend that indicated blue collar workers were clearly part of a declining minority. Job opportunities in these areas are rapidly becoming virtually extinct. The outlook for those skilled occupations such as tool and die making, machinist, and pattern and sheet metal work that have formed the "aristocracy of labor" is at best uncertain.

At the same time that blue collar jobs are being decimated, a similar but much slower process is at work in the upper white collar and lower- and middle-level managerial occupations. This change is due to that phase of automation called "cybernetics." Cybernetics is a term applied to the simulation of human cognitive activities by machines, particularly computers. Already, computer programming of operations involved in activities such as financial records, payroll accounting, cost and quality control, and personnel records has drastically changed the occupational opportunity structure in industries such as banking and insurance, and in industrial management generally. As computer methods are applied to decision-making activities in purchasing, marketing, production control, investment management, and countless other business and industrial activities, more and more individuals in "middle-management" positions will be eliminated.

Thus, technological developments now underway threaten to destroy the two classes that benefited most from the earlier phases of the Industrial Revolution: the "blue collar" class and the "managerial" class. Neither manual dexterity nor relatively unspecialized and untrained human intelligence are particularly valuable economic assets in the new industrial system.

The Changing Occupational Structure

The impact of the new technologies upon the occupational structure will be enormous. Even though various kinds of socially induced pressures will lessen the impact of these changes on the labor force generally, very little can be done to soften these effects upon young workers entering the labor market in the next two decades. Job seniority and other labor union devices, earlier retirements, shorter hours, longer vacations, etc., will represent attempts to cushion the impact of automation on those already established in the labor force. None of these devices will be of much help to those who may really never have an opportunity to enter the labor force in more than a very marginal way.

The net effects of technological change may well be to dichotomize the occupational structure into two fairly discrete categories. The first and more fortunate of the divisions might well be called the "ego-involving occupations." These occupations, although technologically very diverse, will have in common an intense degree of lifelong commitment to the occupation. This commitment will be such that it will be difficult for the worker to sort out, psychologically, concepts such as work and leisure. The total life style of the ego-involved worker and his family will be intertwined with the career in very powerful and complex ways. Concepts such as preparation for a career will have little meaning for such workers. Education will be lifelong and continuous in both a formal and an informal sense. Material rewards will be fantastic by present standards. Life satisfactions will be great and varied, but will almost all center directly or indirectly around the worker's career. The great unanswered question is what percentage of the population will have opportunities to enter the ego-involving occupations. The balance of political, economic, and social power will almost certainly be in the hands of this group.

The non-ego-involving occupations will probably constitute that part of the occupational structure open to the majority of the population. These jobs, while varied in setting and function, will be characterized by more and more routinized functioning. Levels of formal education may be relatively high for some of these jobs, even though that education may have little relevance to the actual job itself. The nature of such jobs will be subject to very rapid changes. In this part of the occupational structure, the concept of career may become meaningless. The individual will seek *employment* rather than a *career*. The life style will be built largely around non-vocational determinants such as climate, location, hobbies, and family size. The working day, the working week, and the working life will shrink inexorably. Vacations will be measured in months rather than weeks. Retirement will move back from the sixties to the fifties or even earlier. Leisure will be available on an unprecedented scale.

Counseling Implications

The implications for counseling regarding these changes are enormous. The counselor will have to be prepared to work with developmental processes that will culminate in a world that is largely unforeseeable. For many people, the greatest social and economic asset will be the ability to commit themselves deeply on a lifelong basis; the ability to respond flexibly and intelligently to extremely rapid change processes; and the ability to be fresh, creative, and original in their approach to problems, people, and situations.

For still another group, optimum development may mean the ability to organize life outside the mainstream of economic activity. The ability to utilize vast amounts of leisure time in creative, personally satisfying and socially worthwhile but not essentially economic ways may be the primary challenge.

Helping individuals meet these kinds of challenges will necessitate a greater understanding of social processes on the part of the counselor. For this reason, the discussion of social and technological change factors undertaken here will deal with some of the changes that are already taking place in our culture and the impact that they have for the present as well as the future.

CHANGES IN HUMAN RIGHTS

One of the sweeping tides of change that must be taken into account by counselors is the massive revolution in human rights. The central focus of this revolution has been around the struggle of black Americans to throw off the shackles of centuries of oppression and assert their fundamental rights of citizenship and claim truly human status in a racist society.

As this struggle proceeds, it imposes heavy responsibilities on developmental counselors to help people newly freed from the constraints of discrimination and oppression to utilize newly won opportunities to grow and develop.

The revolution in human rights has not, of course, been confined to black people. Many, many groups (American Indians, Chicanos, and others) have joined this epic struggle.

A vital part of the struggle has involved the change in attitudes of women. An irresitible, ever-mounting pressure is operating in the society to change the traditional roles and status of women. Old, irrational beliefs and attitudes about women are steadily crumbling.

Perhaps there is no single area of human experience that is presently more crucial to be understood by counselors than the ferment of the struggle of American women to grow and develop on an equal basis in the society.

If the revolution(s) in human rights has any truly imperative meaning to developmental counselors, it is that they must begin to search their own feelings, beliefs, and attitudes to find out if they nurture racist or sexist stances that render them useless or destructive in their work with clients. Before counselors can begin to join and advance the tremendous breakthrough in human development represented in these struggles, they must first get themselves together."

CHANGES IN VALUES

Social values have usually been taken for granted within particular cultures because the rate at which they change is generally so slow that transitions are barely if at all perceptible to members of any one generation. Even though many societies have been chronically convinced that their younger generations were bound for perdition, this has usually been merely symptomatic of the struggle between generations for influence and independence (3).

In the changing world of the twentieth century, Western culture has indeed changed so rapidly that profound shifts in cultural values have become obvious to all who care to perceive them. Cultural values in our society are in fact changing rapidly, although perhaps not as rapidly as a reasonable harmony of those values with the real world would indicate.

The values within American culture that were dominant for the first one hundred and fifty years of our history as a nation were born amid an agricultural economy of scarcity, a pioneer and immigrant society, a sparse and widely distributed population—in short, within a whole series of conditions that no longer exist.

Seeley (7) discusses a number of basic changes in values under the label of what he calls "the psychology of scarcity." He points out that the facts of economic scarcity under which our society was born have dictated a wide range of thought patterns, values, and perceptual processes that inevitably shape behavior.

In our society, for example, the highest words of praise are terms such as "achievement," "accomplishment," or "fulfillment." Hobbies essentially become ways of working without appearing to do so. Premiums are set upon discipline, order, and exactness. The human being is essentially perceived as an economic unit and is valued very largely in terms of his economic productivity. Idleness, contemplation, and passivity are adhorred or despised. Self-fulfillment unless expressed in terms of economic acquisitions is largely meaningless.

The economic realities upon which this psychology of scarcity were based have largely disappeared. Material goods are abundant, so abundant that artificial barriers to production and stimulation of consumption by planned obsolescence have to be imposed lest an economic system based upon scarcity could not survive the deluge. Just as much endangered as the economic system of scarcity is the psychological system of scarcity.

When all human motivations are gauged in terms of scarcity, what kinds of goals and purposes can be felt worthwhile in an affluent society? How can people value each other within a system that measures a man by his productivity, when that productivity has been taken over by machines? How can man develop an identity in a society that offers no economic scarcities against which he can pit himself, yet that measures his worth and value in these terms.

The problems of developing an identity in such a society are great. The most insidious kind of cultural lag prevails—the lag between those values on which a man can measure himself and the opportunities and challenges that are available to him. In this kind of society, counselors can expect increasingly to find individuals who are struggling to develop feelings of commitment and self-worth.

People will be struggling to find systems with which they can evaluate themselves and each other that will provide challenge and meaning to life. Just as millionaires now have to contend for political power as a basis for self-fulfillment, so do thousands of others have to find essentially non-economic paths to self-realization.

Traditional and Emergent Values

Spindler (8) examines this kind of cultural lag from the standpoint of the anthropologist. He sees a shift in core values within the culture that has profound implications for counselors and other educators.

Spindler has attempted to study value shifts through open-ended response instruments that try to get at core values. He sees from these studies two distinct sets of values operating within the culture that are quite dissimilar and in some cases incompatible. He calls these two sets of values "traditional" and "emergent."

Traditional values include such concepts as "puritan morality," "work–success ethics," "achievement orientations," and "rugged individualism." In contrast and even in opposition to these kinds of values are "emergent" values, which include "sociability," "moral relativism," "group conformity," and "immediate gratification."

The schism that is involved in commitment to one versus the other of these sets of values has great consequences for society. When contradictory views of life are held by differing groups, their ability to communicate and to cooperate toward common purposes is limited (8).

The school and the counselor by virtue of their institutional and individual learning histories are likely to be representative of "traditional" values. The developing youngsters who move through the school are more and more likely to be committed to "emergent" values.

The developmental counselor cannot forsake his own values because they are not those of his clients. He must recognize, however, the emerging value systems of clients if he is to be able to communicate with them. He must also recognize that his own values are not timeless and unquestionable and must be willing to let clients work through value questions in ways that are relevant to their needs and their times.

CHANGES IN POPULATION

One of the most potent social change factors at work in the world is what has been popularly termed the "population explosion." Quite aside from the economic consequences of rapid population growth, the effects in patterns of interpersonal behavior will be tremendous.

As population pressures in our society inexorably push people closer and closer together, the patterns of behavior that govern interpersonal relationships will inevitably change. Increasing population will almost inevitably mean increased *interdependency* and consequently increased *social control.* Traditional values based upon rugged individualism are already obviously giving away before these pressures. Grave questions exist around the survival of individual responsibility, freedom, and excellence in a society where socially induced pressures for conformity become stifling.

At the same time that physical proximity is making people more interdependent, the growth of urbanization and suburbanization together with the decline of kinship is actually *decreasing* intimacy. As we approach a society characterized by *high interdependency* but *low intimacy,* social controls of a very overt and oppressive kind may become inevitable.

Oriental societies, which have experienced high population densities for centuries, have evolved patterns of extreme politeness and deference that serve to lubricate frictions involved in living close together. Hsu (6) points out that both Chinese and Hindu cultures in different ways provide cohesion within the culture that can withstand strong pressures.

Hsu points out, however, that interpersonal patterns of American society do not provide the same kind of cohesive basis. Marriage in our society, for example, is built on the ideal of "romantic love." This ideal stresses freedom of choice, exclusive possession, and freedom for the partners from outside interference. This combined with other core values of self-reliance and the worship of the young, which Hsu believes are characteristic of our society, do little to promote cohesiveness.

Kinship as an institution that unites the generations through time or that binds groups together in fraternal bonds is not particularly characteristic of our culture. Opportunities for intimacy outside the immediate marital relationships are thus limited. The culture operates to heighten distinctions between self and non-self and to reduce feelings of affiliation and belongingness as compared to some other societies.

The consequences of this kind of value structure and consequent behavior patterns in a society in which interdependence is rapidly increasing are very serious. Highly publicized incidents in which women have been raped and murdered while neighbors or passersby refused to intervene are symptoms of the non-adaptive characteristics of this kind of value system.

The developmental counselor will be increasingly involved in helping people obtain growth-producing levels of independence, separateness, and personal excellence in a mass society that tends to submerge the individual. At the same time, however, counselors will be equally concerned with helping people to establish patterns of interpersonal relationships, group affiliations, and value orientations within which they can feel responsibility, involvement, and commitment in a depersonalizing kind of society.

CHANGES IN FAMILY LIFE

Reuben Hill (5) in an article on the modern American family uses this statement as a point of departure.

> At the turn of the century, most people had the greatest respect for the institution called the family, yet they were loath to learn much about it. The family was taken for granted, ignored, shunted aside, and expected to do the nation's patching and mending without reward or attention. According to the cherished beliefs of the period, all husbands and wives lived together in perfect amity and all children loved their parents, to whom they were indebted for the gift of life. Moreover, even if one knew that these things were not true, he ought not to mention it! [5, p. 76.]

The shift from this naïve view to a more realistic one has been painful. All sorts of ills, real and imagined, in our society have been blamed on the family. A number of important changes in family structure and patterning have occurred and are occurring that have great significance for our culture. Two such important shifts are as follows:

1. *Changes in economic roles.* The family has been gradually shifting away from its role as a self-contained economic unit. From 1890 to 1970, the proportion of American families subsisting through farming declined from almost half to less than one-tenth (5). As this pattern changed, the authoritarian power relationships that had made the father a kind of shop foreman changed with it. The family became much less self-reliant and more dependent upon outside agencies for services such as schooling, religious instruction, recreation, and medical care. The family has become more of a specialized agency concentrating on the personality development of its members and providing warmth, love and security, and sanctuary from the depersonalization and anonymity of mass urban living than it had ever been before.

2. *Changes in family structures.* As the family has changed from an economic to a social-centered unit, the differentiation of roles built upon an economic model have changed. There is less sex differentiation in division of labor, in responsibility for decision-making, and for spending and earning than before. These changes were the result of shifts in size and spacing of families. There is a present tendency to bunch children into the earlier years of marriage. The average mother in 1970 completed childbearing before age twenty-six. There has been a steady increase in the number of married women ages thirty-five to forty-four in the labor market in the past ten years (5). As this occurs, traditional differences in male and female roles tend to be shaded out of existence (1). These changes will be accelerated by the struggle of women discussed earlier.

Companionship in marriage has tended to replace economic interdependency as the central motivation. The model for marriage and family in America has become what Goode (4) calls the "conjugal family."

The conjugal family is a model in which family stability is almost totally dependent upon the emotional relationship between husband and wife. In this pattern, the family system does not emphasize concentrating family lands or wealth. There is little continuity in the family between generations, since the central focus of family life is in the marriage relationship itself rather than the larger kinship group (4). Great freedom of choice is built into the system with resulting wide ranges of consequences for good or harm attached to the possible outcomes. The conjugal model thus does not emphasize stability as a value. It does contain great possibilities for personal development and enhancement of the partners and children when optimal conditions prevail. It also contains great possibilities for harm and impairment of those involved when the marriage fails to meet the high expectations set for it in the conjugal model.

The conjugal family model yields high expectations for the family. When the failures of this level of expectation are reflected in high divorce rates, some people in our culture tend to panic and believe that the whole system is breaking down. The fact that divorce rates are lowest among professional groups offers some indication that the "conjugal model" of marriage and family can be made to work where educational levels are high.

Developmental counselors will increasingly be involved in marriage and premarriage counseling. Preparing students to cope with the demands of a family pattern that has both great risks and great rewards in terms of personal development will be a vital role for education. Successful marital realtionships in our society are increasingly vital determinants of optimum development. Counselors must become competent to give help in this area.

CHANGES IN EDUCATION

Dramatic changes in a society of the kind discussed in this chapter cannot fail to be accompanied by equally dramatic changes in that society's educational system. It is often more difficult to appreciate the magnitude of changes that will affect us intimately than it is to understand changes from which we are more safely detached.

For this season, a frankly visionary attempt will be made here to describe in some detail a few changes that the author believes will probably impinge upon education. They are presented not as a demonstration of prowess in the art of crystal ball gazing, but rather as an attempt to confront the reader with some possible changes in education that are sweeping enough to jar loose the preconceptions that may limit his ability to deal with the future.

Programmed and Packaged Learning

Two major technological developments will govern the future of education. The first of these is the development called "programmed learning." Almost all kinds of material that we now term academic content will be presented in terms of programmed learning principles.

These materials will be organized not alone by teachers, but also by highly qualified experts in the psychology of learning, acting in consultation with recognized leaders in the subject matter fields. The organization of these materials will thus reflect great sophistication in psychology of learning and great understanding of the basic structure of knowledge. Virtually all human knowledge will eventually be organized, packaged, and programmed so that it may be presented in appropriate ways at various levels and stages of development.

These programs will be presented by a wide range of ingenious mechanical and audio-visual devices. These devices will permit almost totally individualized instruction. Concepts of grade levels or school years will become antiquated. Children and adults will visit schools to work through appropriate programs as their needs and family schedules dictate. Precocious ten-year-olds will work on the same programs as twenty-year-olds. There will be no basic discontinuities in education as now represented by elementary, junior high school, high school, and college. Education will increasingly become an integral part of the life style of many people on a continuous and lifelong basis. A teaching machine will be just as much a part of the paraphernalia for a family recreation room as a power saw or a slide projector.

Classroom teaching as we now know it will disappear. The school will contain very competent library staffs to organize and dispense materials, and will have a few technicians adept at servicing complicated educational machines.

The key professional educator will be the "educational programmer." The educational programmer will be a descendent of today's counselor. His background will be in educational psychology, probably at the doctoral level. As each youngster enters school, he will be intensively interviewed and tested. From evidence obtained, the child's educational development will be carefully programmed in a totally individual way. These programs will be periodically reviewed and modified as the child moves through the programmed materials prescribed. Wide ranges of alternative educational programs will be available.

Group Counseling

The dehumanizing possibilities of this kind of education are obvious and threatening. They will be eliminated through the second of the technologies to be discussed. Once academic subject matter can be presented in ways unparalleled for efficiency and effectiveness, the second great task of education will be recognized as facilitating total human development. The technology involved will be drawn from knowledge of group dynamics and personality development and will most closely resemble activities that would now be called group therapy.

The teacher of the future will essentially be a small group leader adept at developmental counseling with small groups of youngsters or adults. These group sessions will be aimed at facilitating total human development and human effectiveness. They will be structured around vastly improved knowledge about developmental tasks, coping behaviors, and social roles. Helping relationships will be systematically provided through these groups and the individual contacts that supplement them.

The school of the future will thus be a combination of programmed learning laboratory and community mental health center. It will also probably include a recreational center where art, music, games, sports, and hobby activities will be coordinated. The counselor of the present will be the professional ancestor of both the educational programmer and the developmental group leader. This kind of educational system can become truly developmental in scope.

This type of school will be radically different in concept. It will be one way in which man will attempt to cope with the challenge of change.

Brown, *et al.* describe the challenge that lies ahead for man in this way:

> Behavior scientists are just beginning to uncover some of the principles of human behavior. This knowledge will undoubtedly grow in the years ahead, and as it grows it can be used to rear healthier children and to help adults achieve their full potentialities. . . . Our knowledge of the nature of creative thought processes, of imagination, and of intuition will increase. More knowledge of group dynamics, of social and political behavior, and of means for controlling feelings and emotions can help man achieve his constructive, socially helpful goals and divert him from hostile, destructive action.

. . .

. . . man can, if he wills it, create a world where people can lead lives of abundance and creativity within the framework of a free society. . . . The future . . . revolves around the question of whether man can learn to live with man. [2, p. 153.]

This is the challenge facing the developmental counselor in the age of change.

REFERENCES

1. BRIM, O. G., JR. Personality development as role-learning. In I. Iscoe & H. W. Stevenson (Eds.), *personality development in children*. Austin: University of Texas Press, 1960.
2. BROWN, H., BONNER, J., & WEIR, J. *The next hundred years*. New York: Viking, 1963.
3. EISENSTADT, S. N. *From generation to generation: age groups and social structure*. New York: Free Press, 1956.
4. GOODE, W. J. *World revolution and family patterns*. New York: Free Press, 1963.
5. HILL, R. The American family today. In E. Gunzberg (Ed.), *The nation's children*. Vol. 1. New York: Columbia University Press.
6. HSU, F. K. *Kinship and culture*. Chicago: Aldine, 1971.
7. SEELEY, J. R. Guidance and the youth culture. *Personnel Guidance J.*, 1962, 41:302–310.
8. SPINDLER, G. D. Education in the transforming American culture. In *Education and culture*. Holt, Rinehart, 1963.
9. The Corporation for Economic & Industrial Research. *World-wide and domestic economic problems and their impact on the foreign policy of the United States*. For the U.S. Senate Committee on Foreign Relations, 1959.
10. WRENN, C. G. *The counselor in a changing world*. Washington, D.C.: American Personnel and Guidance Association, 1962.

RECOMMENDED READINGS

BARDWICK, JUDITH M. *Psychology of women*. New York: Harper and Row, 1971.
DRUCKER, P. F. *Age of discontinuity: guidelines to our changing society*. New York: Harper and Row, 1969.
DRUCKER, P. F. *New society: the anatomy of industrial order*. New York: Harper and Row, 1971.
EISENSTADT, S. N. *Comparative persepectives on social change*. (Comparative Perspectives in Sociology Series). Boston: Little, Brown, 1968.
EPSTEIN, CYNTHIA F. *Women's place: options and limits in professional careers*. Chicago: University of Chicago Press, 1971.
EPSTEIN, C., & GOODE, W. (Eds.). *Other half: roads to women's equality*. Englewood Cliffs, N.J.: Prentice-Hall, 1971.
FIRTH, R. *Essays on social organization and values*. (Monographs on Social Anthropology No. 28). New York: Humanities, 1970.
FITZGERALD, LAURINE, & HARMOND, LENORE. Counseling women, *The counseling psychologist*. 4, 1, 1973 (Special issue).

GANS, H. J. *Levittowners: ways of life and politics in a new suburban community.* New York: Pantheon Books, 1967.

GANS, H. J. *People and plans: essays on urban problems and solutions.* New York: Basic Books, 1968.

GOODE, W. J. (Ed.). *Contemporary american family.* Cleveland, Ohio: Quadrangle Books, 1971.

GOODE, W. J. (Ed.). *Dynamics of modern society.* Chicago: Aldine Publishing, 1971.

GRIER, W. H., & COBBS, P. M. *Black rage.* New York: Basic Books, 1968.

GRIER, W., & COBBS, P. M. *Jesus bag.* New York: McGraw-Hill, 1971.

HAVIGHURST, R. J. *Comparative perspectives on education.* Boston: Little, Brown, 1968.

HAVIGHURST, R. J., & LEVINE, D. U. *Education in metropolitan areas.* 2nd ed. Rockleigh, N.J.: Allyn and Bacon, 1971.

HAVIGHURST, R. J., & NEUGARTEN, B. L. *American Indian and white children: a socio-psychological investigation.* (Double-Page Reprint Series). Chicago: University of Chicago Press, 1969.

HAVIGHURST, R. J., et al. (Eds.). *Society and education: a book of readings.* 2nd ed. Rockleigh, N.J.: Allyn and Bacon, 1971.

HILL, R. *Family development in three generations.* Cambridge, Mass.: Schenkman Publishing, 1971.

HUBER, JOAN, (Ed.) Changing women in a changing society. *American journal of sociology.* 78, 4, Jan. 1973. (Special issue).

JENCKS, C., & RIESMAN, D. *Academic revolution.* Garden City, N.Y.: Doubleday, 1968.

LEWIS, O. *Study of slum culture: backgrounds for La Vida.* New York: Random House, 1968.

MEAD, M. *Family.* New York: Macmillan, 1971.

MILES, M. B. *Learning in social settings: new readings in the social psychology of education.* 2nd ed. Edited by W.W. Charters Jr. Boston: Allyn and Bacon, 1970.

PETTIGREW, T. F. *Profile of the black american.* 2nd ed. New York: Van Nostrand-Reinhold, 1971.

RIESSMAN, F. *Strategies against poverty.* New York: Random House, 1969.

SHERIF, M., & SHERIF, C. W. (Eds.). *Problems of youth: transition to adulthood in a changing world.* Chicago: Aldine Publishing, 1965.

TOFFLER, A. *Future shock.* New York: Random House, 1970.

8

DIAGNOSIS, PREDICTION, AND THE COUNSELING USE OF TESTS

One of the oldest and most unfruitful sources of disagreement in counseling has grown up around the question of whether to diagnose or not to diagnose. Part of the disagreement has probably stemmed from the fact that, as a term, the word "diagnosis" was drawn from medicine and has a strongly medical connotation.

Diagnosis in medicine and diagnosis in counseling are *not*, however, basically similar processes. For the physician, the process of diagnosis is aimed at discovering a specific *disease entity*—measles, mumps, etc.—for which he can then prescribe a particular differential treatment or therapy. Diagnosis in this sense involves the study of symptoms, use of laboratory tests to identify pathological agents, and so forth. Diagnosis necessarily precedes treatment and represents a discrete stage in the total process.

Even in medical settings, attempts to apply this type of process to those problems of human behavior termed "mental illnesses" have not been notably successful. The nature of disease entities in so-called functional illnesses has not proved to be the same as in those types of pathology for which positive organic bases can be established (4).

Evidence regarding the low reliability of independent psychiatric diagnoses even in terms of such gross constructs as neurosis, psychosis, depression, anxiety, etc., has suggested to Eysenck (4) that the whole notion of disease entities in the area of functional mental abnormalities needs to be banished. Menninger (10) also has suggested that traditional methods of diagnosis based upon the illusion of disease entities be replaced by what he calls a "unitary" system of diagnosis.

For counselors, the problem of disease entities has not been the same kind of limiting factor as has been the case in psychiatry. A number of attempts have been made in counseling, however, to establish systems of mutually exclusive diagnostic constructs (12). Many such systems have not proved particularly useful for counseling practice for somewhat the same basic reasons that the concept of disease entities has not been helpful in psychiatry. Unfortunately, clients are simply not cooperative enough to fit themselves into the tidy little pigeonhole provided by narrow diagnostic constructs and then stay there. Human behavior is often too complex and the interaction effects among the various behavioral determinants too intricate for a simple set of diagnostic constructs tied to causal factors to be adequate.

LEVELS OF EFFECTIVENESS

For the developmental counselor, one kind of diagnostic construct may be somewhat useful. It is based upon a vertical functioning dimension and is not tied to any presumed set of causal agents. This concept is the *level of human effectiveness* at which an individual is functioning at any particular time.

As Menninger (10) points out, this is essentially a unitary concept of diagnosis. The dimension of human effectiveness is largely defined by the degree of control that the individual can exert over his environment and his affective responses. The lowest possible level of control is of course represented by the suicidal person. Five levels of human effectiveness are described below.

Panic

This level is characterized by actual loss of control over affective responses and/or loss of control over the immediate and short-term environment. The individual is usually institutionalized or needs institutionalization to protect himself and others. He may have intense feelings of being out of control, of being at the mercy of hostile and uncontrollable forces. He may make active attempts at suicide or may become violently aggressive or show extreme withdrawal behavior.

Inertia

In this level, there is some control of short-term immediate aspects of environment. There is little or no control over long-term or wide-reaching aspects of environment. While the individual is not institutionalized, he is unlikely to be economically or socially self-sufficient or independent. He tends to react to environmental demands in ways to avoid immediate punishments or failures, or to secure very immediate gratifications. He is unable to develop and carry through goal-oriented plans that require organized, controlled behavior. He has difficulty accepting responsibility for his behavior or its consequences. He tends to project responsibility for his difficulties upon others. He often feels at the mercy of fate and tends to show indifference and distrust.

Striving

In this level, the individual has some degree of control over long-term and wider aspects of environment and is actively seeking more. He has some degree of control over his affective responses, but is likely to alternate between feelings of hope and confidence and feelings of resignation and despair. Behavior is planful and goal-oriented to a limited degree, but the individual's life is likely to consist of a series of crises and emergencies that are preventable if planning and organization were more effective.

Coping

At this level, there is control of large segments of long-term environment and over major components of behavior including emotional responses. Behavior is planful and very largely goal-oriented. The individual reacts to life as a challenge rather than with defeatist attitudes. Considerable anxiety may be present over outcomes of ego-involving events. This anxiety does not extinguish appropriate risk-taking behavior, however.

Mastery

This level represents the highest degree of human effectiveness. The individual is in active control of large and important segments of the environment. He characteristically enters into active, planful interaction with environment rather than merely reacting to it. He has feelings of adequacy, mastery, and security in most of his roles. He finds life full of zest and meaning. He feels involved with and committed to values and projects that transcend his own existence.

The five constructs listed above seem useful to the developmental counselor for several reasons. They offer some guideposts with which to establish goals that are appropriate for the creation of developmental contracts with clients. The client who is operating at the inertia stage will probably not immediately enter a developmental contract aimed at finding values with which he can identify to find greater meaning for life. The kinds of contracts that are feasible are tied to the level of functioning of the client and his consequent motivations.

The nature of appropriate counselor behavior may also depend upon the client's level of functioning. The degree of client responsibility that can be structured, the degree of counselor response to emotional versus intellectual factors that is helpful, and the degree of ambiguity that is appropriate may depend upon the client's level of functioning.

For example, it may be quite inappropriate to begin a contact with a client at the inertia level by asking him to free associate, or by giving him information. Such approaches might well be appropriate for a client attempting to move from the coping to the mastery levels.

The constructs used in this system really are tied to the way in which the client perceives his world and relates himself to it. If the counselor's behavior is not based upon some understanding of this, he will find it difficult to be helpful.

In counseling then, the whole concept of diagnosis is of a special order. In counseling, diagnosis refers to *the process through which the counselor comes to understand the client, the client's world, and the meaning that his interaction with that world has for him.* The question of "to diagnose or not to diagnose" simply does not exist if the counselor makes any claim toward a serious effort to understand his client. The extent to which the counselor will use the process to develop a *differential diagnosis* or to assign clients to categories for which *differential treatments* are presumed appropriate will depend upon the particular theoretical orientation of the counselor.

Research on the nature of the diagnostic process in counseling by Koester (7), McArthur (8), Parker (11), and others suggests that diagnosis is most effective when it is *continuous, tentative,* and *testable.* In counseling, diagnosis is not a distinct stage of the counseling procedure. It is a continuous process that permeates the entire counseling enterprise. The ongoing process of diagnosis is concerned with continuous revision and modification. The Pepinskys (13) suggest that diagnosis in effect consists of building a hypothetical model "client." This model client is built from the observations that the counselor makes of the "real" client's behavior.

As these observations are organized and inferences developed from them are drawn, a hypothetical client emerges. It is this hypothetical client that furnishes the actual basis for the counselor's responses. The counselor always responds to the "real client" as though he were like the hypothetical model that exists only in the counselor's mind.

The counselor must always realize that this hypothetical model is just that, hypothetical, and therefore *tentative.* As new samples of behavior are observed and new inferences formulated, the hypothetical model grows and changes. Ideally, it becomes richer and more diverse in characteristics. As new samples of behavior emerge that challenge some of the earlier inferences, the model may have to be drastically changed. If the model is *ever* frozen and new observations shut out, the model may become very different from the flesh-and-blood client and the counselor's responses correspondingly inappropriate.

The method by which the counselor attempts to maintain compatibility between his hypothetical model and his real client is one of *hypothesis testing.* Inferences drawn from observations must be framed as testable hypotheses and verified through subsequent observations before they are allowed to become parts of the hypothetical model. In order to be testable, hypotheses must be framed in rigorously operational terms. In other words, hypotheses must be capable of conversion into predictions that can be verified or rejected. These predictions can be verified through subsequent interview behavior or through independent extra-interview observations such as test results and observations of others.

One of the greatest dangers in the diagnostic process is that hypotheses are not formulated rigorously enough so that negative evidence can be recognized. Often in testing hypotheses in the interview, the counselor unconsciously selects only evidences that support preconceived hypotheses or manipulates situations so that no opportunity for negative "feedback" exists. It is very easy for attempts at hypothesis testing to be unconsciously converted into the form of "self-fulfilling prophecies." For example, the counselor who is convinced that a sexual basis for a client's problem exists may manipulate the interview in a way to exclude other possibilities from being tested.

DEVELOPMENTAL DIAGNOSIS

If the basic concepts related to human development are to have any real value in counseling, they must be useful in establishing appropriate goals and approaches for particular clients. As we have seen, many of the labels derived from abnormal psychology have not had much utility in this area. Developmental psychology as a discipline grew out of the realization that children were neither miniature adults nor passive embryos waiting to become persons, but were growing, active, aspiring human beings with specific needs, concerns, and problems that changed across the entire life span.

In Chapter 4 we traced a chronological approach to development based heavily on Erikson's eight stages, and in Chapter 5 we looked at a hierarchical system built by Maslow to follow the growth of a human being to full self-actualization. As we utilize developmental constructs such as these, we can identify three basic sets of variables that can be employed in understanding or "diagnosing" a client. (2)

Life Stage Factors

Life stage factors are those that are mostly closely tied to chronological age. In many ways the interaction of any human being with essential elements in his environment—family, school, work, leisure, etc.—are influenced by his age. The utility of a life stage concept lies in its ability to focus on the interaction between an individual's maturational capacities or limitations and the social or cultural expectations established for him.

The implications for counseling which grow out of an understanding of life stage factors can perhaps be best communicated through an example. Two boys, one in elementary school and one in high school, are referred to their counselors for the "same problem." In both cases the referring teacher's report that the boys disturb classes by talking, laughing, and other "disruptive behavior." Each time, from the standpoint of the youngster, his problem stems from the way teachers react to his behavior. Both boys have received strong verbal disapproval, lowered grades, and reduction of privileges as a result of the situation.

In both cases the counselors review the cumulative records, contact parents, and examine the student's developmental history. The eight-year-old—Johnny—is in third grade. His parents report that his home behavior seems normal and appropriate. His father thinks Johnny is "all boy" and his mother wishes he would keep his room neater. Both expect their child to attend college and are concerned about this "trouble in school." A check of medical records and teacher observations indicate that physiological development is normal.

The results of the case history of the seventeen-year-old high school junior—Paul—seem very similar. Again physiological development appears normal. Prior school achievement has been satisfactory. Parents report that he is popular with peers, engages in healthy recreational and school activities, that they see him less frequently than they would like and have occasional problems in communication with him, but view this as a normal part of his growing independence. They too expect their son to go to college and are concerned about this problem.

Here we have two seemingly similar presenting problems, and social and family histories alike. Does the developmental counselor, however, proceed in the same way with two clients at quite different life stages? Are either his goals or his approaches the same?

If we consult the chart in Chapter 4, pages 84–85, we find some answers. Our eight-year-old is in later childhood, a stage in which the principal developmental tasks are initiative and industry—learning to delay gratification, control emotional reactions, and develop positive work habits and attitudes. Coping behaviors include appropriate sex role and achievement-oriented behaviors.

The counselor, bearing in mind the developmental tasks and coping behaviors for this stage, first works with the teacher, sharing his understanding of human development. He points out that the situation is an important one, and that either ignoring it or reacting punitively might have serious consequences for Johnny's future development. A major developmental problem at this stage is the development of feelings of shame or inferiority. Use of ridicule or disparagement of his achievements might have very negative consequences for Johnny's future growth.

The counselor consults with Johnny's teacher to establish a plan by which his achievement or work-oriented behavior can be rewarded or reinforced. In interviews with Johnny and his teacher, a set of acceptable rewards are identified and a number of specific situations in which the disruptive behavior occurs are noted. The teacher learns to identify these situations, recognize opportunities for constructive behavior, and reward this behavior appropriately. Johnny, too, becomes aware of the contingency system in the classroom and learns to gain recognition, attention, and approval with positive achievements. The counselor has employed essentially a behavioral approach, but one in which Johnny is treated as a partner who can understand and participate in a process designed to help him grow.

Is a similar approach the most appropriate for our seventeen-year-old, Paul? When we consult the Developmental Table (page 84), under later adolescence we find that key developmental tasks involve moving from peer-dominated relationships to those involving individual responsibility, autonomy, and productivity. Key coping behaviors are reciprocal and cooperative in nature.

In this situation the counselor sees the basic nature of Paul's interpersonal relationships as the focal point. He begins by working directly with Paul and attempting to build a warm, empathic, and trusting relationship. As this relationship develops it becomes clear that Paul is often torn between needs to gain approval from peers—sometimes through behavior that he recognizes as immature and inappropriate—and his needs to feel independent, productive, and competent.

As their relationship progresses, Paul and the counselor agree on a developmental contract with goals focused upon the achievement of a mature and integrated style of interpersonal behavior that can be utilized in relationships with both adults and other adolescents.

We have seen then, two cases representing similar situations but different life stages may be handled quite differently by the developmental counselor.

Life Space Factors

Life stage factors are closely tied to chronological age and related social roles. A second set of factors that must also be included in a "developmental diagnosis" are called "life space" factors. The physical and psychological space of any human being defines his world of reality. This life space represents in a sense the opportunity structure that incorporates the resources and limitations within which his struggle to grow must occur. Developmental counselors cannot afford to ignore the tremendous life space differences represented in the environments of different clients.

There are any number of ways in which the individual's environment of life space may limit his development—for example, the boy who has difficulty relating to male teachers may come from a home in which there is no father. The girl moving from a relatively isolated farm to a large city seems shy and fearful. The college girl from an affluent upper middle-class suburb seems naïve and overprotected to her freshman advisor and he wonders how she will respond to the vastly more heterogneous environment of an urban university campus.

For each of the above examples a set of hypotheses may be established about life space factors and how they will impinge on future growth. As these hypotheses are refined and developed out of careful listening and observing, they may emerge into goals and approaches designed to enhance the client's future growth. Often such goals and approaches involve bridging discontinuities between limitations imposed by past life space factors and opportunities available in present learning environments.

If we examine the histories and present situations, for example, of children from oppressed subcultures, we often find that their experiences handicap them in the institutions controlled by the dominant middle-class culture. For instance, they often must be virtually bilingual; the language they have learned at home is not the standard dialect of the institution. There may be disadvantages in the child's inability to manipulate objects or ideas which are deemed so important by the dominant subculture that they are introduced early in the middle-class child's life. Whether the manipulation involves the contents of a book or an idea about the role of individual initiative rather than fate, the child who is unfamiliar with the object or idea may be disadvantaged in the dominant subculture. In many cases the life space of the middle-class child may be similarly impoverished by overprotection and social stratification in suburban communities.

As we analyze life space then, we are primarily concerned with defining the opportunity structure. By opportunity structure we mean the elements in that environment offering possibilities for future growth and development. The opportunity structure is represented by the available helping relationships, educational programs, peer contacts, job possibilities, financial, moral, and psychological support, etc., that are present and available in the environment.

In one sense the environment represents an objective given. In another sense, however, the opportunity structure is a personal or phenomenological reality that is never the same for any two individuals and hence is part of his life space.

We have often failed to understand the psychological aspects of an environment, particularly in regard to its opportunity structure, because of our naïve notions about human motivation. We have tended in the past to view motivation as a more or less fixed quantity that resides within an individual, rather than as a learned response to a given environmental situation.

Recent formulations (3) have viewed motivation as a more complex construct. Such views tend to focus upon the level of stimulation existing within a given environment and to assess level of motivation in terms of approach–withdrawal behavior. These constructs see the human organism as seeking stimulation and as requiring at least minimal levels of stimulation for normal development. The concept of "stimulus hunger" adds a new dimension to human needs. As we mentioned in Chapters 1 and 4, Heisler (5) has pointed out that when levels of stimulation become too high, the organism tends to retreat or withdraw into situations with which it can cope more comfortably. The level of stimulation with which a child, for example, can engage and cope adequately is a function of his past learning experiences. An overprotected child or a child from a different cultural background may withdraw from levels of stimulation in a classroom that challenge and intrigue another. Still a third child with a very rich stimulus diet may be bored and seek to raise the stimulus level in the same classroom. (See Chapter 7.)

Unfortunately, we know all too little about the nature of stimulus conditions that produce stress in one child and evoke wonder and excitement in another. As we saw in Chapter 1, however, at least four elements in stumulus situations are known to be related to their effects on approach–withdrawal behavior or motivation.

The most obvious of these elements is intensity. The hot stove, the loud noise, the electric shock are obviously aversive stimuli in many situations. Even here, however, wide individual differences in reactions to stumulus intensity exist, as shown by the success of rock bands, psychedelic displays, or even such hobbies as parachute jumping. Many individuals are motivated to seek very high levels of stimulus intensity and even to use drugs or other chemical means to increase the intensity of experience.

Another obvious stimulus element is novelty. New stimulus elements tend to have higher values in raising levels of stimulation than do more familiar ones. Children and adults tend to seek increased stimulation through novel experiences, but they may withdraw from the situation and experience stress reactions when intensity and novelty are both high.

A third element that raises the level of stimulation in a situation is complexity. Games, puzzles, works of art, literature, and music all vary in complexity and attract or repel given audiences as a consequence.

A fourth element that operates in a manner similar to complexity is ambiguity. Considerable social psychological research has demonstrated the existence of differences in tolerance for ambiguity and consequent resistance to such ambiguity-reducing defenses as oversimplification or premature closure.

As we analyze the life space of an individual, we need to assess the levels of stress and stimulation that exist for him in that environment as a function of the match or mis-match that exists between his previously learned capacities to cope with such elements as intensity, novelty, complexity, and ambiguity. Often considerable learning must occur before a given individual is able to utilize the opportunity structure represented by school or community or even peer culture.

Counselors are often called upon to help with what the institution regards as a limitation in the individual's life space. The counselor's response to the institutional request may vary. He may attempt a change in the large environment, gaining family cooperation for a "Big Brother" or training male teachers for an approach to the fatherless boy which the boy himself finds acceptable. He may develop a relationship with the shy or sheltered girl preparing her for a group experience in which personal feelings or interpersonal relationships are discussed. He may design a learning program for a child that takes him successfully through a sequence of study skills or reading exercises. In each case, the counselor must look carefully at the life space of the individual to see what opportunities are needed in the person's life space and learning history, and how the opportunity structure can be reorganized and expanded to stumulate growth-producing motivations.

Life Style Factors

The concept of life style is related Adler's to phrase "Style of Life." (See Chapter 3.) However, we are not thinking as Adler did of a single variable like the striving for superiority which pervades all of an individual's behavior. Life style can be seen as encompassing all of the behaviors that are characteristic of a person, and that have made him an understandable and predictable member of society. Included are the person's characteristic general approaches like moving close to or distancing from others as well as his patterned approaches to specific situations. Life style is a more ideosyncratic quality than life stage or life space. Life style variables are often highly dependent upon the person's subjective view of himself. Some examples will help to define both the life style and the approaches appropriate to particular characteristics of the individual's life style.

A teacher approaches a high school counselor for help with a problem. Mr. Andrews feels that as he ages his students grow more and more distant from him. He and the counselor continue to talk and the counselor helps Mr. Andrews to formulate his concern more explicitly. He fears that he has lost touch with his skills in forming satisfying relationships with his students. The counselor explores Mr. Andrews' feelings about the situation and agrees that his fears are based in reality and in the kind of role and approach that characterizes his classroom behavior. The counselor offers the outline of a different approach and Mr. Andrews decides to engage in a definite program to learn the techniques of that approach. In a series of sessions in which the counselor models the techniques of attending to what students say and responding directly to their feelings and statements, Mr. Andrews and the counselor alternate in the teacher and student roles. Mr. Andrews then decides to enter a teacher effectiveness group engaged in learning more open communications. He begins to try out the techniques he has learned from the counselor and the group with his students, sometimes recording them for the counselor's appraisal. After a while Mr. Andrews finds that students are telling him and others that they feel closer to and more comfortable with him. He and the counselor arrange to keep in touch occasionally, but agree that Mr. Andrews has grown in his ability to relate to students.

The teacher has worked on a fairly general characteristic of life style. In another case we can examine a more specific factor. A counselor in a college counseling center is approached by a student whose freshmen grades have been below those predicted by previous achievement. He does well on term papers but has developed a paralyzing anxiety when taking tests. As Gary and his counselor talk, it becomes clear that he is really doing fairly well except for this specific problem. He is dating happily, enjoys life at the fraternity house, plays on the tennis team, and enjoys skiing. Gary feels that he is learning in school and that his studies are relevant to his vocational plans. Satisfied that the anxiety is genuine and focused on the testing situation, the counselor suggests the technique called desensitization. (See Chapter 3.) The student learns to relax under the counselor's instruction and, when fully relaxed, is presented with a series of images which Gary and the counselor have made into a hierarchical sequence running from images of situations which cause little anxiety to ones that provoke great anxiety, such as waiting for the tests to be handed out in the testing room. When the student has completed the hierarchy of images and remained fully relaxed, he tests his "desensitization to the testing situation" in reality.

We have seen how three sets of developmental factors—life stage, life space, and life style—can be utilized separately to develop hypotheses out of which developmental counseling goals and approaches can emerge. Obviously, in real counseling situations these three sets of factors are integrated in order to provide a set of filters through which important questions and hypotheses can be formulated. We noted earlier that this process should be continuous, tentative, and testable.

Within the developmental framework we are consequently establishing cognitive maps that help us to explore the unknown territory represented in each client's development. We are *not* searching for a set of labels to hang upon him or a group of neat, categorical boxes to put him in. Our diagnostic constructs are open-ended—generating hypotheses, questions, and possibilities out of which we can develop and refine our goals and approaches. They lead to a gradual enrichment and expansion of our levels of understanding or, in other words, our developmental diagnosis of a person who is growing and becoming.

PREDICTION

The counselor is interested in the problem of prediction for two basic reasons. First, he is interested in testing his understanding of a particular client and with it the adequacy of his personal theory of counseling. He is essentially operating as a scientist in using the self-correcting features of the hypothetico-deductive system to improve his own psychological effectiveness. In many cases, however, prediction becomes an important tool for helping clients themselves. Clients may want predictions about probabilities of success in college, persistence in occupations, or any of many other situations.

The predictive problems involved in these two categories are somewhat different. In the first case in which prediction occurs primarily for the purpose of testing and refining the counselor's theory or understanding, the predictive process involves what Meehl (9) terms a "clinical prediction." A clinical prediction is merely one in which it is difficult or impossible to separate the predictor from the prediction. For example, counselor X interviews a high school senior girl regarding college plans. Her record is excellent and she verbalizes high interest in academic fields. After several interviews, however, counselor X is willing to preduct that this client will drop out of college within two years to marry. This prediction arises not out of objective test data, but out of a very subjective process in the counselor's mind. The prediction is completely verifiable. The client will either drop out of college within two years to marry or she will not. A follow-up will verify or reject the prediction. Testing this prediction will essentially be a test of the counselor's understanding or theoretical system, rather than a challenge of an objective system of prediction.

Instead of using a clinical method of prediction, the counselor might instead use an *actuarial* method. He might obtain a set of college aptitude test scores for the client, insert these into an *expectancy table*, and make a prediction based upon the experience of a group of other individuals with scores similar to his client. From such an actuarial prediction, the counselor could determine a level of probability of persistence in college for people with test scores like this client. In this case, an actuarial prediction of college persistence and a clinical prediction might give exactly opposite results.

Research comparing the efficiency of actuarial and clinical methods of prediction in situations where both are equally applicable typically give results heavily in favor of actuarial methods (9). The choice of methods is not altogether easy, however, even in the presence of these data. The counselor needs to continue to make and to test clinical predictions in order to refine his own personal theory. He does not need to impart these predictions to his client unless he has reason to believe, however, that they will be more useful than a similar prediction made from actuarial data. In situations where actuarial data are available, the counselor needs to compare his predictive efficiency with that of actuarial methods and to use with clients the most efficient method.

In many situations, however, actuarial methods are simply not available. In predicting many kinds of behavior, objective experience tables are just not recorded, and the counselor must resort to the subjective "experience tables" that he carries in his head. In other situations even where actuarial tables exist, there is considerable doubt whether a particular client really fits into a cell in the expectancy table. For example, in predicting college success for a boy with a very different cultural or language background than the group represented in the expectancy table, is it proper to enter the client's scores in the table and accept the prediction given?

Another complicating factor in prediction is the problem of *base rates*. Counselor Y operates in a high school in which 90 per cent of the graduates enter college. Follow-up information shows that 80 per cent of the graduates persist in college after one year. A simple "base rates prediction" of persistence in college after one year will tend to be right four out of five times for graduates of this high school. In some situations, actuarial use of test data based on statewide groups with very different base rates may actually reduce the predictive efficiency obtained from base rates alone.

In general, counselors need systematically to make and test clinical predictions to insure their own professional growth. They also need to assemble actuarial data into expectancy tables whenever possible. In making predictions for client use, counselors need to use the predictive methods known to be the most efficient for the particular problem involved.

THE COUNSELING USE OF TESTS

There is perhaps more general misinformation in circulation concerning the use and misuse of tests in counseling than on any other subject in the field. Various opinions have been widely expressed to the effect that tests are good, bad, immoral, unfair, un-American, useless, infallible, etc. The fact is, of course, that tests themselves are none of these things. A psychological test is merely *a sample of behavior taken under standardized conditions from which we infer other behavior.*

Giving or using tests in counseling is no more indicative of a "diagnostic" or "evaluative" attitude than is making any other kind of observation and drawing any other kind of inference. Tests themselves are only devices for making observations. It is only when the users of test information begin to make inferences from these observations that the possibility of being unjust, biased, or just plain mistaken comes into play.

One of the most frequent sources of misuse of tests involves misunderstandings of the basic assumptions and constructs that underlie the use of particular tests. One of the most frequently misunderstood set of assumptions is that involved in the use of aptitude tests. An aptitude is a psychological construct that we invent to explain individual differences in performance. When we witness a superb performance in some activity, we typically explain this in terms of ascribing to the performer an unusual talent or *aptitude.*

Aptitudes can then never be measured directly. Only performances can be directly observed. In designing so-called aptitude tests, therefore, we contrive to observe a *performance* that is always *learned or achieved,* and we then *infer aptitude.* We *measure* achievement and *infer* aptitude. When we move beyond the observation to infer a psychological construct, certain key assumptions must be made. Very often, however, the nature of these assumptions is forgotten.

Since we cannot measure aptitude, but must infer it from a learned performance, we must assume that individual differences in performance are due to differences in the underlying construct of *aptitude* that we intend to infer. This inference is only reasonable at all if we are willing to make the assumption that *all subjects on whom observations are made have had equal opportunity* to learn or achieve the measured performance.

This assumption is probably reasonably true when we compare performances of subjects who have had relatively homogeneous learning histories, family background, cultural experiences, and so forth. When comparisons are made for groups or individuals without homogeneous backgrounds, the assumption of equal opportunity is invalidated almost immediately.

It follows from this that we can measure differences in achievement or performance rather easily. It becomes quite difficult to make safe inferences that explain these differences. All the tests we use measure *only achievement.* No test now available can measure aptitude directly. If such tests ever come into existence, they will almost undoubtedly be *physiological* rather than *psychological,* and it seems doubtful that they would have high correlations with any socially useful criteria. Until the unlikely event that we are able to attach a galvanomenter to a subject's ears and measure the electrical discharge between them, counselors would do well to remember that constructs like "intelligence" or "scholastic aptitude" or "college ability" are dependent upon highly fallible inferences that go well beyond the nature of the actual observations on which they are based.

Another source of misuse of test information stems from loose thinking about the nature of underlying constructs inferred such as intelligence. For many years, efforts have been made to develop so-called culture-free tests of intelligence. Few quests could be more self-defeating in nature. Perhaps the only defensible general definition of intelligence is "overall ability to adapt to environment." The nature of intelligent behavior is *defined by the environment or culture.* The typical college professor thrown on his own in the jungle is probably less fitted to adapt than the football player whom he fails in mathematics and considers stupid.

The nature of environmental *demands* determines the nature of behavior that will be considered *intelligent.* The term "intelligent" is merely a value word applied to behavior. So long as there are individual and group differences between human beings, there will probably be people to apply value judgments to those differences in terms of good and bad, intelligent and stupid, superior or inferior.

Hunt (6) in studying the facts accumulated in an exhaustive review of evidence from a wide range of relevant research concluded that the assumption of a fixed, genetically determined intelligence is simply not compatible with the evidence. Instead he concludes that intellectual development and the explanatory construct, intelligence, grows from the interaction of the child with his environment. In this context, the role of the developmental counselor is not to use tests to attempt to measure some artificially defined set of limits on development, but to help determine the kinds of environmental encounters that will best facilitate optimal development.

Schwebel explains this position when he says:

> . . . the mental functions of human beings develop in the process of

learning. While mastering the experience of mankind the cerebral systems are formed. . . .

The education of the child begins in infancy. Five or six years later those who enter school with inadequately formed or unformed cerebral functions require diagnostic and corrective measures. They must be helped to acquire these functions through the planned actions of teachers who do not just permissively wait around for some pre-determined potential to develop. [11, p. 651.]

The developmental counselor helps to insure that tests are used in the educational setting to facilitate development, rather than to rationalize failures to do so.

Tests can be used in counseling for two general purposes. The first concerns the testing of counselor hypotheses and has been dealt with in preceding pages. The second use involves interpretation of test information to give clients more adequate information of a descriptive or predictive nature about themselves and their possibilities.

Perhaps the most important factor to be remembered in test interpretation is that test information never constitutes an end in itself, but only represents a tool to be used to facilitate some more important counseling goal. Test interpretations should always be *integrated* into the context of a counseling interview in a way to insure maximum meaning to the client in terms of the client's particular situation. Test interpretations should always *involve* the client in an active consideration of the meaning of the test information *to him*.

Interpretation of test results to clients involves at least minimal understanding of several crucial measurement concepts. The first and most crucial of these is *validity*.

Before we pass to the technical questions that are involved in psychological testing we should reaffirm the importance of very basic understandings. The misuse of psychological tests has probably been connected with more human tragedy than any aspect of modern behavioral science. The systematic oppression of and discrimination against millions of minority children and adults has often been partially sanctioned by the use of tests.

The reader is urgently asked to read very carefully the recommended readings on testing of minority members. A thorough understanding of this literature is virtually an ethical and moral imperative for the developmental counselor.

Validity

Validity involves the degree to which a given instrument measures what it purports to measure. A number of concepts are involved in a discussion of validity. At least four aspects of validity have been identified (1). These include *predictive validity, concurrent validity, content validity,* and *construct validity.*

The type of validity with which the counselor is more typically concerned is *predictive validity.* Predictive validity is the ability of an instrument to predict some future event or events, as for example, grade point averages of a group of high school seniors after one year of college. Predictive validity is usually obtained by computing the correlation coefficient between a distribution of test scores obtained at an earlier time against a distribution of scores on some later criterion measure.

Concurrent validity differs from predictive validity only in the factor of time. It is usually measured by the calculation of a correlation coefficient between the distribution of test scores and some concurrently existing criterion measure. For example, concurrent validity for a standardized test in American History might be obtained by correlating a set of test scores on students with their present grades in history.

The important factor in these two concepts is that they are not interchangeable. A test's ability to predict future events cannot be demonstrated by its correlation with a concurrent criterion measure.

A third aspect of validity is *content validity.* In many kinds of tests, particularly achievement tests in subject matter fields, it is important to demonstrate that the items of the test are representative of a universe of items that is comprehensive enough to represent the presumed objectives of the content field. Content validity differs from predictive and concurrent validity in that it is determined essentially by the process through which the items were *selected.* For example, a test publisher might obtain a universe of several thousand items developed by eleventh-grade American History teachers to measure their course objectives. These items might be reduced to several hundred by eliminating overlapping content. From this pool, a test of one hundred items might be drawn by random or stratified random sampling. This test could then claim content validity on the basis that it is representative of a universe of items deemed by experts to define the relevant content of American History at a particular level.

The fourth and generally most confusing aspect of validity is *construct validity.* Construct validity is not of great concern to most practicing counselors. Construct validity is a concept that is useful in research in areas where knowledge is so limited that usual kinds of criterion measures are of little value. For example, the psychologist who is interested in investigating the phenomenon of "anxiety" is likely to find a number of measures of anxiety exist, but that none of these really represents a comprehensive measure of the construct as it is inferred from personality theory. He devises an instrument in terms of how much the results obtained fit the theoretical formulations that undergirded its development. If the results are relevant to the theoretical base and help to develop or elaborate the theory, the test can be said to have construct validity.

It should be remembered that the practicing counselor need not be impressed with claims of construct validity for tests to be interpreted to clients. Unless tests can demonstrate predictive, concurrent, or content validity, it is usually of little value to interpret them to clients. Tests are typically interpreted to clients in order to help them understand better the probability of future events (predictive validity), how they compare with some relevant group (concurrent validity), or how completely they have mastered some field of knowledge (content validity). See Table 8–1.

Another concept of validity that is often erroneously conceived is *face validity*. Face validity is the degree to which the items of a test *appear* to measure something. Face validity is, of course, no validity at

TABLE 8–1

Types of Validity Measures and Relevant Criteria

Type of Validity	Type of Criterion
Predictive	Correlation of present set of scores with a set of future events
Concurrent	Correlation of present scores with some other observation of present behavior
Content	Representativeness of items of some well-defined universe of content
Construct	Compatibility of results with some theoretically derived hypothetical model

all in an empirical sense. For example, a test that seems to measure mechanical ability and is replete with items about gears, pulleys, vectors, etc., may have no empirical validity of any kind. Another personality test, for example, that is composed of many "subtle" items that have no apparent relevance can have substantial empirical validity.

Reliability

Another major concept involved in using tests is *reliability*. Reliability refers to the consistency of a measurement. The two major aspects of reliability are consistency of measurement over time, which is usually determined by test–retest reliability, and consistency between two similar measurements, which is usually termed "parallel forms" or "split-half" reliability. These two aspects of reliability are not the same since the kinds of consistency being measured are quite different.

Test–retest reliability is the type of reliability in which counselors are usually most interested. It is usually computed by calculating the correlation coefficient between two distributions of test scores obtained at two different times on the same population. The time interval between administrations is the relevant factor in evaluating the consistency of the test. For example, a test may have a test–retest reliability of .90 for two administrations one month apart. This gives a meaningful measure of its reliability over time.

Test–retest reliabilities are obviously expensive and difficult to obtain. Because of this fact, test publishers may use measures of internal consistency in place of test–retest reliabilities. For example, the test-builder may take a set of test items and divide them in two parts through some random method such as odd and even numbered items. He may then correlate the scores obtained from each half or form of the test to obtain a measure called a "split-half" or sometimes a "parallel forms" reliability. This measure only tells the user the extent to which the two halves or forms of the instrument perform in the same way or, in essence, measure the same things. It *does not* measure the consistency of the measurement over time in any way.

Occasionally, the nature of the construct to be measured is such that high test–retest reliability is not desirable. For example, a "mood scale" intended to measure fluctuations in emotional reactions would not be expected to possess reliability over time because the underlying construct is not presumed to be stable over time. Achievement tests or tests of "mental age" or other time-linked constructs would not be expected to have great reliability over *long* periods of time. On the other hand, constructs such as aptitudes are usually considered relatively stable over time even though the evidence for this is far from conclusive.

Since nearly all psychological tests, like other kinds of measurements, are not perfectly reliable, the degree of imprecision caused by this factor has to be considered in any use or interpretation of scores. In using psychological tests, this imprecision is accounted for in what is commonly called a "band interpretation." A band interpretation in contrast to a "point interpretation" recognizes the fact that, because of unreliability of measurements, a particular score would not probably be repeated on a subsequent administration of the test. Instead, by converting the reliability coefficient into what is called a "standard error of measurement," we can calculate the width of the band in which subsequent scores can be expected to fall at some level of probability—in this case, approximately two times out of three. For example, if the standard error of measurement of a particular test is plus or minus five raw score points and we have an obtained raw score of 85, we can expect that, upon retesting, about two-thirds of the time scores would fall between 80 and 90.

A few other relatively simple injunctions regarding the use of tests need to be kept in mind by counselors. Some of these are listed below:

1. Test scores must always be interpreted in the context of *all* available information regarding the client. Information regarding the cultural background, health, motivation, and educational skills of clients, among other variables, are essential factors in placing the meaning of test scores in perspective.
2. Predictions from test scores obtained through actuarial or "expectancy" tables are always for groups, never for individuals. The prediction should always be made in the third person plural: "For people with scores like these . . ."
3. Success in almost any endeavor is determined by a complex of factors that certainly include motivation and self-control as well as ability. Ability may be a necessary factor but is almost always not a sufficient condition for success.

Tests are useful instruments for making observations and, in some cases, predictions about human behavior. The nature of the inferences that can be legitimately drawn from test data is limited. It is very unlikely that clients can be adequately described by test data alone. Such data, when skillfully combined with other observations, can be useful to a counselor. If the counselor is to use tests as an important part of his set of professional techniques, he must become expert in their use. Such expertness comes only through intensive study and wide experience with the instruments to be used.

REFERENCES

1. AMERICAN PSYCHOLOGICAL ASSOCIATION. *Technical recommendations for psychological tests and diagnostic techniques.* Washington, D.C.: American Psychological Association, 1973.
2. BLOCHER, D. H., & SHAFFER, W. Guidance and human development. In Cook, D. R. (Ed.). *Guidance for education in revolution.* Boston: Allyn and Bacon, 1971.
3. BUTLER, J. M., & RICE, L ADIENCE, self-actualization and drive theory. In Wepman, J. & Heine, J. (Eds.). *Concepts of personality.* Chicago: Aldine Publishing, 1962.
4. EYSENCK, H. J. Classification and diagnosis. In H. J. Eysenck (Ed.), *The handbook of abnormal psychology.* New York: Basic Books, 1961.
5. HEISLER, VERA. Toward a process model of psychological health. *J. counsel. Psychol.,* 1961, 11 (1), 59–62.
6. HUNT, J. McV. *Intelligence and experience.* New York: Ronald, 1961.
7. KOESTER, G. A. A study of the diagnostic process. *Educ. psychol. Measmt,* 1954, 14:473–486.
8. MCARTHUR, C. Analyzing the clinical process. *J. counsel. Psychol.,* 1954, 1:203–208.
9. MEEHL, P. E. *Clinical vs. statistical prediction: a theoretical analysis and review of the evidence.* Minneapolis: University of Minnesota Press, 1954.
10. MENNINGER, K. *The vital balance.* New York: Viking, 1963.
11. PARKER, C. As a clinician thinks. *J. counsel. Psychol.,* 1958, 5 (4), 253–262.
12. PEPINSKY, H. B. *The selection and use of diagnostic categories in clinical counseling.* Applied Psychol. Monogr., 1948, No. 15.
13. PEPINSKY, H. B., & PEPINSKY, PAULINE. *Counseling: theory and practice.* New York: Ronald, 1954. Pp. 233–250.
14. RIESEN, A. H. Stimulation as a requirement for growth and function in behavioral development. In Fiske, D. W., & Maddi, S. R. (Eds.). *Functions of varied experience.* Homewood, Ill.: Dorsey Press, 1951.
15. SCHWEBEL, M. Learning and the socially deprived. *Personnel Guidance J.,* 1965, 43 (7), 646–653.

RECOMMENDED READINGS

Diagnosis in Counseling

KOESTER, G. A. A study of the diagnostic process. *Educ. psychol. Measmt,* 1954, 14:473–486.

McArthur, C. Analyzing the clinical process. *J. counsel. Psychol.*, 1954, 1:203–208.
Meehl, J. The cognitive activity of the clinician. *Amer. Psychologist*, 1960, 15 (1), 19–27.
Menninger, K. *The vital balance.* New York: Viking, 1963.
Miller, H., & Bieri, J. An informational analysis of clinical judgment. *J. abnorm. soc. Psychol.*, 1963, 67:317–325.
Parker, C. As a clinician thinks. *J. counsel. Psychol.*, 1958, 5 (4), 253–262.
Robinson, F. P. Modern approaches to counseling diagnosis. *J. counsel. Psychol.*, 1963, 10:325–333.
Witryol, S., & Boly, L. Positive diagnosis in personality counseling. *J. counsel. Psychol.*, 1954, 1:63–69.

Prediction in Counseling

Cautela, J. R. The low probability hypothesis. *Personnel Guidance J.*, 1964, 42:670–673.
Endler, N. S., & Steinberg, D. Prediction of academic achievement at the university level. *Personnel Guidance J.*, 1963, 41:694–699.
Juola, A. E. Predictive validity of five college-level academic aptitude tests at one institution. *Personnel Guidance J.*, 1960, 38 (8), 637–641.
Lewis, E. C., & MacKinney, A. C. Counselor vs. statistical predictions of job satisfaction in engineering. *J. counsel. Psychol.*, 1961, 8 (3), 244–230.
Meehl, P. E. *Clinical vs. statistical prediction.* Minneapolis: University of Minnesota Press, 1954.
Meehl, P. E. Wanted—a good cookbook. *Amer. Psychologist*, 1956, 11:263–272.
Rinsland, H. D. Actuarial prediction in guidance. *J. educ. Res.*, 1961, 54:168–172.
Towbin, A. When are cookbooks useful. *Amer. Psychologist*, 1960, 15 (2), 119–123.

General Considerations in the Counseling Use of Tests

American Psychological Association. *Technical recommendations for psychological tests and diagnostic techniques.* Washington, D.C.: Author, 1973.
Bauernfeind, R. H. The matter of ipsative scores. *Personnel Guidance J.*, 1962, 41:210–217.
Bechtoldt, H. P. Construct validity: a critique. *Amer. Psychologist*, 1959, 14 (10), 619–629.
Berdie, R. F., Layton, W. L., Swanson, E. O., & Hagenah, Theda. *Testing in guidance and counseling.* New York: McGraw-Hill, 1963.
Bernardoni, L. C. A culture fair intelligence test for the ugh, no, and oo-la-la cultures. *Personnel Guidance J.*, 1964, 42:554–557.
Cheers, Arlynne Lake, & Sherman, Dorothy M. Response pattern differences of selected Negro and white subjects on S.C.A.T. *Personnel Guidance J.*, 1963, 41:582–589.
Cooper, J. G. The culture-free intelligence test in a college of the western Pacific. *Personnel Guidance J.*, 1962, 41:123–125.
Gough, H. The relationship of socio-economic status to personality inventory and achievement test scores. *J. educ. Psychol.*, 1946, 27:527–540.
Guilford, J. P. Three faces of intellect. *Amer. Psycholgist*, 1959, 14 (8), 469–479.
Humphreys, L. G. The organization of human abilities. *Amer. Psychologist*, 1962, 17:475–483.
Jones, M. The polarity of psychological tests. *J. consult. Psychol.*, 1958, 22 (1), 25–29.

KLINEBERG, O. Negro–white differences in intelligence test performance: a new look at an old problem. *Amer. Psychologist*, 1963, 18:198–203.

SPIKER, C. C., & MCCANDLESS, B. R. The concept of intelligence and the philosophy of science. *Psychol. Rev.*, 1954, 61:255–266.

SUPER, D. E. The multifactor tests: summing up. In G. Farwell, & H. Peters (Eds.). *Guidance readings for counselors*. Chicago: Rand McNally, 1959.

TYLER, LEONA. *Tests and measurements*. Englewood Cliffs, N.J.: Prentice-Hall, 1971.

Interpreting Tests to Clients

BERG, I. A. Test score interpretation and client confusions. *Personnel Guidance J.*, 1956, 34:576–578.

Faries, MIRIAM. A therapeutic approach to test interpretation. *Personnel Guidance J.*, 1957, 35:523–526.

GUSTAD, J. W., & TUMA, A. H. The effects of different methods of test interpretation on client learning in counseling. *J. counsel. Psychol.*, 1957, 4:313–317.

KAMM, R. B., & WRENN, C. G. Client acceptance of self-information in counseling. *Educ. psychol. Measmt*, 1950, 10:32–42.

RUDIKOFF, LYNN, & KIRK, BARBARA. Test interpretation in counseling. *J. counsel. Psychol.*, 1959, 6 (3), 223–229.

Interest Measurement

EWENS, W. P. Relationship of interest to aptitude by profiles and by interest areas. *Personnel Guidance J.*, 1963, 42:359–363.

LAYTON, W. *Counseling use of the strong vocational interest blank*. Minnesota studies in student personnel work no. 8. Minneapolis: University of Minnesota Press, 1958.

STRONG, E. K., JR. *Vocational interests of men and women*. Stanford, Calif.: Stanford University Press, 1943.

STRONG, E. K., JR. *Vocational interests eighteen years after college*. Minneapolis: University of Minnesota Press, 1955.

SUPER, D. E. The measurement of interests. *J. counsel, Psychol.*, 1954, 1 (3), 169–171.

Testing Minority Members

ROBERTS, JOAN. (Ed.). *Children in the Urban slum*. New York: Free Press, 1967.

WILCOX, R. C. *The psychological consequences of being a black American*. New York: Wiley, 1971.

(These two books of readings are musts for counselors who work with minority children.)

9

DEVELOPMENTAL RELATIONSHIPS

Whitaker and Malone (20) define counseling as an interpersonal relationship that accelerates the growth of one or both participants. For the developmental counselor, such a definition has obvious relevance. The central question that is involved in such an approach, however, concerns the essential nature of growth-accelerating relationships (1, 2, 12, 14).

CHARACTERISTICS OF DEVELOPMENTAL RELATIONSHIPS

Carl Rogers (15) and other client-centered counselors have written extensively about the nature of helping relationships. Rogers believes very strongly that the formation of helping relationships depends not upon any set of techniques that the counselor may or may not have mastered, but rather upon the kinds of attitudes that the counselor holds about himself, his client, and the nature of their interaction. Rogers' approach to the nature of helping relationships can perhaps best be summarized by paraphrasing a number of questions that he says the counselor might ask himself as he approaches the counseling relationship (15). These include the following.

1. Can I *be* in some way that will be perceived by the other person as dependable or consistent in some deep sense?
2. Can I be expressive enough as a person that what I am will be communicated unambiguously?
3. Can I let myself experience positive attitudes toward this person—attitudes of warmth, caring, liking, interest, and respect?
4. Can I be strong enough as a person to be separate from the other? Can I be a sturdy respector of my own needs as well as his?
5. Am I secure enough within myself to permit him his separateness?
6. Can I let myself enter fully into the world of his feelings and personal meanings and see these as he does?
7. Can I be acceptant of each facet of this other person that he presents to me?
8. Can I act with sufficient sensitivity in the relationship that my behavior will not be perceived as a threat?
9. Can I free him from the threat of external evaluation?
10. Can I meet this other individual as a person who is in the process of *becoming*, or will I be bound by his past and by my past?

These questions represent one of the most thoughtful approaches to the nature of counseling relationships available in the literature. Rogers has essentially distilled these questions further in defining three factors that he considers essential conditions for learning in counseling (16). These are: "congruence," "unconditional positive regard," and "empathic understanding." Each of these concepts deserves some thoughtful and critical attention.

Congruence

Congruence is generally considered the quality of being one's self, not playing a part or a role or being artificial. As we have seen, however, the very fact that we live in a complex society means that we play many roles. Does the fact that a counselor's behavior in a counseling relationship may be somewhat different from his behavior in a social conversation, for example, mean that he is not being congruent? How different can the counselor be within various roles without being "phoney" or artificial? Is counseling really a generalized "way of life" rather than a professional specialty? These are very significant questions for the counselor in preparation.

Perhaps the most useful concept of the distinction between entering a specialized professional role and being an artificial or "phoney" person is that supplied by Grinker (9). He points out that some counselors may advocate playing particular artificially assumed roles for the supposed benefit of particular clients or particular occasions. This kind of artificially assumed role is usually detected as such by the client. The spontaneity of the relationship under these conditions is quickly destroyed, and the client loses trust and confidence in the counselor. The counselor who tries deliberately to be "reassuring or supportive" today and "objective and analytical" tomorrow is obviously playing a set of parts for the client's benefit and, no matter what his artistry as an actor, will eventually be recognized as an actor and nothing more.

Grinker distinguishes between this kind of acting and the entering of *social roles*. These roles do not imply the artificiality of stage acting because social roles refer to *automatic* patterns of behavior *deeply internalized* through social learning. These roles and the behavior that they elicit are a *deep* and *genuine* part of personality. Being able to enter the role of "helping person" in the sense that Rogers conceptualizes it does not necessarily mean that the individual has not internalized other social roles and is capable of being "congruent" in them as well. As Grinker points out, social roles may be conceived of as bridges between personality and social behavior. They are derived from *unconscious* attitudes and are governed by many complex motivations rather than a simple desire to make a specific impression upon an individual at a particular moment in time.

Unconditional Positive Regard

Unconditional positive regard is the term that Rogers has used to define the quality of acceptance. Acceptance has a long and confusing history in the literature of counseling. Although most writers in the field have repeated the usual clichés about the importance of acceptance, few have done much toward clarifying its nature. Several kinds of definitions or approaches to acceptance can be identified.

Perhaps the most common approach to acceptance has been to define it as the absence of evaluation or moral judgment. This approach has typically held that external evaluation is bad and that counselors are accepting when they do not evaluate or judge human beings or their behavior.

Several practical problems are attached to this approach. First, how is the absence of evaluation or judgment different than an attitude of indifference or laissez faire, neither of which is generally considered a useful attitude in counseling? Second, if, as Arbuckle (3) says, it is impossible to distinguish between evaluating an individual and evaluating his behavior, how can counselors who have value systems of their own be genuinely accepting? Is the effective counselor a shadowy, truly valueless, neutral person?

Another approach to acceptance is that implied by Rogers' term of unconditional positive regard. This implies a generalized belief in the dignity and importance of all human beings regardless of their behavior. As an abstraction, this philosophical approach is probably given lip service to by most individuals in our society. In practice, in face-to-face relationships with individuals, what does unconditional positive regard really mean. Does believing in the worth and dignity of all human beings imply ignoring all individual differences? Are all human beings equally worthwhile? These are some of the questions left unanswered by this approach.

Working through answers to questions like these are part of the necessary professional development of every counselor. They are based upon deeply held philosophical convictions about the nature of man, religious beliefs, etc. For this writer, however, acceptance implies the following meanings, which may or may not be helpful to another counselor.

First, acceptance does *not* mean the absence of moral judgment about a client's behavior. Judgments about behavior are an inescapable part of being a valuing human being. Acceptance does mean a belief in the worth of a client. It means that this client is specifically worth all the attention, skill, and understanding that the counselor is able to focus upon him. Essentially, acceptance means *interest in* and *concern for* a client, *not judgment about* clients. The most significant signs of non-acceptance of clients are not moral judgments, but feelings of boredom, disinterest, and lack of caring.

Empathic Understanding

Empathic understanding is another term that is not without difficulty. For example, the concept of empathy is difficult to differentiate from commonly used terms like sympathy and understanding and from psychological concepts such as projection, identification, and transference (13). Projecting one's own feelings on others or overidentifying with a client's problems may obviously limit one's ability to help. On the other hand, it is possible to have a rather clear and accurate perception of dynamics of behavior without being able to enter a helping relationship. For example, a psychologist in a prison may interview a criminal and understand rather thoroughly the dynamics of his behavior without being able to reach him psychologically within the context of what could be called a helping relationship.

Empathy then involves at least two components. One is a cognitive component that involves psychological understanding. The other is an affective component of feeling *with* a person.

Perhaps the best discussion of what empathy means in counseling is that given by Buchheimer (4). He discusses empathy within the context of several dimensions of the counseling process. The interaction of counselor and client in terms of these dimensions serve essentially as operational definitions of the empathic qualities of the counseling relationship. These dimensions are:

1. *Tone*. This is an expressive and often non-verbal dimension based upon nuances of expressions of warmth and spontaneity.
2. *Pace*. This involves the appropriateness and togetherness of timing in the interview.
3. *Perception*. This relates to the counselor's ability to abstract the core of the client's concerns and to formulate them in acceptable terms to him.
4. *Strategy*. This relates to the predictive or role-playing aspect of the interview. It relates closely to Pepinsky's "model client."
5. *Leading*. This relates to the resourcefulness of the counselor in formulating a set of leads that will move the interview in the direction of the client's concerns.

For Buchheimer, then, empathy involves a great deal more than a simple understanding of the client's verbalizations or even of a warm or sympathetic attitude toward him.

Trust

This is another difficult concept in counseling. Does trust mean that the client believes that the counselor will always put his allegiance to the client above all others? Does it mean that ethical obligations such as confidentiality must be absolute? How is trust developed and communicated in a counseling relationship?

In terms of the writer's experience, trust has a rather specific meaning. Trust in this sense consists of an individual's feeling of inner certainty that he can predict another's behavior under a given set of circumstances. The client is able to trust when he believes that he can predict the counselor's behavior. Trust then does not depend upon how well the client will *like* the counselor's behavior in a given situation, but how well he feels he can predict that behavior.

Trust thus is based upon consistency rather than compatibility. A client must have available some sample of counselor behavior upon which to base his judgment of predictability. It is very difficult to predict the behavior of a shadowy, neutral, unreal person.

Clients need to be able to trust counselors in this sense if they are to risk revealing themselves in any really significant way. Counselors too need to trust clients if they are to be able to behave consistently and confidently. The ability of the counselor to predict client behavior is more than a psychological game by which he tests his own sophistication. Understanding, tested by prediction, is a basis on which the counselor can approach a client with openness and trust.

One of the most difficult problems for the student counselor is how to synthesize the complex set of concepts and abstractions that are used to describe the relationship aspects of counseling into some set of attitudes and understandings that will be personally useful in actual counseling situations (6, 7, 18). No one can ever fully understand the meaning of a counseling relationship by reading about it. Experience in a wide range of interpersonal relationships and a real desire to become aware of and sensitive to the quality of one's interpersonal relationships are probably the necessary conditions for developing the capacity to be a helping person.

The kinds of learnings that are involved in this process are as much or more of an emotional nature as of a cognitive type. For many people, the process of critically examining their interpersonal behavior and opening themselves to "feedback" in terms of how they are perceived by others is a very threatening and painful experience. The counseling practicum and the group and individual relationships that surround it are effective largely in terms of the opportunities that they offer for this learning to take place.

A number of generalizations about the nature of counseling relationships may be helpful in assisting the counselor who is preparing himself to enter practicum experiences.

1. The capacity to develop counseling relationships is more attitudinal and personal than cognitive and technical. As a rule, techniques alone are not adequate for building relationships.

2. There is no single formalized "counseling relationship." Rather,

each counselor has to discover the particular kind of interpersonal relationship that will enable *him* to be most helpful to clients.

3. The key to developing effective counseling relationships lies more in sensitivity to others' reactions and flexibility of responses rather than in rigidly trying to implement a preconceived stereotype of what the counselor should be.

RESEARCH ON DEVELOPMENTAL RELATIONSHIPS

Perhaps some discussion of the very limited research available on relationships in counseling will cast further light on these generalizations. The most often quoted study in this area is that done by Fiedler (8). Fiedler attempted to answer two questions: (*a*) Do therapists with divergent theoretical views differ in their concept of an ideal therapeutic relationship? (*b*) Is the concept of an ideal human relationship unique to psychotherapy, or does it simply represent a general view of good interpersonal relationships?

In attempting to answer the first question, Fiedler had groups of experienced and inexperienced therapists from several theoretical orientations (psychoanalytic, non-directive, Adlerian, and eclectic) sort a set of statements describing the ideal therapeutic relationship. In analyzing these data, he found greater agreement among experienced therapists of different theoretical persuasions than between experienced and inexperienced therapists of the same theoretical orientation.

In answering the second question, Fiedler compared the sorts of non-psychologically trained raters with those of the therapists. He found that non-psychologically trained raters had very high agreement with therapists in describing the nature of an ideal therapeutic relationship.

Fiedler concluded that therapists of different orientations do not differ from each other or from laymen in describing the nature of an ideal therapeutic relationship.

Another interesting set of studies are those by Truax and Carkhuff (19) who reported a series of studies that analyzed interviews of clients ranging from college students to hospitalized schizophrenics. Personality test results and other criteria were used to determine improvement or deterioration. When interviews of both improved and deteriorated subjects were analyzed, those subjects who were judged as improved were found to be in counseling relationships with therapists whose behavior was rated significantly higher on *empathy, unconditional positive regard,* and *self-congruence.* Patients who were judged as deteriorated were correspondingly found in relationships with therapists judged low on all three variables.

Truax and Carkhuff conclude that counseling relationships may operate as two-edged instruments capable of either hurting or helping clients, depending upon the nature of the relationship.

A study by Combs and Soper (5) is relevant to the counselor personality characteristics associated with counseling effectiveness as judged by a counselor education staff. They evaluated protocols obtained from twenty-nine counselors in training. These protocols came from papers submitted by the students describing a "Human Relations Incident." These protocols were scored by judges on the basis of twelve perceptual constructs based on how the subject perceived himself and others and the nature of counseling. Scores on these constructs were then correlated with counselor education staff judgments about the effectiveness of the students at the end of training. Ten of the twelve correlations were significant at the .01 level of confidence. High correlations were with the following constructs:

1. Sees people as able rather than unable
2. Sees counseling as freeing rather than controlling
3. Sees people as friendly rather than unfriendly
4. Sees self as identified rather than unidentified
5. Sees self as revealing rather than unrevealing

Combs and Soper interpret their results to indicate that counselor attitudes and perceptual processes are the important determinants of counselor effectiveness.

These studies seem to support the general proposition that the development of effective counseling relationships is determined more by the counselor's personality than by his theoretical orientation or repertory of techniques.

Counseling then is not primarily a rigid mold of behavior that a counselor puts on and takes off. Rather, it is a relationship appropriate to a given task of helping another person grow that leaves the counselor as a natural and spontaneous person.

As Wyatt says:

> It is actually a sign of professional maturity when the therapist begins to drop role and gesture and undertakes to be himself. He will have found out then that he can only do his work best in his own way and with the resources of his own personality. [21, p. 307.]

Clark Moustakas says much the same thing when he describes the important factor in any helping relationship as the encounter or confrontation between two people.

> In the true confrontation, the relationship unfolds into more and more meaningful expression of the self, release of feelings and resolutions of issues and conflicts toward growing insights and awareness and toward a sense of responsibility. In such a confrontation the teacher is all there, fully committed as a person. It is sheer nonsense to consider whether, in the moments of the full human exertion of a confrontation, the teacher can adapt himself to the role of the educator, or therapist, or disciplinarian. The teacher is there as a total person engaged in a meeting in which all dimensions and resources of self converge, in which the whole being comes to grips with an impelling human conflict. [11, p. 262.]

In another publication, Moustakas writes again of his own development as a therapist.

> I saw that I must stop playing the role of the professional therapist and allow my potentials, talents, and skills, my total experiences as a human being to blend naturally into the relationship with the child and, whenever possible, to meet him as a whole person. Thus, I came to realize that one person, a direct, human-loving person, a unified personal and professional self, meets another person, a loving or potentially loving child and, through a series of deep human encounters, waits for and enables the child to come to his own self-fulfillment. [10, p. xiii.]

The counseling relationship does not come about, then, by putting on a professional cloak or pulling out a bag of tricks. It is more a product of *encounter and confrontation,* of *interest in* and *caring about* people than of techniques and abstractions (17). It arises out of being a real person within the framework of a human encounter between a client and a professional person who is deeply genuine and warmly human.

OTHER ASPECTS OF COUNSELING RELATIONSHIPS

Limits

Like all human relationships, counseling relationships have limits. Limits on the relationship govern the behavior of both counselor and client. The counselor's behavior is governed by a set of ethical obligations, for example. The client, on the other hand, is limited in terms of time of appointments, length of appointments, the nature of interaction with the counselor, and so forth. Sometimes it becomes difficult for clients to accept some limits on the relationship.

Dependency

Some clients develop feelings of *dependency* on the counselor. They may feel a need for the counselor to give more and more of his time, to break appointments with other clients to see them, to conduct interviews by telephone or in non-professional settings, or for the counselor to give them advice or take responsibility for their decisions. Such demands are evidences of client dependency. Although the client may genuinely experience these feelings as needs, it is obvious that long-term dependency of this kind in a counseling relationship is seldom growth producing. The counselor generally faces the task of accepting the client's feelings of need for special favors or setting aside of limits without acceding to them in a way that will foster immature dependency or will be disruptive to the counselor's professional activities.

Transference

Another relationship phenomenon is *transference*. At times within a counseling relationship, either a client or a counselor may develop feelings toward the other of an irrational or disturbing nature. Dealing with these feelings before they reach proportions that destroy the relationship is important. Transference feelings may be either positive or negative. In either case, they should be brought into the open and *worked through*.

Such a working-through process may be painful and threatening to both counselor and client. If strong feelings are present, however, ignoring them will not be a satisfactory solution for either counselor or client.

Resistance

Another phenomenon involved in the relationship is *resistance*. Resistance consists of client behavior that seems aimed at hindering progress within the counseling process. Examples of client resistance may consist of turning away from subject matter that seems highly relevant, being distracted or inattentive, or it may take the form of being late for appointments, missing appointments, failing to follow through on assignments, and so forth.

Resistance phenomena can be classified as *unconscious* or *conscious*, depending on the client's ability to recognize and to verbalize. Often when the counseling process begins to touch a very sensitive or painful area of the client's life, he tries to protect himself from the resulting anxiety without really being aware of what he is doing. In such cases, the counselor may need to accept the resistance but help the client become aware of what is happening. In other situations, the client may be aware of what he is doing in terms of resistance. The counselor again may need to accept his right to resist, but may need to work through why the reluctance exists in terms of the nature of the relationship.

There are several problems that exist in handling resistance. First, the counselor may have negative feelings of impatience, hurt feelings, or feelings of inadequacy as resistance phenomena appear. It may be very difficult to accept the client who seems to resist attempts to help him. Working through these feelings as they appear may be better than letting them build up, however.

Another difficulty is, of course, that what the counselor sees as resistance is possibly merely the result of his own clumsiness or misperception. When the client wants to talk about something that seems less productive to the counselor, it is very possible that the latter's judgment is simply in error. It may also be that the counselor is misperceiving the nature of the relationship in that the client does not really have the security and trust necessary to talk about threatening areas. Both of these hypotheses should probably be tested before the counselor makes even a tentative judgment about client resistance.

There are no general pat solutions or techniques that will solve relationship problems. The best approach to most of these relationship phenomena is one of direct, open, and honest reaction to the client. If the counselor can be secure enough to deal with the relationship in these ways, some of this security will usually be communicated to the client and will help him to be more open, trusting, and confident.

Working through relationship problems as they occur is generally an activity of high priority and in order at almost any stage of the counseling process. Postponing dealing with such problems or ignoring them altogether usually simply frustrates the entire counseling effort.

The developmental relationship has two basic purposes: *to support* and *to stimulate*. The supporting function is aimed at restoring a sufficient level of security or homeostasis to an individual to free sufficient energy for differentiation or growth processes to move forward. The relationship also serves to stimulate the client toward new growth experiences and toward alternative ways of behaving that will facilitate further growth in desired directions. The function of the relationship is to change levels of *security* and *motivation* in order for optimum development to occur.

REFERENCES

1. ANDERSON, R. P., & ANDERSON, G. V. Development of an instrument for measuring rapport. *Personnel Guidance J.*, 1962, 41:18–24.
2. ARBUCKLE, D. S. Client perception of counselor personality. *J. counsel. Psychol.*, 1956, 3 (2), 93–96.
3. ARBUCKLE, D. S. *Counseling: Philosophy Theory and Practice.* Boston: Allyn & Bacon, 1961. 2nd ed., 1971.
4. BUCHHEIMER, A. The development of ideas about empathy. *J. counsel. Psychol.*, 1963, 10 (1), 61–71.
5. COMBS, A. W., & SOPER, D. W. The perceptual organization of effective counselors. *J. counsel. Psychol.*, 1963, 10:222–226.
6. DRASGOW, J., & WALKER, R. A graphic description of counseling relationships. *J. counsel. Psychol.*, 1960, 7 (1), 51–55.
7. FARSON, R. E. The counselor as a woman. *J. counsel. Psychol.*, 1954, 1:221–223.
8. FIEDLER, F. E. A comparison of therapeutic relationship in psychoanalytic therapy, non-directive and Adlerian. *J. consult. Psychol.*, 1950, 14:436–455.
9. GRINKER, R. R., MACGREGOR, HELEN, SELAN, KATE, KLEIN, ANNETTE, & KOHRMAN, JANET. *Psychiatric social work: a transactional case book.* New York: Basic Books, 1961.
10. MOUSTAKAS, C. E. *Psychotherapy with children: the living relationship.* New York: Ballantine Books, 1970.
11. MOUSTAKAS, C. E. Confrontation and encounter. *J. existent. Psychiat.*, 1961–62, 2:266–269.
12. O'HERN, JANE S., & ARBUCKLE, D. S. Sensitivity: a measurable concept? *Personnel Guidance J.*, 1964, 42:572–576.
13. PATTERSON, C. H. A note on the construct validity of the concept of empathy. *Personnel Guidance J.*, 1962, 40:803–806.
14. REEVES, MARY E., & ARBUCKLE, D. S. The counseling attitudes of deans of women. *Personnel Guidance J.*, 1963, 41:438–441.
15. ROGERS, C. R. Characteristics of a helping relationship. *Personnel Guidance J.*, 1958, 37:6–16.
16. ROGERS, C. R. *On becoming a person: a therapist's view of psychotherapy.* Boston: Houghton Mifflin, 1961.
17. STANDAL, S. W., & CORSINI, R. J. *Critical incidents in psychotherapy.* Englewood Cliffs, N.J.: Prentice-Hall, 1959.
18. STEFFLRE, B., & LEAFGREN, F. A. Mirror, mirror on the wall: a study of preferences for counselors. *Personnel Guidance J.*, 1964, 42:459–462.
19. TRUAX, C. B., & CARKHUFF, R. *Toward effective counseling and psychotherapy.* Chicago: Aldine Publishing, 1967.
20. WHITAKER, C., & MALONE, T. *The roots of psychotherapy.* New York: McGraw-Hill, 1953.

21. WYATT, F. The self-experience of the psychotherapist. In J. McGowan and L. Schmidt (Eds.), *Counseling: readings in theory and practice.* New York: Holt, Rinehart & Winston, 1962.

RECOMMENDED READINGS

COMBS, A. W., *et.al. Helping relationships: basic concepts for the helping professions.* Rockleigh, N.J.: Allyn and Bacon, 1971.

KELL, B. L., MUELLER, W. J. *Impact and change: a study of counseling relationships.* New York: Appleton-Century-Crofts, 1966.

MOUSTAKAS, C. E. *Personal Growth: the struggle for identity and human values.* Cambridge, Mass.: Howard Doyle, 1969.

PIETROFESA, J. J., LEONARD, G. E., & VAN HOOSE, W., *The authentic counselor.* Chicago: Rand McNally, 1971.

ROGERS, C. *On becoming a person.* Boston: Houghton Mifflin, 1961.

10

DEVELOPMENTAL
INTERVIEWS

Discussions of interviewing are usually concerned with questions of technique. In the sense that developmental counseling primarily involves an interpersonal relationship, there are no cut and dried techniques of *counseling*. Rather, there are some techniques of *interviewing* that may be used to maximize communication between counselor and client, and consequently to enhance opportunities for worthwhile learning to take place within the counseling relationship.

Probably the most serious danger for the beginning counselor in approaching the interview situation is that he may become *fixated* with problems of technique. Often, when a counselor becomes preoccupied with trying to use some set of techniques, he loses the very qualities of sincerity, spontaneity, and concern for the client that make possible the establishment of genuine counseling relationships. One of the remarkable phenomena associated with the use of interview techniques in counseling is that often they are effective only when the counselor is no longer conscious of using them; that is, techniques are helpful only when they are *internalized* by the counselor and *incorporated* into his *natural pattern of counseling behavior*.

Too often, beginning counselors view techniques as ends in themselves rather than as means to ends. For example, they may become preoccupied with some relatively difficult technique such as reflection of feeling and make this a purpose for the interview rather than using it for the needs of the client. Another pitfall of technique is that counselors tend to apply value connotations to techniques themselves. Techniques are never *good or bad in themselves*. They can only be evaluated in terms of some set of goals that has been set up for the counseling interview itself.

FORMULATION OF GOALS

The first consideration in any discussion of counseling interviews concerns the formulation of goals. Without some formulation of goals or purposes, it is impossible for a counselor to assess his own progress or the degree of progress with a particular case or the effectiveness of the approaches that he uses.

Formulation of goals in developmental counseling comes from two major sources. The first of these is the counselor's own personal theory and philosophy of counseling. From this standpoint, goals are based upon the counselor's professional value system and upon the way he conceptualizes human development in terms both of process and outcome. Preceding chapters of this book have attempted to provide some resources for students of counseling to use in building such a personal theory and philosophy.

The second source of goals, however, comes from the client. While counselors need generalizable goals, ultimately, every goal statement must be formulated in terms applicable to the life situation of a particular client. This process then requires the active participation of the client in helping to work out, in partnership with the counselor, the tentative, ever-changing but still recognizable statements of goals called the "developmental contract." The developmental contract is the tangible, operational outcome of the counseling relationship. Without it, the conditions of *mutuality, trust,* and *empathy* that characterize counseling relationships simply do not exist.

The developmental contract is based upon both counselor values and client needs. It is not a fixed or static kind of agreement. The developmental contract can be expected to grow and change as the client's perception of his needs grows and changes. The presenting concern that a client brings to the counselor is obviously not always the only one with which he needs help, nor is it often even the central one. It is, however, the *beginning point* in counseling. Without agreeing to consider and attempt to be of help with a presenting concern, no matter how trivial, the counselor can hardly expect to see the developmental contract broadened to incorporate other more central kinds of concerns. The counselor who confronts all clients with some abstract set of highly generalized goals is not likely to enter developmental contracts with clients whose purposes are based upon specifically felt and immediately perceived needs in *their life situations.*

Structuring

The technique aspect of the formulation of goals or developmental contracts is the process called "structuring." The concept of structuring in counseling is one of those that has been often used and seldom understood. Structuring is essentially the process of *communicating and sharing expectations* about the nature of the counseling process itself. Structuring is not an *event* or even a *stage* in counseling, but rather an ongoing part of the counseling process. The purpose of structuring is to provide the basis for *mutuality,* that is, the sense of commonness of purpose. It also helps to promote *empathy,* the quality of thinking and feeling together. These are essential conditions for the counseling relationship. Structuring in developmental counseling is not an arbitrary telling a client what he is here for, or is it a subtle manipulation based upon persuading him to agree to what is supposed to be good for him. Rather, structuring involves a direct, honest, and clear *communication* of expectations by both participants about the *nature of the relationship,* the *content of the interview,* the *kinds of procedures* involved, and the *types of goals* to be selected.

Structuring is not an *event* that is terminated after the first five minutes of the initial interview. As counseling progresses toward new goals or redefines old goals, or as the nature of the relationship itself is elaborated, structuring or restructuring continues. Whenever either client or counselor senses a breakdown in *mutuality* or *empathy,* further structuring has the highest single priority in the interview.

Structuring involves both direct verbal responses and non-verbal communications. The counselor needs to have worked through his own expectations of the counseling process adequately enough to communicate them clearly to an inexperienced client. One of the reasons that many beginning counselors have trouble with structuring is that they have never really worked through in their own minds what counseling is all about. These counselors tend to defer structuring with a client in the hope that if they wait long enough something magical will happen that will give purpose and meaning to the interview. Curiously enough, this sometimes happens in that some clients are highly motivated or intelligent enough to structure the situation for the counselor in spite of himself. In most cases, of course, this does not happen.

Even though direct, clear verbal structuring is desirable, some of the nuances of the counseling relationship are hard to communicate verbally. For example, the counselor structures the relationship in terms of warmth and concern not by saying, "I am going to be warm and concerned," but by demonstrating this in his total behavior. Structuring can only occur successfully when the counselor's verbal structure and his total behavior are congruent. For example, he cannot structure verbally a high degree of responsibility for the client and then proceed to assume full responsibility himself. Nor can the counselor structure a degree of openness or ambiguity in the counseling situation and then turn away from the client when he responds to this. An amusing example of this kind of double communication is seen in the following exchange taken from a tape recording of an initial interview between a beginning counselor and a client.

> COUNSELOR: This is your hour. I want you to feel free to talk about anything at all that may concern you.
> CLIENT (*somewhat hesitantly*): Well, I guess what I'd really like to talk about is that I hate my mother.
> COUNSELOR: Is there anything *else* you'd like to talk about today?

For the counselor, then, the ability to structure the counseling process is based primarily upon his knowledge of himself, his values, his goals, his attitudes, and his limitations. He cannot structure either verbally or non-verbally those things about which *he* is unclear, ambivalent, or afraid. Only by becoming more and more aware of himself and his own counseling behavior can the counselor learn to communicate a consistent, clear structure of the kind that will be conducive to those counseling goals to which he subscribes.

The structuring process of course also includes receiving communication from clients. The client's goals, expectations, doubts, and fears are of great significance for structuring the kind of counseling process that will be growth-producing for him. The counselor must be sensitive and perceptive to client communications. Some clients will have experienced negative or even punishing situations with someone who called himself a counselor. Others will have never encountered a relationship with an adult that was not essentially authoritarian in nature. Still others will have never experienced a situation in which it was not only permissible, but desirable to talk freely and frankly about themselves. Some clients will have grave doubts about the degree and nature of confidentiality that is involved in the counseling process. The counselor must be sensitive to these kinds of client expectations and deal with them in a shared and open structuring process that continues throughout the course of counseling.

DIMENSIONS OF THE COUNSELING PROCESS

There are several possible dimensions along which the counseling process can be structured. Three that seem to have particular relevance are discussed below.

Division of Responsibility

One of the more naïve myths pervading the field of counseling is that counselors are "directive" or "non-directive" in an either–or sense. A more useful approach is to view counseling through the dimension of division of responsibility. As in any interpersonal process, many decisions or choices have to be made in counseling. Examples of these include choice of subject to be discussed, use of procedures such as testing, length and number of interviews, assignments of tasks for "homework," and many others. The fact that the counselor shares in responsibility for these kinds of process decisions does not mean that he imposes his views or values on the client for other kinds of *outcome decisions* such as choice of an occupation, development of a set of values, or other long-term decisions that confront the client.

In practice, for most experienced counselors, responsibility for "process decisions" is shared with the client. In this sense, the division of responsibility may fluctuate from time to time and from one circumstance to another. At one point, the client may decide that he wishes to discuss a particular concern at this moment; at another point both counselor and client may share a decision about whether test information would be useful; once such a decision is reached, the counselor may decide the exact tests to be used.

Techniques that reduce counselor responsibility include simple acceptance, the nod of the head or "Uh-huh," the use of silence, or simple restatement of content. Techniques that increase counselor responsibility are explaining, interpreting, or questioning. Techniques that change the topic of discussion also increase counselor responsibility.

Division of responsibility for process then is a continuum along which counselors move from case to case and from time to time in the same case. A few observations are in order about the nature of this continuum. It is usually easier to move in the direction of increased counselor responsibility than to return in the direction of greater client responsibility. A considerable degree of client responsibility in the counseling process is necessary if the client is to remain an active and involved learner and if the counseling process is to be a model through which he can grow in responsible independence. The exercise of counselor responsibility is neither good nor bad in itself, but it must be used with judgment and discretion by the counselor in terms of his immediate and long-term goals.

Ambiguity

A second useful perspective through which to view the counseling interview is what Bordin (1) calls the ambiguity dimension. Ambiguity was discussed briefly in Chapter 3 under the cognitive model. The term "ambiguity" in counseling refers to the degree of openness or uncertainty that exists in the minds of both counselor and client regarding what is supposed to happen next. The ultimate in ambiguity for the client is free association, that is, saying anything that comes into his mind. The minimum of ambiguity is created by the continued use of "yes" or "no" questions. In this case, the nature of the client response is severely limited—virtually to a choice of two monosyllables. Ambiguity can be increased through the use of more open-ended questions of the "how" or "why" category and through very general leads that give the client considerable latitude in responding.

Techniques that move the interview along the dimension of ambiguity in either direction are not necessarily good or bad in themselves. Their value depends entirely on the results that are obtained. Many beginning counselors, however, overwork techniques of the narrow "yes or no" type and are unable to use the more imaginative leads that increase ambiguity. Continued use of closed questions may seriously hamper communication. On the other hand, the use of completely uncontrolled ambiguity may be threatening to both counselor and client under some circumstances.

The Affective-Intellectual Dimension

It is possible to view counseling along a dimension from dealing entirely with cognitive material to responding only in terms of emotions. Neither end of this continuum has any particular merit in itself. A completely uncontrolled expression of emotion may be a helpful release for a client under certain circumstances, but is seldom if ever a solution to his problems. On the other hand, a flat, rigidly intellectualized approach to situations that are fraught with emotional connotations is not useful. Techniques that move the interview toward the affective end of the continuum include reflection of feeling, which simply communicates to the client that the counselor is aware of the emotional aspects of the communication. Reflection of feeling is a difficult skill because most counselors are unable to perceive emotion in others. Many beginning counselors work so hard to develop this skill that they become enamored with it and tend to use it indiscriminately as though it were a universally useful technique or even an end rather than a means.

Restatement, on the other hand, is a technique that communicates understanding of cognitive content. It is a very easy technique to learn that is occasionally useful when the client may be unsure whether the counselor is following his thinking. Often, beginning counselors confuse these two techniques and use restatement of content when they are trying to reflect feeling. The resulting series of reiterations of the obvious is very distracting and annoying to the client.

The skillful counselor is able to help the client move the interview along this continuum from cognitive to affective as his needs and the goals of the interview demand.

The three dimensions of the counseling process discussed above may provide perspectives for examining the application of techniques. Techniques help move the interview along these dimensions. Sudden or abrupt moves along any of these dimensions may be threatening or disconcerting to clients and may require restructuring.

PERCEPTUAL SKILLS

The primary interview skills of the developmental counselor are not involved in learning to *say* the right thing. Most beginning counselors are so preoccupied with trying to think of the right thing to *say* that they are unable to concentrate on the really important task of *perceiving* the significant aspects of the client's communication. Counselors almost always say the wrong thing because they have not perceived the right thing.

Listening

The most basic skill involved in the counseling interview is the task of *listening.* Listening is a form of perception. Listening in the counseling sense is difficult because, like other forms of perception, it is *selective.* Few people in our society are good *total* listeners. Instead, they have been conditioned to be *selective* listeners. Learning to be a listener as a counselor often means breaking down deeply ingrained habits of selective perception. Most individuals have been conditioned to be selective listeners on at least three dimensions that have to be reversed for successful counseling. These three dimensions are:

1. *Personal need-relevance.* Most people are conditioned to perceive only communications that tie in with their *own* existing preconceptions. They are conditioned to "tune out" communications that are irrelevant or disturbing to their own need structure. In counseling, this kind of selective perception often makes it impossible to hear what a client is really saying or is really concerned about.

2. *Ideational rather than affective selection.* Most people are conditioned to selectively perceive communications on an ideational or cognitive level and to screen out communications of an emotional or affective nature. Reacting to an expression of feeling is in many ways a cultural taboo in our society. The polite, well-bred thing to do, in our society, if someone is uncouth enough to express strong feelings, is to ignore it much as one might a loud belch. In counseling, of course, this cultural prescription is almost exactly reversed. Communications of an affective nature are often the most significant ones that must be recognized and responded to if communication is to be kept open. Beginning counselors often have great difficulty with the technique of reflection of feeling because of this selective perception phenomenon.

3. *Positive rather than negative communication selection.* Another cultural restraint on perception is the one that encourages perception of positive rather than negative feelings or ideas. In those rare instances when affective responses are recognized, these are much more likely to be communications of positive rather than negative feelings. This phenomenon is readily seen in a roomful of people when one person begins to cry. Most individuals will studiously ignore the crying and proceed as though it simply did not happen. In counseling, it is often important to recognize and respond to negative feelings or ideas before the client is able to go on to more positive communications. The counselor must be able to perceive and respond to negative expressions without undue anxiety.

There are many other dimensions of selective perception that interfere with listening in counseling. The same kinds of phenomena are involved in other kinds of observations. Most people tend to shut out stimuli that communicate feeling tone such as blushing, rate of breathing, postural changes, and facial expressions. These non-verbal communications are important clues to the effective counselor.

Changing one's status as a "selective perceiver" and moving toward the ideal of being a "total perceiver" is not accomplished by reading books. It can usually best be accomplished by involvement in actual interpersonal situations where the possibility for "feedback" or correction of perception is possible. In group situations where there is an open and secure climate and where members are consciously attempting to improve their sensitivity, this kind of "feedback" can take place.

Perhaps the most useful way to conceptualize the problem of communication and selective perception is in terms of Kelly's (34) "personal construct." A personal construct is a way that an individual uses for construing differences and similarities in people, objects, or events. Values, for example, are constructs for construing good and bad. Constructs are bipolar, such as good and bad, dangerous and safe, ugly and beautiful. Communication with another person involves to some extent coming to understand the nature of the constructs through which he communicates those meanings. When a counselor selectively screens out much of the meaning that the client is attempting to communicate, it becomes difficult or impossible for him to understand the client's personal constructs or private world of meaning.

No set of techniques will enable the counselor to achieve this kind of understanding. Preoccupation with techniques only dissipates energy and attention that is better devoted to perceptual tasks.

RESEARCH ON THE INTERVIEW

The research available on the use of interview technique is extremely limited. A number of studies are relevant, however, to the position taken here. Two studies by Strupp (8, 9) throw some light on the use of interview techniques by therapists with different backgrounds and different levels of experience. In one study, Strupp (9) compared the responses of twenty-five psychiatrists, seven psychologists, and nine psychiatric social workers to a series of twenty-seven client statements taken from actual interviews. All of the therapists had a generally psychoanalytic orientation. Although some differences among professional groups were found, the most striking finding was that the response profiles were remarkably similar across professional groups. When comparisons were made between experienced and inexperienced therapists, results generally showed that experience and training are associated with *greater diversification* of techniques.

In a second study, Strupp (8) compared the responses of Rogerian and psychoanalytically oriented therapists in much the same way as outlined above. In this study, sharp differences were found between theoretical orientations with Rogerian therapists using a significantly greater number of reflective responses. When comparisons were made between experienced and inexperienced Rogerian therapists, however, the experienced therapists showed a significant *decline* in the number of reflections. Strupp concluded that exclusive reliance on one technique appears to be a correlate of inexperience (8).

A similar study by Robert Wrenn (10) compared responses of fifty-four counselors to a set of client statements deliberately chosen to highlight theoretical differences. Counselor's theoretical orientations were categorized by judges in terms of phenomenological, analytic, neobehavioral, eclectic, and others. The only significant differences were those between analytic and phenomenological and analytic and eclectic on the dimensions of reflection. Results thus were similar to those obtained by Strupp.

Very few studies have attempted to study relationships between counseling effectiveness and techniques. Landfield and Nawas (5) studied cases of thirty-six college student clients working with six different counselors. They were particularly concerned with examining the relationship between client improvement and counselor–client communication. Using a method developed by Kelly (4), they studied the relationship between the personal constructs that clients and counselors used in understanding others. Judgments on improvement were made by experienced judges on the basis of case materials. Results indicated that communication between counselor and client as measured by similarity between their personal constructs was significantly associated with improvement. This study implies that communication between counselor and client is an important variable in counseling effectiveness. A study by Mendelsohn and Geller (7) similarly indicated that clients have greater commitment to counseling when the counselor is similar to them in cognitive-perceptual orientation.

Forgy and Black (3) did a three-year follow-up study of clients at a university counseling center. They found no differences in terms of client satisfaction between clients who had received counseling from counselors with different technique orientations. Callis, Polmantier, and Roeber in a five-year study of the counseling process concluded that counselor experience and training is more significant in terms of counselor effectiveness than theoretical or technique orientation (2). McGowan in reviewing the research on counselor techniques sums up his conclusions in this way:

> It would seem advisable for educators engaged in the training of counselors to give less emphasis to the development of response techniques, identified with a particular school of counseling, and to encourage students to develop response methods in line with their own past experiences and natural style of speech. [6, p. 371.]

The problem of acquiring interview techniques is often overemphasized by students of counseling. There are no counseling techniques as such. Techniques are only aids that provide counselors with varied and flexible ways of responding to client communications. Techniques cannot be useful unless they are based upon accurate perceptions of client communications. The primary areas in which counselors must develop skills are in perceiving total client communications in terms of those relevant constructs through which the client views his world and assigns meaning to his perceptions. Research indicates that experienced counselors are more varied and flexible in their use of techniques than are neophytes. Research also supports the position that effectiveness in counseling is at least partially a function of communication and understanding.

The purpose of the developmental interview is to help the client find and try out new and alternative ways of behaving that will be goal-oriented for him. The interview must provide maximum communication between counselor and client, and must lead to plans, tasks, and actions that can provide a basis for changes in behavior. The developmental interview then is characterized by *communication, openness,* and *action.*

One reason that interviewing skills are difficult to learn is that they are complex. Too often, the beginning counselor finds it difficult to focus in on a set of specific skills and measure his progress on them. Below are four simple rating scales which have been found useful in counselor training and assessment. They are based upon constructs such as those discussed earlier in this chapter and in Chapter 9. These constructs are titled Openness of Communication, Sensitivity in Communication, Consistency of Communication, and Involvement in Communication. The scales were developed by the author and Dr. Herbert Burks.

The scales have been related to ratings of counseling effectiveness and effects of training. They are given here not as a rigid mold for technical development, but rather as a very general guide for self-improvement and assessment that a beginning counselor can use in listening to his interview recordings.

One of the advantages of these scales is that they are anchored in specific counselor behaviors. A beginning counselor may choose to work on three or four behaviors from a particular scale at any specific time. He may then move on to include more of the responses in a given scale until he has mastered the total construct.

It is again important to repeat that the techniques represented in the scales are *not* ends in themselves, but are merely tools that may be helpful in particular interview situations.

Openness of Communication

The counselor is a person to whom a client comes to get a fresh and different perspective about himself and his concerns. In meeting this need, the counselor may be able to respond in creative and divergent ways that reflect his "cognitive-flexibility" or openness of communication.

As viewed here, there are three aspects to the dimension: (a) the degree of tentativeness that characterizes the counselor's attempts to understand the client, (b) the openness or ability to entertain new hypotheses or data about the client that the counselor maintains, and (c) the diversity of techniques or approaches that the counselor uses in working with the client.

Observation of Specific Behaviors: The following are some of the behaviors from which openness of communication may be inferred. For convenience in performing the overall rating at the end of this scale, the specific behaviors to be observed have been grouped according to the three components. For *each* behavior:

Circle "YES" if the behavior occurred in this interview.
Circle "NO" if the behavior should have occurred in this interview, but did not.
Circle "N/A" (for "Not Applicable") if the behavior failed to occur because it was irrelevant to this interview.

Tentativeness

1. Suggests tentative causal relationships between client's past experiences and present situation.   YES   NO   N/A

2. Uses and tests clinical hunches. For example, explores the possibility that a client's hostility toward authority is related to feelings about parents.   YES   NO   N/A

3. Tentatively suggest an approach or solution to the problem under discussion which the client has not considered.   YES   NO   N/A

4. Gives tentative summaries of interview material that invite the client to add to or correct his impression.   YES   NO   N/A

5. When restating content or reflecting feeling, the counselor frequently asks if his understanding is correct with a question such as, "Is this how you feel?," or "What I hear you saying is . . ."   YES   NO   N/A

6. Use test scores and other data to generate probability

statements. Does not make absolute or final statements from such data.   YES   NO   N/A

Openness

7. Phrases questions in an open-ended manner that gives the client a variety of possible responses, rather than simple yes or no replies.   .   YES   NO   N/A

8. Counselor continues to gather relevant information throughout the interview and continues to enrich and add to his picture of the client. He avoids premature closure in terms of his diagnosis of client problem or client characteristics.   YES   NO   N/A

9. The counselor asks the client how he would like to change his behavior or what his goals are.   YES   NO   N/A

10. The counselor restructures the interview or the relationship when new information shows that he and the client have different expectations or goals.   YES   NO   N/A

11. The counselor combines data from different sources to form a psychologically rich picture of the client. For example, the counselor relates test scores to other information such as grades, interests, or satisfaction.   YES   NO   N/A

12. The counselor calls attention to conflicting or incompatible aspects of the client's behavior. He helps the client to form a new cognitive structure that can incorporate these elements.   YES   NO   N/A

13. The counselor achieves movement in the interview. There is an evident and understandable progression of topics rather than a fixed or rigid perseveration on one narrow aspect of the client's problem or behavior.   YES   NO   N/A

Diversity

14. The counselor uses a wide variety of "leads" to help the client talk about his problem from a number of fresh and new perspectives.   YES   NO   N/A

15. The counselor deals with both the feeling and content aspects of the client's remarks.   YES   NO   N/A

16. The counselor shows that he is aware of and using as data both the verbal and non-verbal behaviors of the client.   YES   NO   N/A

17. The counselor deals with past, present, and future aspects of the client's situation or problem.   YES   NO   N/A

18. The counselor is able to relate aspects of the client's past behavior to his behavior in the immediate interview situation. In other words, the counselor works in the "here and now" as well as the "there and then."   YES   NO   N/A

19. The counselor uses some relatively infrequent or original technique or approach such as role playing, role reversal, drawing or diagramming, or dealing with dreams or fantasies.   YES   NO   N/A

Overall Rating on Openness of Communication: Considering the definition of this dimension and the specific behaviors observed in the interview, circle a number on the following scale to indicate your overall rating of the counselor on openness of communication. Bear in mind that the three components of this dimension are: (a) tentativeness, (b) openness, and (c) diversity.

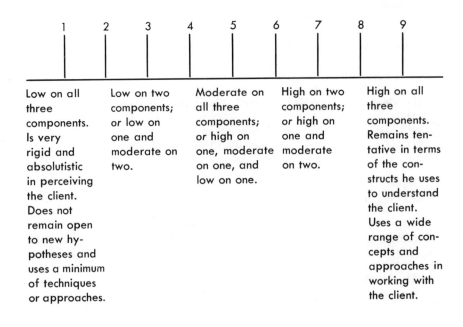

1	2	3	4	5	6	7	8	9
Low on all three components. Is very rigid and absolutistic in perceiving the client. Does not remain open to new hypotheses and uses a minimum of techniques or approaches.	Low on two components; or low on one and moderate on two.		Moderate on all three components; or high on one, moderate on one, and low on one.		High on two components; or high on one and moderate on two.		High on all three components. Remains tentative in terms of the constructs he uses to understand the client. Uses a wide range of concepts and approaches in working with the client.	

Sensitivity in Communication

Part of the counselor's task is to listen and comprehend what the client is communicating. Client communications vary from overt, simple verbal expressions to very subtle, non-verbal communications which are expressed through changes in voice quality, facial expression, gestures, nervous mannerisms, and the like.

Observation of Specific Behaviors: The following are some of the behaviors from which sensitivity in communication may be inferred. For *each* behavior:

Circle "YES" if the behavior occurred in this interview.
Circle "NO" if the behavior should have occurred in this interview but did not.
Circle "N/A" (for "Not Applicable") if the behavior failed to occur because it was irrelevant to this interview.

1. Listens carefully to and remembers what the client has said, rather than having to be corrected or refreshed on such matters later in the interview.   YES   NO   N/A

2. Behaves in a manner apparently consistent with the client's mood (for example, smiles when the client smiles, etc.).   YES   NO   N/A

3. Apparently tries to see things from the client's point of view.   YES   NO   N/A

4. Appears alert to the *feelings* which are expressed in the client's remarks—both negative and positive.   YES   NO   N/A

5. Makes statements apparently intended to convey his understandings of the client's feelings (or, states that he understands how the client feels).   YES   NO   N/A

6. Suggests how the client feels about an event which he (the client) has mentioned.   YES   NO   N/A

7. Seems able to perceive and sort out ambivalent and conflicting feelings on the part of the client.   YES   NO   N/A

8. Responds to negative as well as positive feelings of the client; does not "move away" from negative feelings.   YES   NO   N/A

9. Does not get fixated at one problem level, but stays with client.   YES NO N/A

10. Follows client shifts in topic.   YES NO N/A

11. Usually responds to the "core" of a long, confused or ambivalent client statement.   YES NO N/A

12. Responds to subtle cues regarding client attitudes, goals, etc.   YES NO N/A

13. Responds to non-verbal cues on the part of the client, such as posture, tone of voice, and facial expression. YES NO N/A

14. Avoids premature, defense-arousing interpretations.   YES NO N/A

15. Uses a level of vocabulary (word difficulty) similar to that of the client.   YES NO N/A

16. Supplies a key word or phrase for which the client is unsuccessfully groping.   YES NO N/A

17. When the client appears bored, unconcerned, or otherwise "resistant" in the interview, the counselor discusses this with him.   YES NO N/A

18. The counselor's reflection or restatement of a client's response is an accurate representation of what the client says.   YES NO N/A

Overall Rating on Sensitivity in Communication: Considering the definition of this dimension and the specific behaviors observed in the interview, circle a number on the following scale to indicate your overall rating of the counselor on sensitivity in communication.

1	2	3	4	5	6	7	8	9

| Hardly ever receives overt client communications, and never receives the subtle ones. | Receives some of the overt client communications, but none of the subtle ones. | Receives most of the overt communications of the client, and a few of the subtle ones. | Receives nearly all of the overt client communications, and most of the subtle ones. | Receives all of the overt communications of the client, and all or nearly all of the subtle ones. |

Consistency of Communications

The counselor communicates with the client in verbal and non-verbal ways. He sends out "signals" to the client by means of (1) what he says verbally, and (2) his voice inflection, facial expression, posture, gestures, and mannerisms. The counselor's consistency of communication can be ascertained by observing the degree to which his verbal and non-verbal behaviors are compatible, that is, the extent to which they convey the same meaning.

Observation of Specific Behaviors: The following are some of the specific behaviors from which consistency of communication may be inferred. For *each* behavior:

Circle "YES" if the behavior occurred in this interview.
Circle "NO" if the behavior should have occurred in this interview but did not.
Circle "N/A" (for "Not Applicable") if the behavior failed to occur because it was irrelevant to this interview.

1. When his facial expression or other non-verbal behavior indicates he is puzzled or unable to understand or answer the client's question, he admits his ignorance.   YES   NO   N/A

2. When his facial expression or other non-verbal features suggest that he does not agree with the client, he states his disagreement verbally.   YES   NO   N/A

3. When his non-verbal behavior (for example, looking away from the client, "startled" facial expression) suggests that he is shocked or offended by something the client has said, he states his feeling to the client.   YES   NO   N/A

4. When he makes a humorous remark to the client, he smiles.   YES   NO   N/A

5. When he states that he does not comprehend what the client is saying, he looks puzzled.   YES   NO   N/A

6. When he states his disapproval of something the client has said, he frowns.   YES   NO   N/A

7. When he looks perplexed by something the client has said, he mentions his confusion to the client. In such situations, he does *not* nod or say "Um-hum," "I see," "I understand," etc.   YES   NO   N/A

8. Tone of voice is compatible with the verbal content of his responses. For example, when he says "I understand how you feel about this problem," his voice tone communicates an earnest "I *really* know how you feel," rather than a business-like "I know how you feel; I've seen many others who felt the same way; now, let's get on with the interview."   YES   NO   N/A

9. When he turns from a "lesser" topic to a more serious one, his tone of voice becomes more concerned (that is, softer, slower, deeper).   YES   NO   N/A

10. When he looks shocked or angry, his voice quality mirrors these feelings (for example, his voice is agitated, louder, etc.).   YES   NO   N/A

11. When his remarks suggest a feeling of greater psychological closeness to the client, he moves physically closer to him.   YES   NO   N/A

12. Gives the overall impression of "being himself" in the interview; does not put on a professional front or facade; is not a pretender, a phoney, a "glad-hander," or a "con-man."   YES   NO   N/A

Overall Rating on Consistency of Communication: Considering the definition of this dimension and the specific behaviors observed in the interview, circle a number on the following scale to indicate your overall rating of the counselor on consistency of communication.

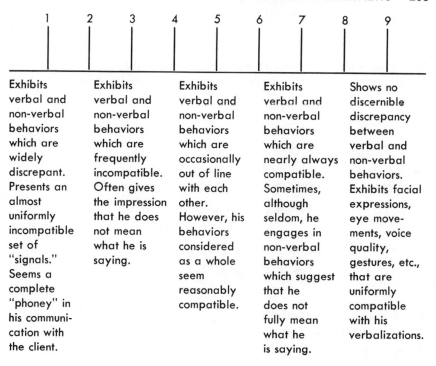

1	2	3	4	5	6	7	8	9
Exhibits verbal and non-verbal behaviors which are widely discrepant. Presents an almost uniformly incompatible set of "signals." Seems a complete "phoney" in his communication with the client.		Exhibits verbal and non-verbal behaviors which are frequently incompatible. Often gives the impression that he does not mean what he is saying.		Exhibits verbal and non-verbal behaviors which are occasionally out of line with each other. However, his behaviors considered as a whole seem reasonably compatible.		Exhibits verbal and non-verbal behaviors which are nearly always compatible. Sometimes, although seldom, he engages in non-verbal behaviors which suggest that he does not fully mean what he is saying.		Shows no discernible discrepancy between verbal and non-verbal behaviors. Exhibits facial expressions, eye movements, voice quality, gestures, etc., that are uniformly compatible with his verbalizations.

Interpersonal Involvement in Communications

One of the counselor's assets is his ability to enter into a close, spontaneous relationship with the client. There are two main aspects to this dimension of counseling: (a) the extent to which the counselor shows a genuine feeling of acceptance and caring for the client, and (b) the extent to which the counselor reveals himself frankly and openly as one human being to another.

Observation of Specific Behaviors: The following are some of the behaviors from which interpersonal involvement in communication may be inferred. For *each* behavior:

Circle "YES" if the behavior occurred in this interview.

Circle "NO" if the behavior should have occurred in this interview but did not.

Circle "N/A" (for "Not Applicable") if the behavior failed to occur because it was irrelevant to this interview.

1. Uses the client's first name.	YES	NO	N/A
2. Usually looks at client.	YES	NO	N/A
3. Focuses his attention on the client, rather than appearing detached, disinterested, or preoccupied.	YES	NO	N/A
4. Has an open and receptive facial expression.	YES	NO	N/A
5. Has an animated, overtly responsive manner in the interview, not "deadpan."	YES	NO	N/A
6. Seems at ease with the client; has a relaxed posture; does not appear tense or exhibit nervous mannerisms.	YES	NO	N/A
7. Smiles as an expression of cordiality toward the client.	YES	NO	N/A
8. Smiles when the client makes a humorous remark.	YES	NO	N/A
9. Leans toward the client apparently as an expression of interest.	YES	NO	N/A
10. Makes casual physical contact with the client as an expression of affection.	YES	NO	N/A
11. Shows consideration for the client's physical comfort (for example, asks whether client is physically comfortable, offers a more comfortable chair, adjusts window for client's comfort, hangs up client's coat, etc.).	YES	NO	N/A
12. When the client directs negative feelings toward him, the counselor invites a frank discussion of these feelings.	YES	NO	N/A
13. Deals directly and openly with a client request to know his opinion, value, attitude, or feelings.	YES	NO	N/A
14. When a client statement obviously challenges one of the counselor's values, he talks about this with the client.	YES	NO	N/A

Overall Rating on Interpersonal Involvement in Communication: Considering the definition of this dimension and the specific behaviors observed in the interview, circle a number on the following scale to indicate your overall rating of the counselor on interpersonal involvement in communication.

1	2	3	4	5	6	7	8	9

1	2 3	4 5	6 7	8 9
Gives no evidence of genuine acceptance or caring for the client. Almost uniformly distant, guarded, and overly "professional" in manner.	Usually quite remote in the relationship, although there are a few indications that he would like to get "closer" to the client.	Usually communicates his acceptance and caring for the client, but at times seems somewhat distant and impersonal. Shares himself openly with the client on some occasions, but at other times tries to appear neutral or noncommittal.	Communicates his acceptance and caring for the client at all times. Shows some reluctance to share his personal feelings, attitudes, or opinions in response to a client need.	Communicates his acceptance and caring for the client at all times. Reveals himself quite frankly and openly in response to a client need.

REFERENCES

1. BORDIN, E. S. Ambiguity as a therapeutic variable. *J. counsel. Psychol.*, 1955, 19:9–15.
2. CALLIS, R., POLMANTIER, P., & ROEBER, E. Five years of research on counseling. *J. counsel. Psychol.*, 1957, 4:119–123.
3. FORGY, E. W. & BLACK, J. D. A follow-up after three years of clients counseled by two methods. *J. counsel. Psychol.*, 1953, 1:1–9.
4. KELLY, G. A. *A theory of personality: the psychology of personal constructs.* New York: Norton, 1963.
5. LANDFIELD, A. W., & NAWAS, M. M. Psychotherapeutic improvement as a function of communication and adoption of therapist's values. *J. counsel. Psychol.*, 1964, 11 (4), 336–341.
6. McGOWAN, J. Developing a natural counseling style. In J. McGowan & L. Schmidt (Eds.), *Counseling: Reading in theory and practice.* New York: Holt, Rinehart, 1962.
7. MENDELSOHN, G. A., & GELLER, M. H. Effects of counselor–client similarity on the outcome of counseling. *J. counsel. Psychol.*, 1963, 10:71–77.
8. STRUPP, H. H. An objective comparison of Rogerian and psychoanalytic techniques. *J. consult. Psychol.*, 1955, 19:1–7.
9. STRUPP, H. H. Psychotherapeutic technique, professional affiliation and experience level. *J. consult. Psychol.*, 1955, 19:97–102.
10. WRENN, R. L. Counselor orientation: theoretical or situational? *J. counsel. Psychol.*, 1960, 7 (1), 40–45.

RECOMMENDED READINGS

Dimensions of the Counseling Interview

BERKOWITZ, L., & DANIELS, LOUISE R. Responsibility and dependency. *J. abnorm. soc. Psychol.*, 1963, 66:429–436.

BORDIN, E. S. Ambiguity as a therapeutic variable. *J. counsel. Psychol.*, 1955, 19:9–15.

COOK, J. J. Silence in psychotherapy. *J. counsel. Psychol.*, 1964, 11 (1), 42–46.

DANSKIN, D. G., & ROBINSON, F. P. Differences in "degree of lead" among experienced counselors. *J. counsel. Psychol.*, 1954, 1 (2), 78–83.

DIPBOYE, W. J. Analysis of counselor style by discussion units. *J. counsel. Psychol.*, 1954, 1:21–26.

ELLSWORTH, S. G. The consistency of counselor feeling-verbalization. *J. counsel. Psychol.*, 1963, 10:356–361.

HOFFMAN, A. E. An analysis of counselor sub-roles. *J. counsel. Psychol.*, 1959, 6:61–67.

LANDFIELD, A. W., & NAWAS, M. M. Psychotherapeutic improvement as a function of communication and adoption of therapist's values. *J. counsel. Psychol.*, 1964, 11 (4), 336–341.

LAYTON, W. L. Constructs and communication in counseling: a limited theory. *J. counsel. Psychol.*, 1961, 8 (1), 3–8.

ROBINSON, F. P. A cubist approach to the art of counseling. *Personnel Guidance J.*, 1963, 41:670–676.

ROGERS, C. A process conception of psychotherapy. *Amer. Psychologist*, 1958, 13 (4), 142–149.

Studies of Interview Variables

CAMPBELL, R. E. Counselor personality and background and his interview subrole behavior. *J. counsel. Psychol.*, 1962, 9:329–334.

GRATER, H. A. Client preferences for affective or cognitive counselor characteristics and first interview behavior. *J. counsel. Psychol.*, 1964, 11 (3), 248–350.

GRIGG, A. E. Client response to counselors at different levels of experience. *J. counsel. Psychol.*, 1961, 8 (3), 217–223.

KEMP, C. G. Counseling responses and need structure of high school principals and of counselors. *J. counsel. Psychol.*, 1962, 9:236–328.

MENDELSOHN, G. A., & GELLER, M. H. Effects of counselor client similarity on the outcome of counseling. *J. counsel. Psychol.*, 1963, 10 (1), 71–77.

POHLMAN, E., & ROBINSON, F. Client reaction to some aspects of the counseling situation. *Personnel Guidance J.*, 1960, 38 (7), 546–551.

STEFFLRE, B., KING, P., & LEAFGREN, F. A. Characteristics of counselors judged effective by their peers. *J. counsel. Psychol.*, 1962, 9:335–340.

STEFFLRE, B., & LEAFGREN, F. A. Mirror, mirror on the wall: a study of preferences for counselors. *Personnel Guidance J.*, 1964, 42:459–462.

STRUPP, H. H. An objective comparison of Rogerian and psychoanalytic techniques. *J. consult. Psychol.*, 1955, 19:1–7.

STRUPP, H. H. Psychotherapeutic technique, professional affiliation and experience level. *J. consult. Psychol.*, 1955, 19:97–102.

WEITZ, H. Counseling as a function of the counselor's personality. *Personnel Guidance J.*, 1957, 35:276–280.

Other Significant Studies

GOLDSTEIN, A. P., HELLER, K., & SECHREST, L. *Psychotherapy and the psychology of behavior change.* New York: Wiley, 1966.

TRUAX, C. B., & MITCHELL, K. M. Research on certain therapist interpersonal skills in relation to process and outcome. In BERGIN, A. E., & GARFIELD, S. L. (Eds.). *Handbook of psychotherapy and behavior change.* New York: Wiley, 1971.

11

DEVELOPMENTAL GROUPS

No particular reason exists to believe that the learning processes involved in what we have called developmental counseling are confined to one-to-one situations, or indeed that such situations are even necessarily the most desirable. Instead, what we do know about human behavior strongly suggests that such behavior is heavily influenced by the individual's group memberships. Attempts at behavior change that ignore the motivational possibilities inherent in group structures appear to be discarding one of the most powerful tools available for behavioral intervention. Cartwright points out the change potential inherent in groups in these words:

> To begin with the most general proposition, we may state that the behavior, attitudes, beliefs, and values of the individual are all firmly grounded in the groups to which he belongs. How aggressive or cooperative a person is, how much self-respect and self-confidence he has, how energetic and productive his work is, what he aspires to, what he believes to be true and good, whom he loves or hates, and what beliefs and prejudices he holds—all these characteristics are highly determined by the individual's group memberships. In a real sense, they are properties of groups and of the relationships between people. Whether they change or resist change will, therefore, be greatly influenced by the nature of these groups. Attempts to change them must be concerned with the dynamics of groups. [3, p. 11.]

Said another way, it is obvious that the kinds of behavioral changes with which the developmental counselor is most concerned are those that occur in social situations. Any attempts to change behavior outside the social contexts in which those changes are expected to persist will depend for effectiveness upon some degree of transfer of training. The history of attempts at influencing behavior have not been reassuring about the extent of this kind of transfer. Churches, for example, have been attempting to get people to abide by the Ten Commandments for centuries. They have been quite successful in one sense. Hardly anybody violates the Commandments—in church. The transfer between the in-church behavior and out-of-church behavior has been considerably less than satisfactory.

Precisely the same situation exists with regard to counseling. It is one thing to see changes in behavior, primarily verbal, occur in the counseling interview, but it is quite another to cause the same kinds of changes to transfer to the social contexts within which the client operates in everyday life. The developmental group has the great advantage of serving as what Vinacke (10) calls "the miniature social situation." In such a situation, many of the dynamics of the client's life settings are duplicated, and much less transfer of learning need occur.

Despite the rather obvious advantages of group counseling models, movement has been relatively slow toward the utilization of those approaches in field settings. A number of reasons may account for this. The earliest use of group work in the student personnel area was in what was familiarly called group guidance. In most of these group guidance situations, the emphasis was heavily upon information-giving. In many situations, the movement toward individual counseling was a real milestone of progress toward professionalization and individualization of personnel services.

The modern movement toward group work is not at all a return to the group information-giving programs of yesteryear. It is a highly sophisticated program of utilizing the dynamic potentials of group situations as catalytic ingredients to promote the very same kinds of behavioral goals that are inherent in individual counseling. Group counseling is *not* being advocated here as a cheap expedient that can do almost as good a job for a lesser expenditure of time and resources. A few minimally knowledgeable people still advocate it as this. Actually, there is little evidence that group counseling saves time. Instead, group counseling is recommended as a positive approach utilized for its own sake that can be coordinated with individual counseling to provide an effective combination of developmental treatments.

DYNAMICS OF DEVELOPMENTAL GROUPS

Perhaps the first step in a discussion of developmental groups is to review briefly some of the knowledge that is available about group dynamics. Goldman (5) points out that many counselors have become disenchanted with group projects because they have been unable to distinguish between two essential aspects of group interaction—*content* and *process*. Content, of course, refers to the topics or materials or ideas that are being discussed by groups. Most individuals in our society are conditioned to be aware of the content inherent in group interactions. Often, however, these same people are very insensitive to the *process* of group interactions. By process, we mean the roles being played by group members, the ways in which the group meets the needs of its members, the degree to which members are free to express their feelings and attitudes, the extent to which members experience feelings of belonging or rejection, and so forth. The counselor who wishes to use groups as an effective part of his professional competence must learn to be sensitive to *group process*, and must have some knowledge of group dynamics.

Trow *et al.* (9) list a number of basic propositions that are supported by research in group dynamics and that are important to those who wish to use groups constructively. These include:

1. The attitudes of individuals have their anchorages in groups. It may be easier to change the attitudes of individuals in the group by changing the group climate than by attempting to address intervention directly to the individual.

2. All groups demand a certain degree of conformity from members. The closer and more cohesive the group, the more power it has over the behavior of members.

3. When decisions are made by a group, the commitment of members is much greater than when the decision is arbitrarily imposed from outside the group.

4. Highly cohesive groups can overcome greater difficulties and frustrations in pursuit of group goals than can less-cohesive groups.

5. Group cohesiveness is largely a function of the degree to which members feel the group is meeting their needs.

6. People tend to be more effective learners when they are acting as group members in a training situation than if they are acting as individuals in an audience situation.

7. The amount or nature of verbal interaction among members is a function of group factors. For example, in cohesive groups, views, opinions, and behaviors that are quite deviant from the concensus of the group are likely to be ignored, rejected, or punished.

8. Cooperation and communication are greatest in groups where goals are mutually defined, accepted, and understood.

9. The group climate or style of group life can have an important impact on the personalities of members. The behavior of members may differ greatly from one group climate to another. The individual who seems hostile, aggressive, or disruptive in one group situation may behave very differently in another situation where the group climate is different.

Cartwright (3) lists another set of principles of group dynamics that must be understood by those interested in using groups to change behavior. These include:

1. If the group is to be an effective medium of behavior change, those who are to be changed and those who are attempting to influence change must have a strong sense of belonging to the same group.

2. In attempts to change attitudes, values, or behavior, the more relevant these are to the purpose of the group, the more influence the group can exert on them.

3. The greater the prestige of a group member in the eyes of the other members, the greater the influence he can exert.

4. Efforts to change individuals to deviate from the norms of a group will encounter strong resistance.

These principles seem deceptively simple and self-evident. They are violated systematically, however, in many of the attempts to change behavior that are representative of professional practice.

How many times do educators, for example, attempt to change groups without making any real effort to become a part of them? How many times are groups set up for purposes that are not really relevant to the kinds of changes that are supposedly to result from their formation. For example, how often are athletic groups set up for the purpose of winning, while all sorts of supposed character changes entirely irrelevant to the goal of winning are supposed to occur in some sort of magical way?

The counselor who wishes to learn to use groups effectively will need to be aware of elementary group principles of the kinds listed above. He will need further to become extremely sensitive to group process in order to insure that principles such as these are really utilized in group interaction.

THE STRUCTURE OF DEVELOPMENTAL GROUPS

As Gordon (6) points out, a group may be defined as two or more people who have a psychological relationship to each other. In other words, a group is made up of people whose behavior has direct influence upon the behavior of other members. Groups thus are dynamic in that changes in the behavior of any one member produce changes in the behavior of other members and of the total group.

As changes take place, the group attempts to cope with them in some way. One basic assumption in regard to developmental groups is that the group's method of coping will be most appropriate when the group utilizes the maximum resources of all its members. Thus, in an effective developmental group, there is maximum participation of all group members, each making his own most effective contribution. This assumption then includes the proposition that groups that contribute most to the growth and development of members are those that involve and commit all members and in which all members feel an active part of the group process.

Leadership in Developmental Groups

The above assumption defines in a sense a particular model of group leadership that is new to many individuals. For many people, the most familiar pattern of leadership is the *authoritarian* model. One common way of conceptualizing the authoritarian leader as he functions best in a society that gives lip service at least to democratic principles is as the *master manipulator*. In this context, leadership embraces the art of getting people to do what you want them to do while making them think it is their own idea. This model of leadership is the one most frequently acquired in our society. It is the basic model of military, political, and even of educational leadership in our culture. It is the one for which there are ample role models available in the culture.

The pattern of leadership appropriate to the developmental group is a very different one, and one for which there are unfortunately fewer role models. The leader in the developmental group is one who facilitates the group in defining, clarifying, and moving toward its *own* goals. This model of leadership involves concern not only for the end point or decision or final solution that the group reaches, but an equal concern that the process by which the group operates is growth-pro-ducing for all its members. In a sense, this pattern of leadership is even more challenging than the authoritarian role.

The developmental leader must learn to be extremely sensitive to the needs of group members and to the ways in which the group interaction is meeting those needs. He is also concerned about the cohesiveness of the group because the ability to help or hurt a group member is almost directly proportional to the degree of cohesiveness and mutuality present in the group.

Characteristics of Developmental Groups

Several characteristics of successful developmental groups can be described.

1. *Mutuality of purpose.* Successful developmental groups are those within which there is a considerable degree of unity of and commit-ment to purposes. Unanimity is not always present as to details, techniques, or approaches, but enough clarity and agreement exist about basic goals that members are willing to abide by majority decisions and tolerate limited degrees of concensus.

2. *Effectiveness of leadership.* In developmental groups, leaders operate as facilitators rather than manipulators. Basically, this means that those exercising leadership genuinely believe that their needs will be met by a process that insures maximum participation in, and responsibility for, decision making by all members of the group. For the effective leader, the question of "How can I be sure the group makes the best decision?" is answered in only one way. The answer is by insuring that all members of the group have a maximum opportunity to participate in and contribute to that decision.

3. *Flexibility of group organization.* The successful developmental group is one that is organized so that members have an opportunity to play a variety of roles that accelerate their own growth and their opportunities to make unique contributions to the group. The structure of the group is not rigid in terms of role opportunities or power distribution. All members are able to assume leadership roles from time to time as their unique contributions determine these opportunities.

4. *Mutuality of climate.* In a developmental group, just as there is mutuality of purpose so is there mutuality in terms of support and caring about group members. The group does not exploit, neglect, or reject a group member. It is sensitive to his needs and provides legitimate ways for these needs to be met within the framework of the group's structure and purpose.

5. *Positiveness of social control.* All groups exercise some form of social control over members. Some kind of group norm exists for most kinds of group-relevant behavior. Forms of social control are exercised by the group when members deviate markedly from these norms. The forms of social control in a developmental group are not those that are designed to hurt, punish, or retard the growth of members. Instead, social control is exercised in open and positive ways that are intended both to help change the deviant behavior and to contribute to the development of the member.

For example, developmental groups are able to deal openly and directly with members' feelings of resistance or non-commitment. They do not have to use subtle rejections or punishments to shape a member's behavior.

GROUP MODELS IN COUNSELING

A number of models are available for establishing and operating developmental counseling groups. The degree of complexity and sophistication involved in these models varies greatly. Five different models will be described that range from a fairly low degree of sophistication in terms of dynamics to a rather high degree of complexity of dynamics.

Common Problems Model

Perhaps the simplest model for group counseling is what Bennett (1) has called the "common problems" approach. As we have seen, individuals at various developmental stages do have common developmental tasks to master. They tend often to encounter similar kinds of difficulties or concerns. One very good way for the counselor who is attempting to move into group work to begin is by utilizing this fact to establish groups.

A developmental counseling group can be established around any goal or purpose that is genuinely representative of a common concern or problem of the group members. Such groups could be established around concerns such as becoming more comfortable in boy–girl relationships, becoming a better student, choosing a college or vocation, wanting to understand self better, increasing awareness of sexual identity, or any of myriad other areas.

One of the most important factors in this model is that the purpose of the group is genuinely an attempt to do something about a real problem of the members. If, for example, a group of underachievers or students with discipline problems are brought together under a guise of doing something else, but with the hope that they can somehow be manipulated around this common factor, little group cohesiveness is likely to be formed, or if the group does become cohesive, it will likely cohere around its resistance to being manipulated by a dishonest leader.

Once a group has "jelled" or become cohesive around a common purpose, it can supply a number of elements to a learning situation that are not available in other counseling situations. These include:

1. *Mutual support.* A cohesive group can support members who find the exploration of a problem area painful and threatening. Group members who may be experiencing similar feelings are often more sensitive to each other's needs than the most skillful counselor. Often, the most terrifying part of working through developmental problems is the feeling of isolation and loneliness that comes from the delusion that no one else has ever experienced the same difficulties. Common problems groups break down these feelings of isolation and replace them with feelings of belonging and mutuality.

2. *Empathy and insight.* In cohesive groups organized around common problems, members are able to have considerable insight and empathy for each other. They can often create a more empathic climate and show greater insight for each other than can even a skillful counselor who has a different set of experiences to draw upon for these factors.

3. *Focus and direction.* The common problems group can quickly establish focus and direction for the counseling process. The distribution of responsibility is often such that real concerns can be discussed and real movement can occur more readily than when responsibility is heavily on the counselor.

The common problems model offers a fairly simple problem for the counselor beginning in group work. His chief concern is to facilitate a climate that permits full participation and involvement of members.

His chief task is to avoid dominating the group and instead to maximize participation. He must be sensitive to group process and to the needs of members. He helps create through his own example a climate of acceptance and permissiveness like that of the individual counseling interview. The main skill of the leader is to facilitate the development of group cohesiveness and trust. When this kind of climate has been established, the leader can often move into the role of member and allow leadership roles to be shared among members as the situation indicates. This model draws upon sources of gain in relationship and cognitive areas primarily.

Case-centered Model

The case-centered model in group counseling is a model at about the same level of dynamic sophistication as the common problems approach. It is somewhat more flexible than the latter approach in that a group can represent a number of different concerns rather than being homogeneous in terms of problems. In the case-centered approach, the group is unified only in terms of its desire to help each other work through real concerns. Hewer (7) has described this approach.

The format of operation in this model is for group members to take turns in presenting their individual concerns, while the rest of the group act as helping persons. The counselor may take a leading role in the earlier phases of this type of group operation, but essentially other group members learn to operate as counselors as the group process emerges.

The pattern of interaction in the case-centered group is a bit more complex than in the common problems approach. The leader will need more skill in creating a climate of cohesiveness within a more heterogeneous group, and in development of a network of helping relationships among the members. In a real sense, he will be a role model for the members as they attempt to become counselors. At the same time, he has to avoid playing a dominant role if the group is to function fully. The case-centered approach has several advantages.

1. *Multiple helping relationships.* In the successful group in this model, a whole network of helping relationships is developed. When a member is functioning as a client, he must learn to deal with several different helping persons. When he functions as a "counselor," he is in a different relationship. Thus, he has to experience a set of new roles

and relationships, and so his opportunities for new kinds of social learnings are enchanced.

2. *Divergent perceptions and attitudes.* Group members may represent quite different perceptions and attiudes. They are forced to test these against others' viewpoints, and to learn to deal with differences in helping rather than competing ways. In a scnse, the group becomes a laboratory in which attitudes and perceptions are tested and tempered in a group whose central purpose is to maintain a climate of warmth, acceptance, and permissiveness.

3. *Individually centered focus.* Even though, as members present their cases, much social learning occurs for all members, a central focus is established on one member at a time that allows the presenting member to meet his needs in a direct and immediate way. Often a central factor in this model is public commitment to goals and group reinforcement for behavior change.

T Group Model

The T group, or training group, is a model of group interaction that has wide applicability for developmental counseling. This group model is an approach based upon knowledge of group dynamics and pioneered by the National Training Laboratory (4). The model has already developed a number of variations and has been widely used in educational, religious, and business settings.

Basically, the central concept of the T group model is that a group of human beings are put in a quite unstructured and ambiguous situation in which they are confronted with the task of creating a new social system through which they can meet their own needs.

The usual components of a social system are absent or ambiguous in the beginning phase of the T group's operation. No definite authority–responsibility structure exists. No fixed set of goals or methodologies for goal-seeking is provided. Roles and relationships for members are not clearly delineated either in the present situation or by analogy from past situations.

In the face of this ambiguity, the group is forced to draw from its own resources to build a social system that can meet the members' needs and from which cohesiveness and mutuality can develop. In a sense, it is an experience in social creativity.

As the T group struggles to cope with the problems created by this unstructured and ambiguous situation, great opportunity is created for members to learn about themselves and how they typically operate in social situations. Since roles are unstructured and relationships are ambiguous, considerable opportunities for "feedback" from others exist.

In this sense, the T group uses the group situation not as a vehicle for solving external problems as in the first two models discussed, but directly to illustrate social interaction phenomena as they are experienced. In a sense, the T group writes its own textbook and reads it at one and the same time. The T group thus has several definite advantages. It is:

1. *A laboratory for social learning.* It creates a social interaction laboratory in which members can learn to understand their own patterns of coping with social situations and in which new patterns of social coping can be learned.

2. *A process-oriented situation.* In the T group, the primary focus is always on group process. The group is the focus of attention rather than merely the vehicle by which content is communicated.

3. *A miniature identity crisis.* In a sense, the T group is a miniature social situation in which each individual is confronted with such an unstructured and ambiguous situation that he must find again his own identity with and through other people.

Successful handling of the T group model requires considerable skill. Perhaps the most important skill of the leader is to refrain from moving in to furnish structure when the group begins to show anxiety and tension. Most counselors tend to operate in social situations to reduce tension and anxiety. In individual counseling situations, the counselor generally provides considerable structure and controls ambiguity at reasonably comfortable levels. In the T group model of group counseling, the counselor must maintain ambiguity and let the group cope with it even though this process may become very frustrating and tension-producing. A good part of the competence involved in this model is simply acquiring the confidence in groups that allows the counselor to "sweat out" the long and uncomfortable and even hostile period in which the group seeks to establish its own structure.

Another important skill of the T group leader is to keep attention focused on group process. He may act as an observer or commentator, or other members may learn to play such roles. This model uses relationship, cognitive, and behavioral sources of gain.

Human Resources Group Model

Herbert Otto (8) has developed an extremely interesting model of group interaction that is based upon theoretical formulations of writers such as Murphy, Maslow, Goldstein, and Fromm in theorizing about the upper limits of human potentialities.

This model differs from others not so much in terms of the format or procedure by which the group situation is structured, but in terms of the entire focus of the group in establishing goals and purposes. In this model, the avowed purpose around which the group is formed is to help members to extend the upper limits of functioning in ways that will be self-actualizing for them. The assumption is made that the average healthy, normal person functions at only 15 or 20 per cent of his full potential. The group is devoted to helping each member extend his functioning toward these upper limits.

Much of the interaction of the groups in this model is typical of other kinds of counseling or therapy groups. Members talk about their fears, concerns, problems, and aspirations. The focus is always kept on the positive potential of members rather than on pathology, however. Two devices used to illustrate how this focus is maintained are:

1. *The multiple strength perception method.* In this method, one member becomes the center of the group's attention for a particular session. He is asked to begin a process of enumerating and sharing with other members the strengths that he sees in himself and the factors in his life that inhibit him from using these strengths fully. Other members then chime in with their perceptions of the "target" person's strengths and limiting factors. Since the group has worked through, prior to this, a consideration of the fact that understanding of these factors are essential to optimum development, this amounts to a warm and empathic sharing of perceptions of strength and limitations that helps the member develop a new identity structure.

2. *Action programs.* Part of the structure of the group in this model is that they are "action groups" rather than "talking groups." Members are urged to develop "action programs" to increase and facilitate the development of strengths. Members then report back to the group their successes or failures in these action programs. When difficulties are encountered, the entire group works to bring their understanding and sensitivity to bear on the problem and so help remove the blocking to further development. Action programs may

begin at superficial levels such as taking art or dancing lessons and move through to quite significant undertakings such as developing greater creativity or deeper personal relationships.

These and other essentially supportive devices are designed to help the group facilitate each member in his struggle to achieve a higher level of functioning. Groups of this type seem to have obvious relevance in a developmental counseling program. The use of public commitment and group reinforcement are major sources of gain in this model.

Transactional Group Models

The most complex group counseling models discussed here are those that utilize the social interaction or transactions of group members as the basic clinical material from which the members derive new learnings and insights. In the T group model, this same type of learning occurs as a result of the group focus on process. In the transactional analysis model, the counselor acts consistently as an observer and interpreter of behavior who systematically analyzes and feeds back to the group the significance of their behavior.

Berne (2) has described the operation of such a group model based on a somewhat psychoanalytic orientation. Basically, the transactional model is built upon the assumption that, in any group situation, people tend to use a given set of social maneuvers or coping behaviors that are characteristic of their particular life style. These characteristic maneuvers Berne calls "pastimes," "games," or "scripts," depending upon their generalizability and complexity. He also conceptualizes three general levels of behavior tendencies in all people, which he terms "parent," "adult," and "child." These have rather obvious relevance to psychoanalytic constructs.

The group interaction in any social situation can be analyzed in terms of these behavior patterns, and social maneuvers can be categorized as "adult," "parental," or "childlike."

As a group begins to operate, its interaction can be examined in terms of the kinds of social transactions present. A situation in which transactions are direct and straightforward is called a "pastime." Common pastimes in social groups are "PTA" and "psychiatry." In "PTA," people talk about and deplore some form of human delinquency. This pastime has the general theme of "Isn't it just awful how they act," or, occasionally when the topic is self, "Isn't it just awful how I act."

Psychiatry is a somewhat similar pastime but one that is centered on interpreting behavior. Its themes may be "You really did that because," or "Why do I do things like that?"

Pastimes are essentially intellectual maneuvers that people play in social situations to protect themselves from threat, guilt, or boredom. They represent the beginning phase of group interaction; but, if they are not recognized, the group may never move beyond them.

Games are social maneuvers that are similar to pastimes except that they are more indirect and self-deceptive in nature. A typical game that is played in neurotic interaction between spouses is "If it weren't for you." In this game, the individual essentially projects responsibility for problems on someone else and so is relieved of guilt or responsibility.

Another game is "Wooden Leg." When a member is confronted with his own inadequacy in some form, his response is "What can you expect of a man with a wooden leg." In other words, he says, "I can't do any better because I'm neurotic, or weak, or lazy, or worthless."

Games are often merely parts of *scripts,* which are larger and more complex ways of coping with general life situations. As the group learns to understand and interpret games, they are able to move on to examination of *scripts* that underlie their general life styles.

An example of a script is the "rescue" fantasy in which an individual may marry or become involved with, one after another, a series of alcoholic, criminal, or neurotic individuals, each time believing that the new person can be saved or reformed or rehabilitated. As each such experiment fails, it is simply repeated in a new set of circumstances.

In a group situation, a member usually tries to cast other members into the roles necessary for his script. He then tries to maneuver the situation to produce the climax that is demanded.

As the group learns to understand the nature of scripts, members can acquire greater insight into their own life styles and begin to modify these through learning new pastimes, games, and scripts with more positive consequences attached to them.

The transactional model is fairly complex and demanding in terms of the psychological sophistication and skill of the counselor. It has, like any approach to behavior change, some inherent dangers. If the relationships in the group setting are not supportive enough, individuals may be hurt. It offers the advantage, however, of using very fully the social interaction within the group as the basic source of material for new learning. It also teaches the basics of a language for interpersonal behavior. It is a heavily cognitively loaded model.

Just as in the discussion of models for individual counseling theory, none of the models given here may fit the purposes and level of skill of an individual counselor. Instead, each offers some significant concepts or approaches that can be incorporated into a personal theory of counseling that has been enriched by extension into the area of group work.

REFERENCES

1. BENNETT, MARGARET. *Guidance and counseling in groups.* New York: McGraw-Hill, 1963.
2. BERNE, E. *Games people play.* New York: Grove Press, 1964.
3. CARTWRIGHT, D. Achieving change in people: some applications of group dynamics theory. *Human Relat.,* 1951, 4:381–392. Also in W. W. Charters, Jr., and N. L. Gage (Eds.), *Readings in the social psychology of education.* Boston: Allyn & Bacon, 1963.
4. DICKERMAN, W. (Ed.). *Report of the second summer session of the national training laboratory in group development.* Washington, D.C.: National Training Laboratories, National Education Association, 1948.
5. GOLDMAN, L. Group guidance: content and process. *Personnel Guidance J.,* 1962, 40:518–522.
6. GORDON, T. The group-centered group. In G. Kemp. *Persectives on the group process.* 2nd ed. Boston: Houghton Mifflin, 1970.
7. HEWER, VIVIAN. Group counseling, individual counseling, and a college class in vocations. *Personnel Guidance J.,* 1959, 37:660–665.
8. OTTO, H., The personal and family resource development programs—preliminary report. *J. Soc. Psychol.,* 1962, 8 (3), 212–226.
9. TROW, W., ZANDER, A., MORSE, W., & JENKINS, D. Psychology of group behavior: the class as a group. *J. educ. Psychol.,* 1950, 41:322–338.
10. VINACKE, W. E. The miniature social situation. In W. Vinacke, W. Wilson, G. Meredith (Eds.), *Dimensions of social psychology.* Chicago: Scott, Foresman, 1964.

RECOMMENDED READINGS

ALPERT, A. Education as therapy. *Psychoanal. quart.,* 1941, 10:469–474.
CARTWRIGHT, D., & ZANDER, A. (Eds.). *Group dynamics: research and theory.* New York: Harper & Row, 1960.
GINOTT, H. *Teacher and child.* New York: Macmillan, 1972.
HARRIS, T. A. *I'm O.K., You're O.K.* New York: Harper and Row, 1967.
KEMP, C. G. *Perspectives on the group process.* 2d. ed. Boston: Houghton Mifflin, 1970.
LIFTON, W. Group therapy in educational institutions. *Rev. educ. Res.,* 1954, 24 (2), 156–158.
ROGERS, C. R. *Carl Rogers on encounter groups.* New York: Harper and Row, 1970.

SCHEIDLINGER, S. Group factors in promoting school children's mental health. *Amer. J. Orthopsychiat.*, 1952, 22: 394–404.

SLAWSON, S. *The practice of group therapy.* New York: International Universities Press, 1951.

SPOTNEZ, H. *The couch and the circle: a story of group psychotherapy.* New York: Knopf, 1961.

TRECKER, H. *Social group work.* New York: Whiteside, 1955.

YALOM, I. D. *The theory and practice of group psychotherapy.* New York: Basic Books, 1970.

12

DEVELOPMENTAL MILIEU

A central thesis of this book has been the view that the counselor has as his central professional role the facilitation of human development. We know that development represents an interaction process between the individual with his inherent dispositions and his environment, particularly that part of his environment that we call society and culture.

In their attempts to intervene in the transactional process between the individual and society, educators, physicians, judges, social workers, and other professional persons almost invariably tend to assume that their intervention must be addressed primarily to the individual. They tend to assume that it is always the individual who must be changed, adjusted, or manipulated to bring him into conformity with the unquestioned and unquestionable demands of groups, institutions, or other socially sanctified components of the culture.

Nearly forty years ago, Lawrence Frank summed up the cultural myopia of the helping professions in these terms:

> In every department and aspect of our social life we find the same pattern of thought about our society: that our social ills come from individual misconduct that must be corrected and punished so that . . . supposed social forces and social laws can operate without hindrance, thereby solving our social problems. . . . If, then, we abandon this social mythology, as a growing number of

individuals are urging, what have we as an alternative? . . . The conception of culture and personality, emphasizing the patterned behavior of man toward his group and toward other individuals offers some promise of help, for it indicates at once that our society is only one of numerous ways of patterning and organizing life and that what individuals do for good or evil is in response to the cultural demands and opportunities offered them. [12, p. 336.]

For the developmental counselor, this point of view offers perspective for a balanced program of intervention and facilitation. The counselor does believe in individual freedom and individual responsibility as vital human values. He is not, however, naïve enough to deny that great amounts of human behavior are directly determined by the environment, and that very often the most effective and productive way to change behavior is by intervention with the environment as well as with the individual.

This concept has great relevance to the formulation of counselor role. Counselors do not exist in a vacuum. Rather, they exist within institutions that are presumably dedicated to human development. In a sense, this chapter could have been called the "Role of the Developmental Counselor," for it deals essentially with the counselor's ability to function as an *agent of change* who can promote human development by intervening in the social milieu in which that development occurs. The counselor is committed to the creation of an environment within which human development is facilitated and stimulated rather than retarded and stagnated.

The developmental counselor is interested in modifying environmental situations both within and without the institutional settings in which he operates. He intervenes in ways that make it possible for clients to relate themselves to the environment and react to it in maximally growth-producing fashions.

A student may be confronted with a family, social, or school situation in which he is rejected for being himself, where he is consistently expected to be something other than that which he feels he is, wants to be, or can be. He can, through counseling or without it, choose to relate himself to such a situation by fighting it actively, by "going numb" and resisting it passively, or perhaps by withdrawing physically. None of these strategies may really be maximally growth producing in terms of his future development. Each may exact a price in terms of developmental restriction that is undesirable.

In such situations, the most significant intervention of the counselor may well be to attempt to change the social situation in school or family or community so that his client may relate to it in more positive and growth-inducing ways.

The model for this kind of environmental intervention has been provided in the movement variously called milieu therapy, preventative, community or social psychiatry, and in programs for the treatment of whole families. Unfortunately, educational institutions, which employ a great percentage of those who are called counselors, have been very slow to profit from the examples of workers in mental health settings. Instead, educational institutions have resisted change forces that have attempted to bring them more in line with the needs of developing individuals. Education has been largely content to settle back comfortably within the mythology of its own omniscience and moral rectitude.

The concept of milieu therapy is a model from which education can learn much. Cohen (9) writes of the hospital as a "therapeutic instrument" in which patterns of human relationships, physical environments, and interactions with the larger society are consciously and systematically attuned to the treatment needs of patients.

In precisely the same way, the counselor is interested in creating a model of the school or college as a "developmental instrument" attuned to needs of growing human beings. Goldsmith, Schulman, and Grossbard in an article on milieu therapy with disturbed children stress the point that a clinical process such as psychotherapy cannot be integrated into an environment that is alien to it. They say:

> To achieve a schematicized environment which can be consistent and therapeutic in all its aspects, there must first and foremost be a common denominator in the functioning of all staff—clinical and non-clinical beginning with the acceptance of a common formulation for the treatment of those disturbed children. The common bond, the thread which runs through the institution, must be the understanding of the nature of the child. It is this understanding which extends the clinical process into all aspects of the environmental setting. This understanding creates identification, sympathy and tolerance. It permits individualization in the handling of children by all concerned. It is this which creates the basic milieu for and of therapy. [15, p. 482.]

The relevance of this approach for the work of the developmental counselor seems undeniable. The creation of a *developmental milieu* for clients is one of the primary goals of the counselor. The developmental milieu may not be quite the same as that of the therapeutic milieu, for the goals and the population served by the former are obviously somewhat different. The common denominator that must run through the developmental milieu is, of course, the understanding of human development and developing humans. Chapter 4 of this book is an attempt to provide a rough framework for such an understanding.

Unless the developing individual can exist in a milieu within family, within school, and within community where some basic understanding of developmental needs and processes can be found, much of the work of the counselor is almost hopeless. One of the basic reasons that so many workers in the helping professions are continually frustrated is that many of the problems they are called upon to solve are themselves merely the products of pitifully imperfect institutional or community organizations.

THE COUNSELOR'S ROLE AS AN AGENT OF CHANGE

If the counselor is to function as an agent of change within the developmental milieu of his clients, he must do so in the clear knowledge of the difficulties that will be met and the competencies that will be needed. It is not useful for the counselor to accept this responsibility purely on the basis that he has accepted so many others, that is, that a need exists. Counselors have already shown that, like nature, they also tend to abhor a vacuum.

Organizational Role

One of the first difficulties for the counselor lies in the ambiguity of his organizational role. Typically, student personnel workers are not in *line* positions in which they have some authority over other groups of professional workers. In a sense, personnel workers are neither fish nor fowl, neither administrators nor faculty members. The concept of *staff* roles in which individuals can make important contributions to decision-making functions in supporting, advising, and research capacities, rather than in authority positions, has been very poorly developed in education.

The administrative model of the hospital, for example, is very different from the administrative model of the school or college. In the hospital setting, the focus of authority is centered in the physician who also has primary responsibility for treatment. In the school or college, such authority is vested in administrators who have become increasingly divorced from the educational process itself and increasingly preoccupied with public relations, business management, and other essentially non-educational problems.

The counselor who moves into this kind of leadership vacuum must have the skills and attitudes to operate effectively in areas where he has little protection in the form of vested authority. He can only suggest, recommend, or advise changes. He must be able to stimulate change in non-threatening ways—a very difficult challenge since change is almost always threatening to many people. The counselor must be able to "rock the boat" when the boat needs rocking, but without getting so many people wet that they reject him as a helping person. In this process, the counselor must use skills of group leadership that allow groups to solve problems effectively on the basis of group concensus rather than administrative fiat.

Counselor Preparation and Background

If the counselor is to be an effective agent of change, it must be on the basis of his possession of clearly useful ideas, facts, understandings, and methods. It is not useful for the counselor to claim moral superiority to other people, whether parents, teachers, or administrators. If all the counselor can bring to the situation is the desire to "help" or "love" people in some abstract sense, then he is in poor position to make any unique contribution. The day of the counselor as a missionary who attempts to convert is about finished. If he is to be other than a benevolent busybody, the counselor must base his attempts at intervention in the environment on a solid understanding of the behavioral sciences and the relevant contributions that they make to his particular situation. In many cases, he must be able to generate research evidence that will be useful for the local and immediate situation. The ability to do this kind of local research is a source of unique power in most educational situations, because so few people are able to do it.

An example of this type of approach is found in the experience of a suburban school system with a large percentage of college-bound, high-ability youngsters. The counselor received consistent "feedbacks" from high-ability youngsters that homework assignments were excessive. Parents confirmed this by reporting many youngsters who were actually incurring health problems in attempting to compete in this situation.

When the counselor attempted to change this situation through faculty meetings, he consistently met the response that only a few "over-achieving" types were working excessively, and that most of the "high-ability" youngsters were hardly being challenged in terms of time.

The counselor undertook a survey of out-of-school activities of students that incorporated a measure of study time. Results clearly showed that average homework time was excessive, that "good students" spent more time than "poor students" in homework, and that the range of time spent was such that some youngsters' total development, including health, was clearly threatened. When this evidence was presented, many teachers were able to change their behavior and move toward constructive steps to change the situation.

If counselors can equip themselves in their role and preparation to make sweeping and constructive changes in environment, they can multiply their influence on optimum human development many times. Shoben throws out this challenge when he says:

> . . . willy-nilly, the school represents a society-in-little. The challenge before it is whether it can transform itself into a developmentally productive one on an articulate and informed basis and, by a regular and planful process of self-appraisal, maintain itself as a true growth-enhancing community. In such an effort to sharpen the impact of the school and to give it greater cogency for individual students, guidance workers can play a key role, forging in the course of it, a genuine new profession. [31, p. 442.]

The following pages will describe several kinds of developmental milieu within which the counselor may attempt to intervene. Some of the processes that are involved and some of the goals toward which intervention may point are described. Any even minimally adequate understanding of the social systems discussed here must go far beyond a book of this kind. The bibliography at the end of this chapter is intended to help the reader enter the literature that is available.

THE DEVELOPMENTAL FAMILY

The social system that has the greatest impact upon development is, of course, the family. Counselors by virtue of the kinds of contacts that they have usually possess great opportunity for constructive intervention into this developmental milieu. Parents in many situations consistently seek out counselors for help with developmental problems. Too often, counselors are reluctant to give this kind of help because they are afraid it is not part of their role. Even more often, they are unable to be of any real help because of their own lack of knowledge and understanding of the family as a social system (1, 14, 20, 33, 34).

The Family as a Social System

The family is the initial social system within which the developing child learns to cope. As he develops in the family and begins to move outside it, the youngster moves through what Lois Murphy (29) calls the "widening world of childhood." Ways of coping learned in the family will be tried out in other situations. Stress experiences sustained as a result of inability to cope with family pressures will inevitably affect developmental opportunities in the larger environment.

The developmental counselor is then intensely concerned with the operation of the family as a social system within which optimum development can occur. In order to intervene effectively when parents and children ask for help in what are essentially family treatment situations, the counselor needs to have certain minimal understandings.

The Concept of the Whole Family

One of the limitations that most counselors have in working with family situations is their inability to conceptualize the family as a total social system. Counselors instead are attuned to think of single relationships, such as father–son, mother–daughter, or in terms of sibling rivalries, parental conflicts, etc., rather than to attempt to view the family as a total system of interrelationships, each of which profoundly affects and is affected by all of the others. A number of workers in several behavioral science disciplines are now studying family phenomena within the total family concept (2, 5, 19).

Family interaction is the concept around which counselors need to approach their understanding and their interventions (30). A knowledge of family interaction depends, however, on a knowledge of family roles and relationships (7). The family is made up of several personalities. Children are not merely dependent variables who react as puppets to parents who pull the strings. Children's behavior helps to shape parent behavior. The result is a complex network of roles and relationships rather than a series of simple cause-and-effect models (3).

Counselors who approach the family from this concept will ask more complex and sophisticated questions. They will attempt to find out how the several personalities in a family relate in a structure that is both sustained and modified through their interaction.

The Family as a Subculture

In many respects, the family is the mediating agent of the culture (4). It is the chief agency for transmitting values and attitudes. When ambivalences and conflicts exist in the culture about values, these conflicts are likely to be reflected and magnified in the family setting. Cleveland and Longaker (8) attempted to study the impact of cultural factors on mental health by analyzing several families with a high incidence of neurotic members. They found within these families conflicts in value orientation that reflected general cultural conflicts, together with a pattern of self-disparagement tied to failure to cope with value conflicts. Children exposed to this kind of conflict are presented constantly with contradictory role models. As they tend to internalize and incorporate aspects of behavior from these models into their own personalities, they also tend to learn to despise and devalue the same elements. For example, the family in which values of social and financial status conflict with competing values of ease and freedom from pressure, members may experience both ambivalence and self-condemnation, no matter how they choose to cope with their life situations.

The family thus reflects and magnifies cultural influences, but it also transforms these influences in ways that make their effects unique. The family is thus in a sense a microculture of its own (22, 23).

In one family, independence may be the dominant value orientation of this microculture (23, 27). In another, competition may prevail. In still another, cooperation or responsibility may be most important. The skillful counselor needs to be able to examine a family structure from this kind of orientation in order to be able to understand the dominant themes and the major conflicts that lead to integration as well as disharmony.

The Family as the Setting for Role-learning

Brim (6) speaks of personality as role-learning. He conceives of personality differences consisting primarily of the different roles that people have learned to play, and the ways in which they have learned to play them. While this may represent some oversimplification, it seems apparent that social role-learning is a major determinant of development, and that the family is one of the major settings in which this learning takes place.

Several aspects of role-learning within the family merit attention. Goode (16) has proposed a theory of "role strain" to explain the kinds of difficulties that individuals experience in multiple role situations. A family can be conceptualized as a network of relationships in which each individual plays several roles. The father, for example, may have roles of provider, leader, arbiter, helper, lover, companion, disciplinarian, friend, etc., at various times and places within the total network of human relationships that comprises the family. Each role relationship typically demands several kinds of activities or responses. For example, when mother's authority is questioned, he may serve as disciplinarian and be expected by her to affirm her authority. At the same time, children may perceive him as an arbiter or even a protector against what they perceive as unreasonable demands. The individual thus faces a wide, distracting, and sometimes conflicting set of role obligations. If he conforms fully to one set of expectations, it will be difficult or impossible to perform adequately within another. The individual is thus in a situation of role strain.

Since role strain is anxiety-producing, the individual typically seeks to reduce it through some kind of coping strategy. Goode lists several types of coping strategies that are often used. These are:

1. *Compartmentalization.* In this strategy, the individual ignores the problem of consistency and simply deals with the role or relationship that is central to the crisis of the moment. In this strategy, for example, the father might react as stern disciplinarian at one moment, when confronted by pressure from the mother for support, and at another moment be a very non-authoritarian "pal" to children, even encouraging or helping them evade maternal authority. Such a father might, of course, be seen as inconsistent, unpredictable, and untrustworthy in many situations.

2. *Delegation.* In this strategy, the individual may attempt to rid himself of uncomfortable role strains by delegating unpleasant responsibility to others. For example, the father who is uncomfortable in trying to be both an authority figure and a "pal" to his son may simply delegate all disciplinary responsibilities to the mother.

3. *Elimination of role relationships.* The individual may simply try to curtail certain relationships. The father who is caught in a role strain

may simply evade the situation by pulling out from some uncomfortable family roles.

4. *Extension.* In this strategy, the individual replaces the uncomfortable roles with other acceptable but less anxiety-producing ones. For example, the father who is having difficulty in his family roles may become very active in PTA or the Boy Scouts. He uses these commitments to avoid the strained roles in his family.

5. *Restriction of role expansion.* The individual resists the expansion of his role system. A father may avoid strain by refusing to enter situations where uncomfortable strains may be incurred. He may refuse, for example, to be a confidant to spouse or child because of the strain this would impose on another role.

6. *Setting up barriers.* In this strategy, the individual remains remote and unapproachable in order to minimize strain from competing roles. The father's aloofness from the family situation may protect him.

The strategies discussed above are not, of course, restricted to the family. They operate in all kinds of social systems. An understanding of the nature of strategies used by various family members to cope with role strain may help the counselor grasp the dynamics of family interaction and intervene accordingly. He may be able to help family members find more growth-facilitating ways of coping with role strain or, by facilitating communication within the family, actually reduce the role strain caused by conflicting expectations.

Sex Role Pressures

Another aspect of role-learning in the family that is important to the developmental counselor concerns sex roles. Ruth Hartley (21) points out that many of the social roles that an individual learns in the family are sex-connected. These roles are largely determined by the culture and interpreted to the developing child through the family. For example, boys are expected to be brave, adventurous, and competitive, while girls in our culture have generally been expected to be timid or fearful in many situations and to be more submissive and compliant.

Ruth Hartley points out that pressures toward sex-connected behavior can be anxiety-producing. Such anxiety-producing situations are particularly likely to occur when pressures in terms of sex role expectations are great, but where opportunities for role-learning through identification with appropriate role models is limited. This kind of situation is particularly likely to exist with absentee fathers in suburban families, with broken homes, or in highly disorganized families. It may also occur in families that are physically intact, but in which neurotic patterns of interaction between parents make it impossible for children to identify clearly with the same sex parent without incurring the disapproval of the other parent.

In many situations, it is important for the counselor to understand the process by which role-learning occurs in particular families. In many cases, it may be necessary for the counselor to help the child find appropriate role models outside the immediate family situation. In some situations, the counselor may help a family form more realistic stereotypes of masculinity and femininity and so change the way in which sex role pressures are interpreted to the child within the family. As Margaret Mead (28) points out, the nature of male and female stereotypes varies within particular cultures and subcultures. Particularly in lower and middle-class American subcultures, such stereotypes may be unrealistic and maladaptive in terms of the larger society.

Patterns of Family Interaction

Hess and Handel (23) in a very interesting study of family interaction have developed a way of conceptualizing family interaction processes in terms of what they call "family themes." A family theme is a characteristic way of handling interaction within a family so as to cope with strains, tensions, and problems. Such patterns of interaction can be identified around several dimensions that are vital components of family functioning. These include:

1. *Separateness vs. connectedness.* In any family, an attempt is made to approach an acceptable balance between separateness, independence, and freedom of family members, and dependence, belongingness, and possessiveness. Families will handle these processes in different ways and arrive at different balances. For the developing child, the way in which the family copes with the needs for independence and separateness of members as well as for their needs for affiliation and belonging will be vital determinants of development. In families where an imbalance occurs in either direction, optimum development may be thwarted and arrested.

2. *Congruence of changes.* Every family attempts to establish some kind of more or less stable and congruent framework through which to view the world. Without some such framework, there is little basis for communication and empathy among members. The framework that

the family selects will determine in considerable degree the perceptions that its members have of people and events. In some families, the
world may be seen as threatening, competitive, and hostile. In others,
it may be viewed as friendly, cooperating, and helping. To understand
the behavior of family members, the counselor will need to understand
the nature of the unspokcn themes that permeate the family's
perceptual processes.

3. *Boundaries of family experiences.* Just as the family establishes a
framework for viewing the world, so does it establish boundaries
around that world. The family in a sense defines those kinds of
feelings, attitudes, perceptions, interests, and experiences that are
considered desirable and legitimate for its members. The development
of any family member is limited by these boundaries. When a
counselor intervenes to support aspirations toward college or professional vocations for a child whose family has walled out these kinds
of interests as outside its world, for example, he encounters these
boundaries. Often, such intervention can only be successful if the
counselor can succeed in expanding the limits for the entire family. In
a sense, this means getting the total family to accept that these
interests and aspirations are legitimate for "people like us."

4. *Biosocial patterns.* In every family, certain patterns of interaction
must be developed for handling family relationships based upon age
and sex. The family develops certain role prescriptions for appropriate
behavior of eldest son, youngest daughter, mother, father, etc. These
role prescriptions define to a large extent the way in which members
may deal with their needs in terms of maturity and sexuality. The
counselor needs to understand what being the middle child or the
eldest daughter means in terms of a particular family—what it means
in terms of interaction with other family members. Vogel and Bell (35)
have pointed out that, in some pathological families, one child is often
selected to be a scapegoat for all the frustrations and tensions that are
built up around its neurotic interaction patterns. For such a child, a
pathological role may be established that will prevent the development of healthy behavior patterns. For example, one child may be
singled out to be the one who always does things wrong, is always
caught and punished, or is always blamed for family misfortunes. It is
improbable that such a child can be helped materially without
changing the entire basis of family interaction.

For the developmental counselor, the problem of working with
whole families to improve the developmental milieu that the family

offers is an exciting challenge. A number of experimental programs aimed at entire families have been attempted (2, 13, 18, 25, 26, 38). Such approaches usually involve the establishment of close working relationships among professional workers such as counselors, social workers, psychiatrists, and ministers. The developmental counselor who wants to exert positive influences on family milieu will usually need to develop close working relationships with other professionals. Virginia Satir's book (see Recommended Readings) is an excellent introduction to family communication systems.

DEVELOPMENTAL SCHOOLS

The developmental milieu within which the counselor has the greatest opportunity to intervene is the one of which he is an integral part. For most counselors, this is the school or college. The school, like the family, is a social system (17). As such, it operates on developing human beings in a variety of ways. If the counselor is to be able to intervene in this social system to convert it into a "developmental instrument," he must at the very least have some knowledge of how the system operates.

The School as a Social System

The school is a social institution operated by the society for the purpose of equipping its younger generation to perform adequately the adult roles that are believed important to the preservation and enhancement of that society. The nature of the school as an institution will depend on the nature of the society that creates it. In a very complex and pluralistic society such as ours, the influences acting upon the school may be very diverse and diffuse. Wallace (36) points out that our society may be termed a "conservative" one; and, consequently, its general value orientation is somewhat balanced in its relative emphasis upon intellectual development, moral development, and technical skill development. In a conservative society that is secure enough to tolerate change without the necessity of repudiating the past, the educational system is allowed to be reasonably flexible in its approaches. In "revolutionary" societies or in "reactionary" societies, there may be much greater pressure to push the "party line" in an effort to mold the younger generation in the direction of values that are believed threatened by either revolutionary or counterrevolutionary forces.

The conservative and pluralistic society then furnishes the framework for an educational system that can be attuned to the developmental needs of individuals. It does not have to be so preoccupied with ideological fervor that individualization must give way to massive indoctrination.

The great opportunity open to American education stems from this fact. Few societies have ever possessed the economic resources, the social and political stability, and the psychological understanding to build an educational system that can be devoted to the large-scale facilitation of individual human development.

Despite the occasional outcries of extremist groups, our society can be open enough and pluralistic enough to encourage and tolerate a rather wide range of human potentialities. In such a society, it becomes permissible to facilitate the emergence of individual development rather than to fix all efforts toward molding and constricting individuals into predetermined patterns dictated by an insecure and monolithic society.

Unfortunately, the American educational system has not taken full advantage of its potential for facilitating this kind of human development. The role of the developmental counselor is to intervene in the social system called the school or college in order to maximize its potential for becoming a truly developmental milieu. To accomplish this goal, the developmental counselor will have to understand the school from several contexts.

The Power Structure of the School

The American school is formally organized on an authoritarian pattern (37). In terms of the actual exercise of power, however, it utilizes a tri-partite model in which power is divided among administrators, teachers, and students. Each of these groups has rather definite built-in limitations to the exercise of power (15).

The school administrator in theory represents the power of the community, or in a sense the society as expressed through its political institution, the school board, board of trustees, regents, etc.

In practice, however, the power of the administrator is significantly limited by a number of factors. The political organization such as the school board from which the administrator derives authority is rarely monolithic in its structure and representation (10). Instead, it is typically pluralistic and diverse in viewpoint. Rarely is the administrator given a clear and definite mandate except perhaps in the direction of keeping educational costs low. Instead, he typically responds to a variety of dimly perceived and variously felt influences that tend to inhibit rather than facilitate his exercise of power (32). Too often, the administrator becomes a kind of human weather vane who can afford few ideals and no convictions. He rarely has the security to exercise power in firm and consisent directions that can really impose long-term effects upon the day-to-day operations of the institution.

Another factor that tends to inhibit the actual power exerted by the administrator is the wide variety of essentially non-professional tasks that he must perform. Much of the administrator's time is taken up with problems of business organization and management and with public relations activities that are not really germane to his role as a supervisor of educational activities. This is further complicated by a concept of span of control that gives the administrator responsibility for direct supervision of what may well be fifty to one hundred professional workers.

The power structure of the school that is ostensibly organized along highly centralized and autocratic lines thus is often in practice an organization in which power is highly *decentralized* and where the actual locus of decision making may be quite difficult to determine.

The second element in the tri-partite power structure is, of course, the teaching staff. Because the actual supervision is quite remote, the teacher inevitably exercises great control over what is taught, how it is taught, and what the classroom climate is like. To retain this level of autonomy, the teacher must operate within certain broad limits that in practice are defined as those that do not create tensions either in the school or community that will be severe enough to disturb the delicate equilibrium of the already insecure and harassed administrator.

To insure this level of tension reduction, the teacher must engage in a series of transactions with the third element in the power structure, the students themselves. Even though the students are usually not recognized at all in the formal power structure as depicted in organizational plans, they do indeed exert considerable power in the actual structure.

Students by giving and withdrawing cooperation are able to shape the behavior of the teacher significantly as well as to affect the operation of the total system. Most attempts at "student government" are not really recognitions of this power base of the student body. Instead, these student government organizations are at worst subterfuges that attempt to deceive students into believing that they are being accepted into the formal power structure, and at best are merely ways of opening communication between administration and students. The result of this blindness to the power of students is that they become in effect the only group in the power structure with little or no responsibility.

When any group exercises considerable power with little or no concomitant responsibility, the chances are very good that this power will be abused. In American education until quite recently, this situation was not terribly critical for two reasons. First, the students have not been very much aware that they had great power. Second, they have not been deeply enough concerned or involved with what happens in the institution to care to exercise their power fully. Both of these situations are rapidly changing.

These changes are now fully apparent at the level of higher education, and will soon be seen in secondary education. Students are becoming much more aware of their power as they become involved in mass action movements such as civil rights demonstrations. They are becoming more and more concerned and committed to action programs as they see the example of such organizations as the Peace Corps.

The problem that these new developments bring is not that students have power, but that the social system of the school and college has not really recognized that power clearly enough to institutionalize it and to provide the responsibility that can harness the constructive potentialities of student commitment and concern about the problems facing the institution and the society.

Students have learned from parents and from the schools and colleges that the old authoritarian patterns of coercion simply no longer work. Our society just does not coerce children and adolescents any longer. Parental and administrative patterns of interaction based solely upon authoritarian relationships have been proved ineffective. As these adults find that their authoritarian methods are ineffective, many simply tend to withdraw to laissez-faire positions and abdicate all responsibility for working constructively with students in new non-authoritarian relationships.

The results of this abdication can be seen in situations ranging from parent groups frantically trying to band together for more support to establish "Teen-Age Codes" to the picture of a president of a great university losing complete control of his campus and his Faculty, if not his *faculties*, and being forced to call in state police to preserve some vestiges of order.

Developmental counselors need to understand the power structure of an institution if they are to be able to see it accurately as a social system. They need to be able to help create institutional patterns that will weld together these elements within the power structure in a coherent and goal-directed way rather than to perpetuate their existence as competing and alienating segments. They also need to understand how institutions react to influential but non-authoritarian people.

The Influence Structure of the School

A second structure in the social system that is just as important as the *power structure* is what might be called the "influence structure." Many people who are not a part of the formal power structure of an institution exercise great influence on decision making by virtue of their personal characteristics, prestige, reputations, and special skills.

Both faculty and student groups contain important leadership elements that are not reflected in the power structure. The influence structure is more complex and more difficult to understand than the power structure because it is so amorphous. People exert influence in situations where they are judged to have particular competence. Sociometric patterns that determine influence tend to shift with situations. The teacher who is particularly influential in determining a policy decision in regard to curriculum may not have the same influence in a decision involving school–parent relationships.

The developmental counselor needs to be sensitive to the way in which the influence structure operates. This means that he must become aware of the points at which various kinds of crucial decisions are made and implemented. He needs also to know both who in the *power structure* has responsibility for the decision and who in the *influence structure* will play important roles in the decision-making process.

The developmental counselor also seeks to become a significant part of the influence structure of the school.

The counselor typically is not and does not seek to become an important part of the power structure. Formal administrative responsibilities may only distract the counselor from his most central roles and may inhibit these roles by destroying his image as a helping person. The counselor then must seek to institute change through influence rather than authority. The sources of influence in a social system are several. The counselor if he is to function as an agent of change must cultivate sources such as these:

1. *Specialized knowledge.* A social system is a group of people organized to facilitate goal-oriented behavior. The person who possesses special information, skills, and techniques that are relevant to the group goals is in a position to make a unique contribution to the group. He is consequently able to assume a role of special influence in the process by which the group defines and approaches its goals. The counselor has several obvious areas in which he should be able to make such contributions. He should be particularly expert in the psychology of individual differences. He should be knowledgeable in the area of causes of behavior and consequently able to predict the behavioral outcomes of courses of action. He should have special competencies in the area of defining and researching educational problems. Finally, he should be particularly expert in the area of human development. If the counselor is genuinely expert in these and other areas, and if he can communicate this knowledge to others in helpful ways, he will have rich sources of influence in the social system within which he operates.

2. *Skills in facilitating group processes.* The counselor should be an expert in the field of group dynamics and process. He should be able to help groups solve problems and arrive at decisions in ways that will insure that these decisions are sound and yet that preserve the integrity and commitment of group members. The person who possesses such skills has an enormous source of influence in a social system like the school and college that operates very heavily in terms of committees and other small groups.

3. *Capacity to enter helping relationships.* The counselor has a rich source of influence simply through his role as a helping person. If he is competent in this capacity, he is seen as a person who can keep confidences, listen attentively, and react in non-punitive ways. He is a person who will be sought out at crucial times by administrators, teachers, parents, and students. As such, he is in a position both to give individual assistance and to help the system operate in ways that will expedite general developmental goals without grinding up individuals in the process. The volume *Guidance Systems,* listed in the Recom-

mended Readings, is heavily devoted to the change agent or consulting role described only briefly here.

THE NATURE OF THE DEVELOPMENTAL SCHOOL

The developmental school is one that is deeply committed to facilitating positive growth of students, and has as its goal the highest possible level of human effectiveness for each of its students. The central characteristic of the developmental school would be its understanding of the processes of human development and its commitment to organizing and patterning all the experiences and activities of the school in the best possible way to facilitate these developmental processes.

The willingness to consciously plan, pattern, and organize activities around knowledge about, understanding of, and faith in developmental processes comes only with a commitment to a developmental view of human nature. Unless there is some commitment to such a view, the school will be organized to construct and control individuals and to protect itself against them.

Karen Horney contrasts conflicting views of human nature when she says:

> Broadly speaking, there are three major concepts . . . of essential human nature. Superimposed checks and balances cannot be relinquished by anyone who believes—in whatever terms—that man is by nature sinful or ridden by primitive instincts (Freud). The goal of morality must then be the taming of the *status naturæ* and not its development.
>
> The goal must be different for those who believe that there is inherent in human nature both something essentially "good" and something "bad," sinful or destructive. It will center upon the insurance of the eventual victory of the inherent good, as refined, directed or reinforced by such elements as faith, reason, will, or grace—in accordance with the particular dominating religions or ethical concept. Here the emphasis is not exclusively upon combatting and suppressing evil, since there is also a positive program. Yet the positive program rests either upon supernatural aids of some sort or upon a strenuous ideal of reason or will, which in itself suggests the use of prohibiting and checking inner dictates.
>
> Lastly the problem . . . is again different when we believe that inherent in man are evolutionary constructive forces, which urge him to realize his given potentialities. This belief does not mean that man is essentially good—which would pre-suppose a given knowledge of what is good or bad. It means that man by his very nature and of his own accord, strives toward self realization, and that his set of values evolves from such striving. Apparently he cannot, for

example, develop his full human potentialities unless he is truthful to himself; unless he is active and productive; unless he relates himself to others in a spirit of mutuality. Apparently he cannot grow if he indulges in a "dark idolatry of self" (Shelley) and consistently attributes all his own shortcomings to the deficiencies of others. He can grow in the true sense only if he assumes responsibility for himself. [24, p. 14.]

When the school is committed to the latter view that Horney elaborates, many of the patterns of organizing and planning educational activities will fall into place. Schools are presently organized in terms of grade levels and subject matter fields. In the developmental school, another type of structure will replace or be superimposed upon the traditional structure. This new developmental structure will view students within the concept of developmental stages and will view learning activities in terms of developmental tasks.

An outline of human development in these terms was given in Chapter 4. It may be worthwhile to examine the nature of developmental schools at various levels in terms of a few of these concepts.

Elementary School as Developmental Milieu

The elementary school finds the child at the end of the early childhood period and follows him through the period of later childhood. Its central concerns are with facilitating the mastery of the developmental tasks that are central to these stages of development. It is the role of the developmental counselor in the elementary school to help other workers understand the nature of these tasks and to help them organize school activities in a way that will best insure youngsters the opportunity to master them.

As we saw in Chapter 4, one of the central developmental tasks of the early childhood period is the building of a sense of autonomy, that is, a sense of the child's own separateness, independence, and responsibility. Entry into kindergarten and the primary grades are obviously important steps in the completion of the process.

Two of the important classes of coping behaviors at this stage are *cooperative behaviors* and *control behaviors*. The elementary school is obviously interested in helping children to acquire these behaviors.

The methods used in shaping cooperative and control behaviors will differ sharply in schools, depending upon their fundamental promises about the nature of the child and their objectives in regard to him. Elementary counselors and teachers in developmental schools need to understand several basic psychological principles.

1. *Punishment in the elementary school.* The use of aversive stimulation *may* reduce the probability of occurrence of the behavior punished; it does not in any way insure the occurrence of new or more desirable behaviors. While punishment may inhibit some forms of undesirable overt behaviors, it may also trigger other responses that are incompatible with desired behaviors, such as concentration, attention, and interest. When punishment is used in a classroom, its effects generalize rapidly to students for whom punishment is not intended. Its effects for these students are precisely the same as for the student punished; that is, it will tend to reduce the probability of the behavior engaged in prior to the punishing stimulus and to produce emotional responses incompatible with many desirable learning activities.

The teacher, for example, who is confronted with a situation in which twenty-nine students are studying diligently and one is misbehaving may only succeed through overt public punishment of the misbehaver in insuring that none of the students will be able to learn effectively for some time after the punishment.

2. *Shaming as a form of punishment.* The use of shame and ridicule as punishments with children, in the elementary school particularly, are among the most psychologically destructive forms of control possible. They are particularly damaging in early and middle childhood when the child is struggling to build positive attitudes and feelings about himself and when he is most sensitive to the opinions of adult figures. In most school systems, teachers are prohibited from using forms of physical punishment. Such punishments are usually actually less damaging developmentally than are shame and ridicule, which are routinely used by many teachers.

3. *The use of extinction and reinforcement in shaping behavior.* Probably the most effective way of eliminating undesirable behavior is by letting it run to extinction. Behavior potential viewed in this way is like a spring that is wound to some degree of tightness. When released, it will unwind and run down of its own accord. So will most behaviors "run down" if they are not wound up again through some kind of reinforcement.

Often, teachers do not have the personal security to allow undesirable behaviors to run to extinction. The teacher feels forced to intervene to preserve some abstract concept of authority or control. Such intervention, unless it is quite expert, may well backfire by simply "winding up again" an otherwise easily extinguished kind of behavior. For example, if a child needs attention, recognition, sympathy from classmates, etc., a teacher intervention meant to eliminate undesirable behavior may actually reinforce it. The teacher has no monopoly on the use of punishment in a classroom. Even very young children have all kinds of ways of punishing adults, including teachers. They can frustrate and torment adults, for example, by refusing to achieve or conform. Many of these resisting behaviors are developmentally costly to the child, but they are effective punishments for the teacher or parent.

Often, undesirable behaviors are such that even the most secure teacher feels that they are too disruptive to allow to run to extinction. Two strategies are available that are usually superior to the use of punishment.

The first is the use of *reinforcement of incompatible responses*. The teacher who is resourceful can very often skillfully reinforce pupil activities that are incompatible with disruptive behaviors. For example, the child who is reinforced by being given special responsibilities or recognition, or intrinsically interesting tasks, cannot at the same moment exhibit both task-oriented and disruptive behaviors.

A second strategy to eliminate undesirable behavior is simply to prevent the occurrence of stimulus situations in which the undesirable behaviors are most likely to occur. When disruptive behaviors are about to occur, for example, at times when students are bored, restless, or uneasy, the skillful teacher can often restructure the stimulus situation by introducing new activities or techniques or by substituting different types and schedules of reinforcement. The use of games, contests, plays, and other such teaching devices are obvious examples of this strategy. The Madsen and Madsen book in the Recommended Readings elaborates on such an approach.

4. *Competition and evaluation in the developmental school.* Competition and evaluation are undoubtedly reality factors in our society. As such, it is probably naïve to assume that they can or should be totally eliminated from the social system of the school. The elementary school, however, works with youngsters at stages to which the greatest threats to optimum development are the establishment of feelings of shame, guilt, inferiority, and worthlessness. When evaluation and competition impinge upon developing youngsters in destructive ways, the social system obviously needs to be changed. Such changes cannot be done by essentially hypocritical and sentimental evasions or euphemisms. Children are quite aware of individual differences on all

kinds of variables. Grouping children on ability and labeling the groups with such disarming euphemisms as "Blue Bells" or "Violets" hardly changes the impact of the practice. A rose by any other name still smells. Nor does the use of a hieroglyphic grading code that is designed to confuse parents enough so that the child is out of elementary school before the parents can comprehend what the symbols mean really change the fact that the children are being graded.

Two more realistic approaches are to broaden the base of individual differences and behaviors that are really valued. When teachers really do begin to value non-academic behaviors such as openness, courage, honesty, warmth, and enthusiasm, they will communicate attitudes of acceptance and worth that cannot be accomplished through the phoney use of faint praise.

Second, when teachers see as the primary challenge the optimum development of each child's *unique* combination of talents and capacities, they will find that few children are really so disadvantaged that they will be destroyed by constructive evaluation and competition. The developmental school will seek ways for all children to *earn* honest praise and recognition through the optimum development of their own unique capacities.

Many of the statements made above are hardly startling or new in terms of good educational practices. They are given rather as some examples of principles that the developmental counselor can constantly reinforce as he works to improve the developmental milieu. Often, the counselor is able to change the milieu by helping teachers acquire greater security and confidence in dealing with children. The counselor may very well help teachers through consultation and even personal counseling. The counselor can also communicate knowledge about behavior that will enable teachers to be both more secure and more expert in working with children. The book by Tharp and Wetzel in the Recommended Readings describes the use of consultation based upon such approaches.

Secondary School as Developmental Milieu

Many of the same comments that apply to the developmental milieu of the elementary school are obviously just as relevant to the secondary school. Perhaps some additional discussion is appropriate here, however, because the central developmental task of adolescence demands special attention.

This central developmental task is the achievement of a personal identity. Much of the planning and organization of educational activities in a developmental secondary school would be focused on facilitating the development of this identity structure.

In the developmentally organized secondary school, systematic attention is given to the following kinds of learning.

1. *Learning about self.* In most schools, few systematic efforts are made to help youngsters learn anything about themselves. Usually, many thousands of dollars are spent in giving tests and maintaining records that are never used to help the students, for whose benefit the school presumably exists. Indeed, the one thing that students are likely to know about these records is that they contain carefully concealed secrets that are so terrible that they must be guarded from the very people they are supposedly designed to help.

In the developmental school, some systematic effort at keeping records *for* students rather than *about* students is made. In this kind of effort, students are encouraged to participate in and reflect upon their developmental history as recorded. Students are encouraged to contribute to such records their own impressions and perceptions in the form of biographical materials, progress reports, anecdotal comments, outstanding achievements, and so forth. Teachers and counselors too would contribute to these records, but always in ways that are designed to add to the student's growth and to help him take an active part in his own development. Test information would always be expressed in the kinds of graphic terms that give scores some meaning to students. Grades or other evaluations would be given in forms that allowed the student to measure achievement in terms of his own developmental progress rather than only in relation to the achievements of others.

Teachers would view as part of their responsibility the development of self-understanding. Questions of "How do I feel about social issues?" or "How do scientific and technological advances change my life?" would have equal precedence to questions of how presumed experts or authorities react or how technical processes can be detached from human values.

2. *Learning about the world of work.* In many schools, guilt about failure to teach students anything useful about the world of work is assuaged by the device euphemistically termed the "Occupations Unit." In practice, this means that some unfortunate teacher or department whose courses are generally singled out for wastebasket

purposes is assigned the onerous task of presiding over a four- to six-week "unit" in which students are forced to trudge to the library to unearth a wealth of largely irrelevant information about a half dozen occupations that they are, of course, totally unsuited for or uninterested in. The net effect of this kind of procedure is about equivalent to moving bones from one graveyard to another.

In a developmental milieu, occupational information is considered part of the curriculum of all courses in all departments at all levels. Counselors serve as resource persons to teachers in identifying new materials, trends, and information that can be incorporated into ongoing courses and programs. Such information is programmed so that students have information appropriate to their levels of vocational development and to the kinds of choices that they are requested to make.

3. *Learning healthy heterosexual roles.* In a truly developmental milieu, the myth of adolescent asexuality would be abandoned. Systematic, overt efforts would be made to teach youngsters to understand, deal with, and control their own emerging sexuality. In communities where resistance to such openness exists, the school would take leadership in changing community attitudes by pointing out the terrible costs of ignorance and hypocrisy. Courses in health, physical education, biology, literature, and so forth, would face directly and candidly the realities of human sexuality in social, humanistic, and physiological terms. Systematic efforts would be made to help adolescents understand, respect, and control their sexual impulses and so channel them into healthy, socially constructive heterosexual roles and relationships.

4. *Learning to live in a multi-racial world.* In a developmental school, major attention would be focused upon intergroup relationships. Every opportunity would be utilized to insure that students learn to relate to people who are different from them in terms of racial, cultural, and national backgrounds. Basic human relations skills and attitudes would be considered to be as fundamental to educational development as reading and writing.

The Psychosocial Moratorium. Perhaps the key element in the developmental milieu of the secondary school is what Erikson (11) calls the psychosocial moratorium. It means, simply, that adolescents are viewed as growing, changing, emerging human beings who are peculiarly subject to errors and foibles. The role of the developmental school is not to prevent the adolescent from making "mistakes" in his quest for identity. Many of these so-called mistakes, even though temporarily painful, are priceless opportunities for further development. The developmental milieu instead creates a climate in which the consequences of mistakes or floundering are not so irreversible or destructive that they close off the paths for further development.

In such a milieu, teachers, counselors, and administrators do not categorize, stigmatize, or brand adolescents because of isolated outbursts or even frequent patterns of behavior, no matter how frustrating or antagonizing such behavior may seem. This does not mean that deviant or antisocial behavior is ignored in a laissez-faire sense. It does mean that behavior is viewed as potentially understandable phenomena that can be coped with in ways that can be developmentally advantageous to the adolescent and congruent with the goals of the developmental school.

Many of the above statements will no doubt seem entirely divorced from reality when viewed in the experience of conselors experienced in traditional school situations. They may indeed be glib formulations of unutterably difficult challenges. They are presented as examples of possible goals for counselors who see their role as that of being true agents of change.

College as Developmental Milieu

Higher education has perhaps the greatest opportunity of any level of American education to achieve a truly developmental milieu. The college typically has control or could have control over very large parts of the total environment of a population of young people with tremendous capacities for development. Historically, higher education in America has accepted a commitment toward total personality development of students that has never been fully operative in public education. In practice, however, the opportunities for the creation of developmental milieu have seldom been realized. Instead, the focus of higher education has actually been narrowed almost exclusively to intellectual development, and this indeed has been largely approached in a sterile and unimaginative way.

The student personnel movement in higher education has the opportunity to do much to revitalize opportunities for the establishment of developmental milieu. Two central developmental tasks that confront the college student are those of establishing *intimacy* and *commitment*.

Intimacy involves the ability to live in close physical and psychological proximity to others in a variety of relationships not necessarily sexual. For many young adults, entrance into college provides the first opportunity to live close to others outside the immediate family situation. Courtship and dating experiences are also likely to provide important situations in which new, more emotionally involving relationships will be encountered.

The settings in which these kinds of developmental tasks will be mastered or failed on the campus are in dormitories, fraternity and sorority houses, student activities groups, and student unions. These are precisely the settings in which the most expert professional help should be centered both to provide the proper developmental milieu and the proper kind of developmental counseling. Unfortunately, in most colleges and universities, the organization of personnel services exactly contradicts the realities of the developmental situation.

Typically, dormitory counselors, for example, are totally untrained and non-professional personnel who are simply using the position as a way of eking out their precarious way through graduate school in some totally unrelated field. Student activities and student unions are generally administered and operated in ways that are totally uncoordinated with the goals of a unified developmental program.

On those campuses where anything that could really be termed professional counseling services are available at all, they are centrally located in some spot remote from areas where students actually live or meet. If we consider a unitary diagnostic dimension such as that proposed in Chapter 8, ranging from psychological panic at one extreme to a very high level of human effectiveness at the other, it may be worthwhile to examine where a typical client of a college counseling center would be likely to fall. In order to become a client, a student must identify the center as a source of help, seek it out, make an appointment with a secretary, often be required to describe the nature of his difficulty, wait a few weeks until he is seen, then broach his problem with a counselor whom he has never before seen. One might well suspect that the person who can do all these things to get help is not operating at the very bottom of any scale of human effectiveness. The question is how many simply drop out of college before they are able to obtain professional help.

In helping create a developmental milieu on the college campus, student personnel workers might do well to focus their attention on the many opportunities for group and fraternal living experiences represented in existing features of college life. When these kinds of activities are coordinated and enriched with additions of truly professional personnel, the college will probably be several steps closer to becoming a developmental instrument.

REFERENCES

1. ACKERMAN, N. W. *The psychodynamics of family life.* New York: Basic Books, 1958.
2. ACKERMAN, N. W. Emergence of family psychotherapy on the present scene. In M. I. Stein (Ed.), *Contemporary psychotherapies.* New York: Free Press, 1961.
3. ACKERMAN, N. W., & SOBEL, R. Family diagnosis: an approach to the pre-school child. *Amer. J. Orthopsychiat.*, 1950, 20:744–753.
4. ARENSBERG, C. M. The American family in the perspective of other cultures. In Eli Ginsberg (Ed.), *The nation's children.* Vol. 1. New York: Columbia University Press, 1960.
5. BOTT, ELIZABETH. *Family and social network: roles, norms and external relationships in ordinary urban families.* London: Tavistock, 1957.
6. BRIM, O. *Personality development in children.* Austin: University of Texas Press, 1960.
7. BURGESS, E. W. The family as a unity of interacting personalities. *Family*, 1926, 7:3–9.
8. CLEVELAND, E. J., & LONGAKER, W. D. Neurotic patterns in the family. In A. LEIGHTON, J. A. CLAUSEN, & R. N. WILSON (Eds.), *Explorations in social psychiatry.* New York: Basic Books, 1957.
9. COHEN, R. The hospital as a therapeutic instrument. In O. MILTON (Ed.), *Behavior disorders, perspectives and trends.* New York: Lippincott, 1965.
10. DAHL, R. *Who governs democracy and power in an American city?* New Haven: Yale University Press, 1961.
11. ERIKSON, E. *Childhood and society.* New York: Norton, 1950.
12. Frank, L. Society as the patient. *Amer. J. Sociol.*, 1936, 42:335–344.
13. FREEMAN, V. J., KLEIN, A. F., RICHMAN, LYNNE, LUKOFF, I. F., & HEISEY, VIRGINIA. Family group counseling as differentiated from other family therapies. *Int. J. Group Psychother.*, 1963, 13:167–175.
14. GINZBERG, E. *The nation's children.* Vol. 1. *The family and social change.* Washington, D.C.: White House Conference on Children and Youth, 1960.
15. GOLDSMITH, J. M., SCHULMAN, R., & GROSSBARD, H. Integrating clinical processes with planned living experiences. In L. GORLOW & W. KATKOVSKY (Eds.), *Readings in the psychology of adjustment.* New York: McGraw-Hill, 1959.
16. GOODE, W. J. A theory of role strain. *Amer. sociol. Rev.*, 1960, 25:483–496.
17. GORDON, C. W. The role of the teacher in the social structure of the high school. *J. Educ. Sociol.*, 1955, 29:21–29.
18. GROTJAHN, M. Analytic family therapy: a survey of trends in research and practice. In J. MASSERMAN (Ed.), *Individual and familial dynamics.* New York: Grune & Stratton, 1959.
19. HANDEL, G. Psychological study of whole families. *Psychol. Bull.*, 1965, 63 (1), 19–41.
20. HANDEL, G., & HESS, R. D. The family as an emotional organization. *Marriage and Family Living*, 1956, 18:99–101.

21. HARTLEY, RUTH. Sex-role pressure and the socialization of the male child. *Psychol. Rep.*, 1959, 5:457–468.

22. HAVIGHURST, R., & NEUGARTEN, BERNICE. *Society and education.* Boston: Allyn & Bacon, 1962.

23. HESS, R. D., & HANDEL, G. *Family worlds: a psychosocial approach to family life.* Chicago: University of Chicago Press, 1959.

24. HORNEY, KAREN. *Neurosis and human growth.* New York: Norton, 1950.

25. JACKSON, D. D. Family interaction, family homeostasis and some implications for conjoint family therapy. In J. H. MASSERMAN (Ed.), *Individual and familial dynamics.* New York: Grune & Stratton, 1959.

26. JACKSON, D. D., & WEAKLAND, J. Conjoint family therapy: some considerations on theory, technique and results. *Psychiatry*, 1961, 24 (2, suppl.), 30–45.

27. JOSSLYN, IRENE. The family as a psychological unit. *Soc. Casewk*, 1953, 34:336–343.

28. MEAD, MARGARET. *Male and female: a study of the sexes in a changing world.* New York: Morrow, 1949.

29. MURPHY, LOIS. *The widening world of childhood.* New York: Basic Books, 1962.

30. PARSONS, T., & BALES, R. F. *Family socialization and interaction process.* New York: Free Press, 1955.

31. SHOBEN, E. J., Jr. Guidance: remedial function or social reconstruction? *Harvard educ. Rev.*, 1962, 32 (4), 430–443.

32. SPINDLER, G. D. The role of the school administrator. In G. D. SPINDLER (Ed.), *Education and culture.* New York: Holt, Rinehart, 1963.

33. STRODTBECK, F. L. The family as a three-person group. *Amer. sociol. Rev.*, 1954, 19:23–29.

34. STRODTBECK, F. L. Family interaction, values and achievement. In D. McCLELLAND, A. BALDWIN, U. BRONFENBRENNER, & F. L. STRODTBECK (Eds.), *Talent and society.* Princeton, N.J.: Van Nostrand, 1958.

35. VOGEL, E. F., & BELL, N. W. The emotionally disturbed child as the family scapegoat. In N. W. BELL & E. F. VOGEL (Eds.), *A modern introduction to the family.* New York: Free Press, rev. ed., 1968.

36. WALLACE, A. F. C. Schools in revolutionary and conservative societies. In F. GRUBER (Ed.), *Anthropology and education.* Philadelphia: University of Pennsylvania Press, 1961.

37. WALLER, W. *The sociology of teaching.* New York: Wiley, 1932.

38. WYNNE, L. C. A study of intrafamilial alignments and splits in exploratory family therapy. In N. W. ACKERMAN, FRANCES L. BEATMAN, & S. N. SHERMAN (Eds.), *Exploring the base for family therapy.* New York: Family Service Association, 1961.

RECOMMENDED READINGS

Family Milieu

ACKERMAN, N. W. *Family therapy in transition.* Boston: Little, Brown, 1970.

BELL, N. W. Extended family relations of disturbed and well families. *Family Process*, 1962, 1:175–193.

BOSSARD, J. H. S., & BOLL, ELEANOR. *Ritual in family living.* Philadelphia: University of Pennsylvania Press, 1950.

Cousins, A. N. The failure of solidarity. In N. W. Bell & E. F. Vogel (Eds.), *A Modern introduction to the family.* New York: Free Press, 1960.

Eisenstein, V. W. (Ed.). *Neurotic interaction in marriage.* New York: Basic Books, 1956.

Elles, G. W. The closed circuit: the study of a delinquent family. *British J. Criminol.*, 1961, 2:23–39.

Fisher, S., & Mendell, D. The spread of psychotherapeutic effects from the patient to his family group. *Psychiatry*, 1958, 21:133–140.

Grotjohn, M. *Psychoanalysis and the family neurosis.* New York: Norton, 1960.

Haley, J. Family experiments: a new type of experimentation. *Family Process*, 1962, 1:265–293.

Hill, R. *Family development in three generations.* Cambridge, Mass.: Schenkman, 1971.

Mendell, D., & Fisher, S. An approach to neurotic behavior in terms of a three-generation family model. *J. nerv. ment. Dis.*, 1956, 123:171–180.

Robb, J. H. Experiences with ordinary families. *British J. med. Psychol.*, 1953, 26:215–221.

Rosenzweig, S., & Cass, Loretta, K. The extension of psychodiagnosis to parents in the child guidance setting. *Amer. J. Orthopsychiat.*, 1954, 24:715–722.

Satir, Virginia. *Conjoint family therapy.* Palo Alto, Cal.: Science and Behavior Books, 1967.

Elementary School as Developmental Milieu

Alexander, F. "Educative Influence of Personality Factors in the Environment," *Environment & Educ.*, 1942, No. 54. Also in Judy F. Rosenblith & W. Allinsmith (Eds.), *The causes of behavior: readings in child development and educational psychology.* Boston: Allyn & Bacon, 1962.

Beilin, H. Teachers' and clinicians' attitudes toward the behavior problems of children: a reappraisal. *Child Develpm.*, 1959, 30:9–25. Also in Judy F. Rosenblith & W. Allinsmith (Eds.), *The causes of behavior: readings in child development and educational psychology.* Boston: Allyn & Bacon, 1962.

Harris, D. *Emotional blocks to learning: a study of the reasons for failure in school.* New York: Free Press, 1961.

Henry, J. Attitude organization in elementary school classrooms. *Amer. J. Orthopsychiat.*, 1957, 27:117–133. Also in W. W. Charters, Jr., & N. L. Gage (Eds.), *Readings in the social psychology of education.* Boston: Allyn & Bacon, 1963.

Hoehn, A. A study of social status differentiation in the classroom behavior of nineteen third-grade teachers. *J. soc. Psychol.*, 1954, 39. Also in W. W. Charters, Jr., & N. L. Gage (Eds.), *Readings in the social psychology of education.* Boston: Allyn & Bacon, 1963.

Secondary School as Developmental Milieu

Clark, Shirley M., & Clark, J. P. *Youth in modern society.* New York: Holt, Rinehart, 1972.

Coleman, J. S. *Social climates in high schools.* Washington, D.C.: U.S. Office of Education, 1961.

Cordasco, F., Hillson, M., & Bullock, H. A. (Eds.), *The school in the social order.* Scranton, Pa.: International Textbook Company, 1970.

General Studies

BLOCHER, D. H., DUSTIN, R. E., & DUGAN, W. E. *Guidance systems.* New York: Ronald, 1971.

MADSEN, C. H., & MADSEN, C. K. *Teaching*/discipline. Boston: Allyn & Bacon, 1970.

ROGERS, C. R. *Freedom to learn.* Columbus, Ohio: Charles Merrill, 1969.

THARP, R. G. & WETZEL, R. J. *Behavior modification in the natural environment.* New York and London: Academic Press, 1969.

13

ETHICAL CONSIDERATIONS IN COUNSELING

Every professional worker has to be concerned about his ethical responsibilities and obligations. Ethical problems often pose particularly difficult situations for people in the helping professions for several reasons. First, clear-cut, specific ethical practices or codes have yet to be evolved that provide adequate guidelines for ethical behavior in the very wide range of situations encountered in helping relationships. Second, most workers in the helping professions are not in private practice. Their professional operations occur within the context of institutions such as schools, colleges, hospitals, churches, and private agencies whose institutional value systems may be quite different from those of the professional group that the worker represents. Finally, workers in the helping profession are particularly likely to encounter situations where their ethical obligations overlap or conflict. Often, they are working simultaneously with several people who are involved in close interpersonal relationships of their own. Examples of these kinds of "counseling triangles" occur when the counselor is working with husband and wife, parents and child, teacher and student, subordinate and supervisor, and so forth. In such situations, ethical obligations become exceedingly complex.

THE NATURE OF ETHICAL OBLIGATIONS

Ethics are principles or standards of conduct that are based upon some commonly accepted set of values (5). When an aspiring professional group undertakes an activity that involves a considerable element of public trust and confidence, it necessarily has to translate prevailing values into a set of ethical standards that can serve to structure expectations for behavior of its members in their relationships with the public and with each other.

As the group emerges in its development toward professionalization, ethical standards are generally formalized in terms of a code of ethics. Several such codes have relevance for developmental counselors. Tentative codes of ethics were proposed by individuals as guidelines for counselors as long as twenty years ago (5, 6, 8, 9, 11, 14, 15).

These tentative suggestions were followed by formally developed codes of ethics sponsored by professional associations. The American Psychological Association (3, 4), the American Association of Social Workers (1), and the American Personnel and Guidance Association (2) have all published ethical codes relevant to developmental counselors.

Ethical codes generally recognize the fact that counselors have a number of different kinds of ethical obligations. Most counselors would recognize each of the following kinds of obligations.

1. Obligations to clients
2. Obligations to parents of minor clients
3. Obligations to the profession
4. Obligations to employing institutions
5. Obligations to the community or society at large

Making ethical decisions in situations where conflicts between obligations seem to exist is not easy. Codes of ethics may furnish broad guidelines for ethical decisions, but they are seldom detailed enough to apply perfectly to specific ethical situations. Instead, counselors are usually forced to make complex ethical decisions on the basis of their own internalized ethical systems. Such ethical systems are really part of the counselor's personal philosophy of counseling. In essence, an ethical system represents a hierarchy of values that permits the counselor to make choices based upon distinguished levels of good or bad.

When ethical obligations and expectations of important others conflict, the counselor is often faced with situations in which no course of behavior will be such that a perfect reconciliation of values or expectations will occur. Instead, the counselor has to operate in areas where there are many "shades of gray."

The ability to internalize a value hierarchy within which the counselor can operate ethically, effectively, and in good conscience really stems from the counselor's own sense of personal and professional identity. Unfortunately, many counselors have not really decided who they are, or who they want to be. At one moment, they want to be "helping persons" who are deeply committed to assisting one person at a time. At another moment, such counselors want to be "policemen" or guardians of society against the real or supposed transgressions of individuals.

It may be perfectly true that society needs both "helping persons" and "policemen," but it may also be true that, in many situations, it is impossible for one person to behave ethically and consistently in both roles. One of the deepest concerns of the counselor is that he be perceived as a consistent and ethical person. Unless he is perceived in this way, clients will not be able to put the trust and confidence in him that are necessary for establishing helping relationships.

Unethical behavior usually occurs when the counselor communicates himself in a way to establish one set of expectations and then behaves in a way inconsistent with those expectations. For example, the counselor structures the counseling situations verbally or non-verbally in terms of mutual trust, concern, and confidentiality. He then behaves in a way that upsets these expectations because he assigns greater value to another societal role. Such inconsistent behavior is clearly seen as unethical by the client. It often stems from a lack of professional identity on the part of the counselor.

To operate successfully and ethically as a counselor, one must be able to verbalize and to live with a value hierarchy that makes possible consistent decisions that involve obligations to clients versus other obligations. The counselor must be able to understand rather clearly those situations in which the welfare of his client will override other values that may be involved.

When the counselor is unclear and deeply ambivalent about his ethical obligations, he will be perceived as inconsistent and untrust-worthy. When the counselor resolves his value hierarchy but finds that client welfare is not really at or near the top, he will probably no longer be perceived as a counselor. Most ethical misbehavior occurs when workers want to be perceived as counselors, but really assign greater values to other institutional roles such as disciplinary or administrative ones.

CONFIDENTIALITY

The greatest single source of ethical dilemmas in counseling is concerned with questions of confidentiality. Questions of confidentiality are clearer when they are examined in terms of "levels of confidentiality." Confidentiality involves a commitment to retain information that is always *relative* rather than *absolute*. For example, it is hard to conceive of any counselor withholding the information that a client had put a time bomb on an airliner. Three rather distinct levels of confidentiality can be distinguished in counseling.

The first level involves the professional *use* of information. Every professional worker has the obligation to handle information about clients or potential clients *only in professional ways*. Such information, no matter how it is acquired or how trivial it may seem, should never be used loosely in social conversation or in non-professional settings. This includes not only information obtained in counseling interviews, but all kinds of information found in personnel offices. Sources of information should be handled in ways that insure that they do not fall into the hands of persons who might handle the information in non-professional ways.

Records, test scores, and other kinds of information should generally not be released without the client's consent. This precludes furnishing such information to people such as employers, insurance companies, salesmen, newspapers, credit agencies, or even colleges without consent of the client. Whenever there is doubt about release of information, the counselor would do well *not* to release it without obtaining consent of the client. Maintaining this level of confidentiality for all kinds of information is simply good professional practice. It is no different from practices generally subscribed to in other professional settings such as law or medicine. Probably the simplest and best rule for handling information is that it is the joint property of the counseling service and the client, and should not be used in ways objectionable to either. In some situations, it might well be objectionable to give information to a clearly unethical or unprofessional person even with client consent. An example might be a quack who uses a title of counselor or therapist without professional qualifications.

The second level of confidentiality relates to information that arises out of a counseling relationship. In all such situations, the client has a right to expect that information will only be used for *his welfare*. The very nature of the counseling relationship implies this whether it is ever structured verbally or not.

In counseling relationships, however, it is often highly desirable in terms of the client's welfare to share certain information with other persons who are concerned with working with the client and who have a primary concern for his welfare. Such persons may include other counselors, teachers, social workers, psychologists, or parents or spouse. The sharing of information with such persons often poses difficult ethical dilemmas. Often, in order to make referrals or to secure changes in environment that would be helpful to the client, some sharing of information seems essential. On the other hand, clients may be extremely reluctant to have the information shared, even though it is in their best interests. Conflicts that result from this kind of situation often provide the knottiest ethical dilemmas for counselors.

The primary solution to this type of problem is to structure very carefully this level of confidentiality with clients *before confidences are accepted*. If the counselor structures clearly in advance with clients that he will use information only for professional purposes and only in the client's best interests, then many of the ensuing decisions will be professional judgments rather than ethical decisions.

It is possible to base a counseling practice on the two levels of confidentiality discussed above. It is also obvious that, when these are the only levels structured, *some* clients will not bring *some* kinds of concerns to the counselor. A third level of confidentiality is one in which the counselor holds a communication in *complete* confidence except in case of some clear and immediate danger to human life. In this level, the communication would not be divulged without the client's consent even though the counselor felt strongly that it would be in the client's best interest to do so. The only grounds for breaking this kind of confidence would involve an extraordinary circumstance involving danger to human life. The fact that it would be "better" for the client or "better" for society if the confidence were broken is not an ethical reason for breaking a confidence accepted under these conditions. The basis for structuring such a level of confidentiality is simply that it is better that clients have some professionally trained person in whom they can place a confidence, no matter how disturbing it may be, than that no such person be available. The counselor in providing such a person discharges his *primary* obligation to society. His primary role is not to *protect society* by some *direct intervention*, but to protect society including his client by providing a helping, confidential relationship.

The counselor who is not able to accept disturbing and shocking confidences on this basis would do well to structure his relationship with clients accordingly *in advance*. He will need also to accept the limitations that this will impose upon his usefulness. Structuring in advance the level of confidentiality at which a counselor operates is a matter of *professional practice* and *judgment*. Keeping the confidence once it is accepted at a particular level is an *ethical* matter. The counselor who does not keep confidences in an ethical manner will soon have no confidences to keep.

LEGAL RESPONSIBILITIES OF COUNSELORS

One area in which counselors are often confused is in terms of their legal rights and responsibilities. To some extent, the legal status of professional workers varies from state to state and from time to time as new precedents are established (7, 12, 13). Typically, counselors do not have *privileged communication* (13). Privileged communication is a status under law that is given to certain kinds of relationships. A person claiming privileged communication can refuse to testify *against* an individual with whom his relationship is privileged. For example, an attorney cannot be required to testify against his client, or a minister against his parishioner in matters that involve communications arising out of their professional relationships.

Counselors do not presently have this status, largely because they do not represent as homogeneous or readily identifiable a professional group as do lawyers, ministers, or physicians. As the helping professions grow in status, visibility, and homogeneity, they may well acquire privileged communication.

Even though counselors do not typically have privileged communication, they do have certain legal rights as witnesses of which they should be aware. Counselors should keep confidential case notes in the form of memoranda addressed to *themselves* and not available to anyone else. Such personal memoranda cannot typically be subpoenaed as evidence as can formal records. Also, many kinds of client statements constitute "hearsay evidence" and would not be admissible in court. Also, counselors are *not* typically under any legal obligation to voluntarily report a client admission of a criminal act to legal authorities. In some situations, counselors could be guilty of slander or libel if they did report client statements as truth to authorities or others.

PROFESSIONAL HONESTY AND DISHONESTY

An ethical and professional issue that is just as relevant to the developmental counselor as confidentiality is the problem of professional lying to clients. While most counselors would deeply resent the idea that they lie to clients, the fact remains that, as Halleck (10) points out, many professional helping relationships are consciously and unconsciously systematic exercises in deception.

Several major dimensions of professional dishonesty can be readily identified. The first and perhaps the most unfortunate of these concerns the way in which the counselor communicates himself and the world of which he is a part. As Halleck says:

> Professionals communicate a picture of themselves and their world as one in which only the highest type of values and moral standards prevail. The adolescent cannot understand this. His personal experiences, his observational powers, and his intuitiveness tell him that something is wrong. He wants to like and to identify with adults, but he is painfully aware of an inconsistency or basic dishonesty in their approach. He may then come to believe that adults are incapable of being anything but "phoney" and reacts by rebellious behavior or isolation from the adult world. [10, p. 49.]

The type of dishonesty that Halleck describes is not confined to work with children or adolescents. Many counselors tend to behave with all clients as though they were living in a world of make-believe. Any human being, counselor or client, who is literate and intelligent enough to read a daily newspaper cannot avoid the conclusion that the real world is one that is deeply ambivalent about sex, one in which aggressive and hostile urges are constantly acted out against those who happen to be weak and vulnerable, and one in which opportunities for those who are culturally or racially different are systematically restricted.

The counselor who consciously or unconsciously attempts to ignore the unpleasant realities of life can hardly hope to stimulate a client's faith in either his intelligence or his veracity. A counselor can demonstrate a reasoned faith in the future of man without exhibiting a Pollyanna-like insensitivity to reality.

Another dimension of professional dishonesty concerns the implied efficacy of counseling itself. There is no evidence that the counselor or therapist has any curative magic to dispense. Clients cannot honestly be persuaded to enter counseling on the basis that some kind of cure or remarkable personality change will ensue. The only honest approach to counseling is that it is a possibly useful learning experience in which most of the work will be done by the client, and in which the outcome will depend more on his efforts and motivation than on anything else. The most skillful counselor can do little more than facilitate a process of self-help. There is no magic involved in revealing oneself to a counselor, or will there be any magical change in behavior that is sure to accompany efforts at self-exploration. Limitations in environmental and hereditary backgrounds and in social opportunities are real, and no counselor will be able to change them to any great degree. The counselor who consciously or unconsciously communicates a basis for unfounded expectations for counseling only sets up his client for frustrating and embittering disappointments.

The third dimension of professional dishonesty concerns the ways in which contacts with clients are initiated. Many counselors make initial contacts with clients at the behest of teachers, parents, spouse, or administrator. Very often, the counselor feels it necessary to deny or distort the nature of the referral to the client. Counselors typically take refuge in that badly transparent lie "I just wanted to see how you were getting along" the day after the client has been put on probation, for example. It is amazing how many counselors cheerfully begin a counseling contact with a bald-faced lie and then complain that the client is not open and frank with them.

The process of building and internalizing a workable and ethical basis for relating to others in counseling is more than anything else a process of mustering the courage to be painfully honest with one's self. It requires the courage to abandon cherished self-deceptions about one's ability to be all things to all people. Instead, the counselor must find the courage to be consistent within his own limitations and to develop confidence in the worth of his relationships with others. When the counselor really begins to believe that it is worthwhile for the client to have a trusted person who listens and attempts to understand, he will be less likely to try to play other roles that involve inconsistent and unethical behavior. Such a counselor is likely to be too busy helping clients to help themselves to spend his time trying to save clients from themselves.

REFERENCES

1. AMERICAN ASSOCIATION OF SOCIAL WORKERS. *Principles of confidentiality in social work*. Washington, D.C.: Author, 1946.
2. AMERICAN PERSONNEL AND GUIDANCE ASSOCIATION. Ethical standards. *Personnel Guidance J.*, 1961, 40:206–207.
3. AMERICAN PSYCHOLOGICAL ASSOCIATION. Standards of ethical behavior for psychologists. *Amer. Psychologist,* 1958, 6:226–271.
4. AMERICAN PSYCHOLOGICAL ASSOCIATION. Ethical standards of psychologists. *Amer. Psychiatrist,* 1959, 14:279–282.
5. BIXLER, R. & SEEMAN, J. Suggestions for a code of ethics for consulting psychologists. *J. abnorm. Psychol.,* 1946, 41:486–490.
6. CREEGAN, R. Concerning professional ethics. *Amer. Psychologist,* 1958, 13 (6), 272–275.
7. FOWERBAUGH, C. C. Legal status of psychologists in Ohio. *J. consult. Psychol.,* 1945, 9:196–200.
8. GLUCK, S., *et al.* A proposed code of ethics for counselors. *Occupations,* April, 1952, 30:486–489.
9. GOBETZ, W. A proposed code of ethics regarding the announcement of vocational guidance services to the public. *Personnel Guidance J.,* 1955, 33:517–519.
10. HALLECK, S. L. The impact of professional dishonesty on behavior of disturbed adolescents. *Soc. Wk.,* 1963, 8:48–56.
11. HOPPOCK, R., *et al.* A proposed code of ethics for counselors using occupational information. *Occupations,* 1950, 20:466.
12. LOUISELL, D. The psychologist in today's legal world. *Minn. Law Rev.,* 1957, 41:731–750.
13. McCOID, A. H. Privileged communication between psychologist and client. Minnesota Psychological Association, Background paper, No. 1, November, 1963, 1–5.
14. POWELL, W. T. Code of ethics for counselors. *Education,* October, 1944, 65:74.
15. SARGENT, H. Professional ethics and problems of therapy. *J. abnorm. soc. Psychol.,* 1945, 40:47–60.

RECOMMENDED READINGS

Codes of Ethics in Counseling

AMERICAN ASSOCIATION OF SOCIAL WORKERS. *Principles of confidentiality in social work*. Washington, D.C.: Author, 1946.

AMERICAN PERSONNEL AND GUIDANCE ASSOCIATION. Ethical standards. *Personnel Guidance J.*, 1961, 40:206–207.

AMERICAN PSYCHOLOGICAL ASSOCIATION. Standards of ethical behavior for psychologists. *Amer. Psychologist*, 1958, 6:226–271.

AMERICAN PSYCHOLOGICAL ASSOCIATION. Ethical standards of psychologists. *Amer. Psychologist*, 1959, 14:279–282.

BIXLER, R., & SEEMAN, J. Suggestions for a code of ethics for consulting psychologists. *J. abnorm. Psychol.*, 1946, 41:486–490.

GOBETZ, W. A proposed code of ethics regarding the announcement of vocational guidance services to the public. *Personnel Guidance J.*, 1955, 33:517–519.

HOPPOCK, R., *et al.* A proposed code of ethics for counselors using occupational information. *Occupations*, 1950, 20:466.

SUTICH, A. Toward a professional code for psychological consultants. *J. abnorm. soc. Psychol.*, 1944, 39:29–50.

Legal Considerations in Counseling

CARTER, T. M. Professional immunity for guidance counselors. *Personnel Guidance J.*, 1954, 33:130–135.

DIAMOND, B. L., & WEEHOFEN, H. Privileged communication and the clinical psychologist. *J. clin. Psychol.*, 1953, 9:388–390.

FOWERBAUGH, C. C. Legal status of psychologists in Ohio. *J. consult. Psychol.*, 1945, 9:196–200.

GOLDSTEIN, A., & KATZ, R. Psychiatrist-patient privilege: the GAP proposal and the Connecticut statue. *Amer. J. Psychiat.*, 1962, 118:733–735.

GROUP FOR THE ADVANCEMENT OF PSYCHIATRY. Confidentiality and privileged communication in the practice of psychiatry. *GAP Report No. 145*, June, 1960, 89–112.

HENSEN, H. Schools and teachers—tort liability in our changing society. *Univer. Kansas Law Rev.*, 1959, 8:124.

LOUISELL, D. The psychologist in today's legal world. *Minnesota Law Rev.*, 1957, 41:731–750.

McCOID, A. H. Privileged communication between psychologist and client. Minnesota Psychological Association, Background Paper, No. 1, November, 1963, 1–5.

SCHMIDT, L. Some legal considerations for counseling and clinical psychologists. *J. counsel. Psychol.*, 1962, 9 (1), 35–39.

General Ethical Considerations in Counseling

ADAMS, J. F. *Problems in counseling: a case study approach.* New York: Macmillan, 1962.

CREEGAN, R. Concerning professional ethics. *Amer. Psychologist*, 1958, 13 (6), 272–275.

DePALMA, N., & DRAKE, R. Professional ethics for graduate students in psychology. *Amer. Psychologist*, 1956, 11:554–557.

HALLECK, S. L. The impact of professional dishonesty on behavior of disturbed adolescents. *Soc. Wk*, April, 1963, 48–56.

HOBBS, N. Science and ethical behavior. *Amer. Psychologist*, 1959, 14 (5), 217–225.

HOLTZMAN, W. Some problems of defining ethical behavior. *Amer. Psychologist*, 1960, 15 (4), 247–250.

JANOWITZ, M. Some observations on the ideology of professional psychologists. *J. counsel. Psychol.*, 1954, 9:528–532.

LEE, A. M. Social pressures and the values of psychologists. *Amer. Psychologist*, 1954, 9:516–522.

LITTLE, R. Moot questions in psychological ethics. *Amer. J. Psychiat.*, 1956, 113:455–460.

MEEHL, P. E., & McCLUSKY, H. Ethical and political aspects of applied psychology. *J. abnorm. soc. Psychol.*, 1947, 42:91–98.

MOWRER, O. Payment or repayment? The problem of private practice. *Amer. Psychol.*, 1963, 18:577–580.

REZNY, A. A., & DOROW, E. Confidential information and the guidance program. *J. educ. Res.*, 1961, 54 (7), 243–250.

SARGENT, H. Professional ethics and problems of therapy. *J. abnorm. soc. Psychol.*, 1945, 40:4760.

SCHWEBEL, M. Some ethical problems in counseling. *Personnel Guidance J.*, 1955, 33:254–259.

SCHWEBEL, M. Why? Unethical practice. *J. counsel. Psychol.*, 1955, 2:122–128.

WISKOFF, M. Ethical standards and divided loyalties. *Amer. Psychologist*, 1960, 15 (10), 656–660.

WRENN, C. G. The ethics of counseling. *Educ. psychol. Measmt.*, 1952, 12 (2), 161–177.

14

RESEARCH AND EVALUATION IN COUNSELING

Someone has said that counseling is like kissing. It is an activity that is so intrinsically interesting that few people take the time to evaluate its consequences. Astin (1) makes somewhat the same point in what he calls the functional autonomy of psychotherapy; that is, its practice continues in the absence of any evidence of its effectiveness because of its inherent interest. Realistically, however, there are several compelling reasons for carefully studying the counseling process and evaluating its outcomes.

First, research and evaluation are the only vehicles for improving counseling practice. Second, it is necessary to obtain some evidence of the effectiveness of counseling if needed resources are to be obtained from administrators and taxpayers. Finally, research in counseling can provide, as an important by-product, needed knowledge about the development of effective human behavior.

Unfortunately, an examination of the present state of knowledge in counseling research provides relatively little information that is useful in terms of any of the three purposes cited above. The range of sophistication in counseling research is tremendous. The vast majority of the studies that are reported in the literature are simple descriptive or status studies that offer little or no evidence about the effectiveness or lack of effectiveness of procedures used.

PROBLEMS IN EVALUATION OF COUNSELING

A number of reasons exist for the relative dearth of good studies in counseling effectiveness. One of the most fundamental of these problems involves the difficulty of obtaining agreement on definitions of process and outcome that permit meaningful evaluations to be made. Counseling is often defined, for example, as a relationship. Few if any studies, however, distinguish between contacts in which a counseling relationship was developed and contacts in which it was not developed. The most important area of disagreement that clouds the evaluation picture is that of definition of criteria of counseling effectiveness.

The Criterion Problem

Ruth Barry and Beverly Wolf (3) have suggested five necessary conditions in the design of evaluation studies. These include:

1. Definitions of aims and objectives
2. Establishment of criteria against which progress toward objectives can be evaluated
3. Design of techniques or instruments by which the criteria can be measured
4. Collection of data from all available sources
5. Judgments against the criterion about the nature of progress toward achievement of objectives

These conditions seem neither unreasonable nor overstringent. When typical studies are examined in terms of the conditions, however, current difficulties in research become apparent. First of all, there are *no generally accepted* goals or objectives for counseling or psychotherapy. There are approximately as many different goals as there are researchers in the field. Further, many of the stated goals or objectives for counseling are almost completely non-operational; that is, they cannot be converted into behaviors that can be measured as criteria. Goals such as developing self-actualization, building up the integrative power of the ego, or reorganizing the patient's self-structure are a bit difficult to translate into observable behaviors.

On the other hand, most of the operational criteria that have been used are so partial and specific in nature that little agreement could be obtained regarding their adequacy as criteria or perhaps even their desirability as outcomes. Another problem of evaluation is that much of the research has focused upon changes in behavior that are really more part of the process of counseling itself than intrinsically worthwhile or socially relevant outcomes (22).

Kinds of criteria commonly used in evaluation studies can be grouped under several headings. The very wide range of criteria can be seen from the listing below:

Social Adjustment Criteria
1. Adjustment rated by "experts"
2. Reduction in disciplinary offenses
3. Participation in group activities
4. Citizenship grades

Personality Criteria
1. Congruence between self and ideal self-descriptions
2. Changes on personality tests
3. Ratings of personality change or adjustment

Vocational Adjustment
1. Specificity of vocational plans
2. Experts' judgments of realism of plans
3. Job satisfaction
4. Persistence in job
5. Promotions on job
6. Amount of earnings

Educational Criteria
1. Increase in grade point average
2. Correlation between grades and measured aptitude
3. Entrance into college
4. Persistence in college
5. Reduction in scholastic failure
6. Reduction in dropout rate

Other Miscellaneous Criteria
1. Client satisfaction
2. Persistence in counseling
3. Returning to counseling
4. Tendency to use public agencies
5. Self-confidence
6. Optimism about the future

A simple examination of the criteria listed above seems to make obvious the point that at this time there are no fully accepted criteria on which counseling can be evaluated to arrive at definitive statements such as "Counseling is effective" or "Counseling is not effective." Until a class of *behaviors,* as distinguished from non-behavioral constructs, is established that can be judged appropriate for all clients by all schools of counseling, it will be difficult to assign any meaning to the simple questions of generalized effectiveness. Instead, questions of counseling effectiveness must be asked in terms of effectiveness for what? with whom? under what conditions?

The Control Problem

Even if problems of criteria were suddenly eradicated, a very serious methodological problem in counseling evaluation would remain. In any experimental design, an attempt is made to isolate the effects of the experimental variable or treatment by designating a control group of subjects who are like the experimental group in every way except that they do not receive the experimental treatment. Such control groups are best established by randomly dividing a single population into control and experimental groups. If the total group is large enough, differences between groups can be expected to cancel out since they will be distributed randomly. In many studies, however, because of the practical difficulties of randomly assigning human beings to treatment groups, so-called control groups are developed by matching experimental subjects with other individuals who are supposedly similar on certain relevant characteristics. Matching is commonly done on characteristics such as age, sex, I.Q., and socioeconomic status. Since it is virtually impossible to match for more than a handful of the possibly relevant characteristics, matched groups do not really furnish controls of the same type as those obtained through randomization (16). In any experimental study, other variables must also be controlled. Time is an exceedingly important variable in most studies of counseling because subjects can change purely as a function of time rather than treatment (9).

The Problem of Contamination

Another major problem in counseling evaluation is contamination of treatment effects. If a population of subjects is identified who want or need counseling services, and one group is randomly selected to receive treatment, a problem remains of insuring that the control, or non-treated group, does not in fact obtain similar assistance outside the experimental situation. Bergin (4) has suggested that one reason for negative findings in so many studies is that control-group subjects actually do get help from outside sources. This hypothesis is particularly cogent if counseling is viewed primarily as a relationship. There is no guarantee that the therapeutic qualities of counseling relationships are solely confined to relationships that originate in professional settings.

REVIEW OF SELECTED STUDIES

One well-known, if less than encouraging phenomenon, in research on counseling is that an inverse relationship tends to exist between the frequency of positive results and sophistication of research design. In other words, the more carefully designed studies tend to be less-frequently associated with positive results in favor of counseling (14). In view of this factor, it seems worthwhile at this point to review only a few of the most carefully done studies reported in the literature. Perhaps the best way to organize these studies is in terms of the kinds of criteria mentioned earlier. No attempt is made to distinguish between processes called counseling or psychotherapy, but studies are grouped according to the nature of criteria.

SOCIAL ADJUSTMENT CRITERIA STUDIES

Cross (8), in reviewing selected studies on outcomes of psychotherapy, rates the study reported by Teuber and Powers (21) as the most adequate example of experimental design available in the literature. The purpose of this study was to evaluate the effects of counseling in preventing juvenile delinquency. The subjects in this study were 650 six- to ten-year-old boys who were judged by welfare workers to be high juvenile delinquency risks. Subjects were matched in pairs for age, I.Q., grade in school, delinquency rating, and ethnic and socioeconomic background. Pairs were divided into control and experimental groups on a random basis.

The experimental group was given treatment from either psychoanalytic or client-centered therapeutic orientations. The study was conducted for *eight years* with two additional years of follow-up.

The program was developed in this way: For approximately eight years, from 1937 to 1945, a large-scale treatment effort was directed at the prevention of delinquency, by guidance, counseling, and therapy, in a group of over 600 underprivileged boys. By setting up a control group, and by keeping unusually detailed records, this study made provision for quantitative measurements of the effects of therapy and for systematic attempts at an objective description of the therapeutic relationships.

Experimental subjects were given face-to-face individual counseling. Counselors listed about two-thirds of the experimental subjects as having "substantially benefited" from treatment. About half the boys were listed by counselors as "outstanding" in terms of benefit received. More than half the subjects stated that the program had helped them.

When the experimental and control groups were compared for actual delinquency offenses, however, the picture changed. When actual court appearances were compared, it was found that 96 experimental and 92 control subjects were involved. In number of offenses, 264 were committed by experimentals against 218 for controls. Eysenck quotes Teuber and Powers as follows:

> Such an outcome of the delinquency prevention program of the study appears not only negative, but paradoxical. Instead of confirming the expectation that the treatment group would be less delinquent than the matched control group, there is a slight difference in favor of the control group. This apparent advantage of the control group may be offset, however, by other factors, which more detailed statistics seem to reveal. There is a slightly greater incidence of serious recidivism . . . in the control group, and a rating of all offenses according to "seriousness" likewise shows a slight advantage of the treatment cases over the controls; there is a tendency on the part of the controls to commit a proportionally greater number of the more serious offenses. None of these trends, however, are as yet significant. Unless further developments change the picture . . . the direct comparison between T and C groups fails to show that the major hypothesis can be sustained; treatment did not . . . reduce the incidence of adjudged delinquency in the treatment group. [9, p. 703.]

This study seems to cast grave doubt on the efficacy of counseling in "adjusting" clients to societal demands at least insofar as prevention of delinquency is concerned.

PERSONALITY CHANGE CRITERIA STUDIES

Several studies have attempted to assess the effects of counseling or therapy in changing personality. Most of these studies have used some form of personality inventory as a criterion instrument. One major defect of this type of study is that it is in a sense a kind of "process" rather than an "outcome" study since the criteria are not in themselves socially or personally useful. They tend to measure changes in client verbal behavior associated with the counseling process itself. Rosenman (18) has in fact shown that clients tend to make more positive statements about self in the later stages of client-centered counseling.

It may be worthwhile, however, to examine some of these studies. Barron and Leary (2) used changes on the Minnesota Multiphasic Personality Inventory as a criterion instrument to measure personality changes in one hundred and fifty patients who applied for psychotherapy. Twenty-three of the patients were delayed in treatment for three months and so served as a control group. No significant differences were found between groups on any clinical scales either before or after treatment.

Rogers and Dymond (17) in an intensive study used the congruence between self-descriptions and descriptions of ideal self on a Q sort as a criterion instrument for measuring "self-satisfaction."

They used a so-called control group, but since the controls and experimental subjects were not randomly assigned, the control group was not really useful. Also, as Eysenck (9) points out, they did not equate the time periods for the therapy and control groups between criterion measurements.

Rogers and Dymond did show that experimental subjects changed in self-satisfaction significantly more than the so-called controls, and more than the experimental subjects themselves had changed in a sixty-day period prior to therapy.

Rosalind Cartwright and Vogel (7) essentially repeated the Rogers and Dymond study but with time periods equated. Their results as measured by Q sort were not significant even at the .05 level. On the Thematic Apperception Test, no differences were found.

Williams (25) has found that Q sort correlations of the kind reported by Rogers and Dymond can be changed by two interview contacts in educational vocational counseling. He used both a randomly assigned control group and an own control method and obtained significant results after only two interview contacts. Schlien, et al. (20) using the same kind of Q sort criterion variable found that there were no differences in the amount of changes produced in short-term and long-term contacts.

Generally speaking, this evidence is not highly supportive of claims regarding the ability to produce significant changes in basic personality through counseling or therapy. It does appear that it is possible to change the verbal behavior of clients in terms of their willingness to say positive things about themselves. These changes seem to occur regardless of the orientation of the counselor or the number of interviews.

Perhaps the most thorough study of counseling effectiveness using personality criteria was that reported by Volsky et al. (24). In an unusually carefully designed and controlled study, these researchers attempted to evaluate the effects of counseling in terms of personality variables such as anxiety, defensiveness, and personal problem-solving. They were unable to find any positive effects for the counseled group as compared to no-treatment controls.

Overall results of counseling in changing global personality constructs as measured by personality inventories do not seem promising.

VOCATIONAL CRITERIA STUDIES

A number of studies using vocational criteria have attempted to assess the effects of counseling in this area.

A large-scale study by Fairweather et al. (10) evaluated outcomes of four different kinds of treatment on Veterans Administration patients. Treatments included group counseling, individual counseling, and "group living." A control group was used that simply received an individual work assignment. When the patients were followed up after discharge, the only significantly different comparison between treatment and control groups was the per cent of patients employed six months after discharge. This difference was in favor of the experimental group.

Merenda and Rothney (15) did a particularly careful and thorough longitudinal study of the effectiveness of counseling with high school students. They studied 685 high school students who were randomly assigned to counseling and control groups. These students were followed up five years after graduation. Significant differences were found between counseled and control groups in favor of the former on variables that included vocational satisfaction and persistency.

Results of these studies suggest that counseling can affect vocational outcomes, although demonstrated effects consistently tend to be disappointing in terms of magnitude.

EDUCATIONAL CRITERIA STUDIES

Campbell (6) in a twenty-five year follow-up of subjects involved in a study originally done by Bordin and Williamson studied records of approximately four hundred college students who had come for counseling at the University of Minnesota during a three-year period. A matched group of students were used as controls. Results showed that the counseled group rated higher on an Adjustment Scale designed to assess educational-vocational progress and on grade point average. When members of the original control group who subsequently sought and received counseling were followed up, it was found that, after counseling, they resembled the counseled group more than the original control group. When the groups were compared for percentage graduating from college, both counseled groups were significantly higher in per cent graduating than were the controls.

Rothney (19) in another report of the same group reported by Merenda and Rothney also found that greater percentages of counseled students entered and remained in post-high school education.

Research seems to support the claim that counseling can change educational achievement and persistence.

General conclusions that may be drawn from these studies are that little evidence exists to support claims that counseling can effectively change social adjustment or basic personality adjustment. Some evidence does exist that vocational and educational achievement satisfaction and persistence can be brought about through counseling.

BEHAVIORAL STUDIES

One additional group of studies should be cited. These are counseling or behavior therapy studies. The approaches used are drawn from behavioral sources of gain based upon both operant and classical conditioning principles. Successful use of behavior therapy has been reported in a very wide range of presenting problems and clients. This literature is perhaps best reviewed by Eysenck and Beech (10). They present a restrained, but optimistic view of the promises offered by behavior therapy.

The use of behaviorally loaded treatments in a variety of counseling situations has been extensively reported by Krumboltz and Thoreson and their associates (13). Their results strongly suggest that reinforcement principles can be applied to produce significant changes in behavior of clients in the outside environment.

It seems clear that behaviorally loaded approaches offer real promise for improving the power of counseling treatments to yield significant outcomes. Much of the history of behavioral counseling has been clouded by controversy stemming largely from philosophical disagreements.

Krasner (12) says that modern behavioral approaches are based upon the following assumptions which hardly seem controversial: (a) looking at abnormality within a social learning context; (b) extending principles learned in experimental laboratory studies to real life situations; (c) developing experimental attitudes in dealing with clinical problems, and the extension of training of key environmental figures in the community. Such principles as these seem useful and tenable for the developmental counselor.

A MODEL FOR COUNSELING RESEARCH

The very heavy weighting of negative results in research on counseling and psychotherapy in terms of ability to produce personality changes or social adjustment is only devastating if the major goals toward which the counselor works are in these areas. Developmental counseling is not primarily concerned with changing personality. It is, as Leona Tyler (23) says, "minimum change therapy." Neither is developmental counseling aimed at directly adjusting clients to situations or institutions.

Instead, developmental counseling is aimed at facilitating a client in obtaining some degree of control over his subsequent development. Helping a client to persist in high school or college to graduation or to choose a career are certainly important goals within this frame of reference. Obviously, however, much further research needs to be done in order to demonstrate the effectiveness of developmental counseling. To do so will probably require more sophisticated research designs than those presently represented in the literature.

As was pointed out earlier, highly generalized questions about the effectiveness of counseling are rather meaningless. Instead, research questions must be asked in terms of effectiveness of what kind of counseling, with what kind of client, for what kinds of goals. Viewing counseling research in this way is facilitated by conceptualizing three sets of experimental variables that must be considered in any comprehensive program of counseling research.

Input Variables

The first set of variables that must be considered are those that are involved in the counseling situation. These can be categorized in terms of three subsets: counselor variables, client variables, and situational variables. *Counselor variables* include such factors as age, sex, training, theoretical orientation, and institutional role. All of these are relevant to counseling research. It is naïve to assume that all counselors are equally effective or that the same counselor is equally effective with all clients. *Client variables* include such things as age, sex, socioeconomic background, nature of presenting problem, and expectations for counseling. The third subset, *situational variables* include the nature of referral and the physical setting in which counseling occurs.

All of these *input variables* must be considered and controlled in a comprehensive research program. Some counselors may help some clients and be useless to or even harmful to other clients. The setting in which counseling occurs, the way in which clients are referred, and the expectations they have are all extremely relevant. Failure to sort out these important variables could well mask the most important results.

Intermediate Variables

The intermediate or process variables are also extremely important. What actually happens in the counseling situation in terms of the kind of relationship established, number of contacts, and the approaches used are extremely important. It is naïve to assume that, whenever a client enters an office marked "counseling," counseling always takes place. Counseling is a relationship and does not occur automatically when two people look at each other across a desk.

The most important process variable, however, is the *developmental contract*. It has been demonstrated that there is no single class of *behaviors* that are agreed-upon goals for all clients. The particular outcomes upon which a counseling case can be evaluated are idiosyncratic to the client. The process of arriving at a developmental contract is necessary for developing appropriate criteria for evaluating that case. When no developmental contract is identifiable, then developmental counseling has simply not occurred and consequently cannot be evaluated.

The nature of the developmental contract can be specified by counselor and client, formally or through examination of the counseling protocol.

Outcome Variables

The effectiveness of developmental counseling can only be established in terms of changes in behavior that occur outside the interview situation itself. These changes must be relevant to developmental goals established in the counseling situation. The actual behaviors that are goal-relevant for a client cannot be generalized. Four classes of goal-relevant behaviors can be conceptualized to establish a frame of reference for evaluation. These behavioral constructs are similar to those in the human effectiveness model described in Chapter 5.

1. *Commitment.* Client behavior can be evaluated in terms of the degree of commitment shown to the goals specified in the developmental contract. Commitment can be inferred from risk-taking behavior and other kinds of self-involving behavior. For example, enrolling in college, taking a job to finance education, and undergoing training to prepare for an occupation are all examples of commitment.

2. *Competence.* Behaviors that show competence necessary for achieving developmental goals are relevant outcomes of developmental counseling. Such outcomes as grades, study habits, and job skills are examples.

3. *Consistency.* Behaviors that are consistent with goals and values specified in developmental contracts are relevant. These might include taking courses consistent with plans, entering *and* progressing in training programs, or establishing social affiliations or relationships consistent with values expressed.

4. *Control.* Control behaviors could involve managing frustration and aggression appropriately in terms of goals, or meeting physiological and psychological needs in ways appropriate to value systems formulated in counseling.

Outcomes of developmental counseling can thus be identified for each client in terms of the particular developmental contract entered into within the counseling relationship. Behavioral changes can be assessed in terms of new coping behaviors acquired within constructs such as commitment, competence, consistency, and control.

Implementation of the Model

The research model described above can best be implemented within the framework of intensive experimental case studies. As Bergin (5) points out very persuasively in a monumental review of outcome studies, there seems to be little point in continuing the kind of outcome research which we have seen in the past. The input, treatment, and output variables must be individualized and carefully recorded. Appropriate outcomes are necessarily idiosyncratic to particular clients. Counselors are not interchangeable parts, but are unique therapeutic agents. All counselors are eclectic to some extent and the counseling of any client is to a certain degree a unique, non-recurring set of events.

Given these considerations, we are still able to generate useful knowledge about the effects of developmental counseling. Indeed, such knowledge is essential both to the field and to the individual counselor.

The following series of activities can enable a practicing counselor to assess his effectiveness for his own professional growth and for purposes of accountability to those who allocate resources. The model is presented as a flow chart in Figure 14–1.

1. *Group cases by type of presenting concerns and client.* One example would be the counselor in a high school who could initially group all 11th grade boys who are referred for low achievement. This group then would be homogeneous on sex, grade level, low achievement, and condition of referral.

2. *Sub-group cases by treatment category.* The counselor may decide to study his effectiveness with more than one approach. He may, for example, compare a group with an individual approach, or a relationship loaded versus a behaviorally loaded approach, or a direct approach versus consulting with parents or teachers, or some combination.

3. *Determine goals and success indicators for each case.* The developmental contract in each case should yield the goals. Some goals may be harder to behaviorize than others, but any goal should be such that it can be tapped in some way by an observable success indicator. For example, a goal to increase self-esteem might have success indicators such as increasing positive statements or thoughts about self, comparing oneself more favorably with significant peers, commit-

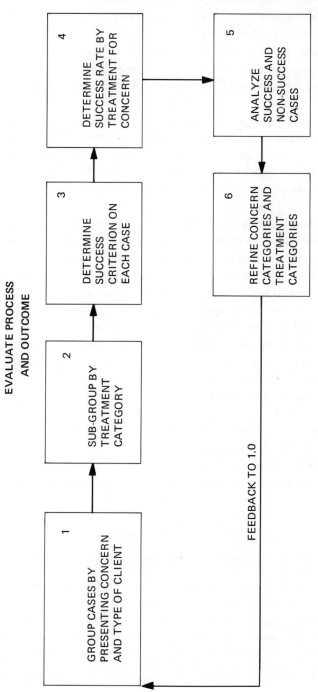

Fig. 14—1. Model for evaluating effectiveness.

ting oneself to realistic educational, vocational, or interpersonal goals as shown by investment and risk.

4. *Determine success rate by treatment for each client-problem category.* Results on success indicators should be carefully recorded and a success ratio percentage computed. For example, with the 11th grade, other-referred low achievers treated by a group relationship-loaded approach might yield success in six out of ten cases. This result can be compared with other approaches.

5. *Analyze success and non-success cases.* Both successful and unsuccessful cases should be carefully analyzed by examining case notes, recordings, or by direct interviews with clients to identify both positive and negative factors.

6. *Refine client-concern and treatment categories based upon data obtained.* Where success is mixed, it may be possible to discover new client-concern groups. For example, the counselor might have success with all middle class boys in the group, but with no lower class boys. For counseling purposes the latter now constitute a separate category for which a new approach is needed. Similarly, the unsuccessful group may all have had reading problems, or parent conflicts, etc.

7. *Refine client-concern categories and treatment approaches.* For example, the counselor might decide on a new client-concern category of 11th grade boys, teacher-referred with parental conflicts. The new treatment might add parent consultations and group counseling.

One of the major values of the above model is that it allows the counselor to get feedback about his results and so improve his own professional skills, as well as provide information for accountability purposes. It becomes a major resource for the counselor's own growth.

REFERENCES

1. ASTIN, A. W. The functional autonomy of psychotherapy. *Amer. Psychologist*, 1961, 16:75–78.
2. BARRON, F., & LEARY, T. Changes in psychoneurotic patients with and without psychotherapy. *J. consult. Psychol.*, 1955, 19:239–245.
3. BARRY, RUTH, & WOLF, BEVERLY. *Epitaph for vocational guidance.* New York: Bureau of Publications, Teachers College, Columbia University, 1962.
4. BERGIN, A. E. The effects of psychotherapy: negative results revisited. *J. counsel. Psychol.*, 1963, 10 (3), 244–249.
5. BERGIN, A. E. The evaluation of therapeutic outcomes. In Bergin, A. E., & Garfield, S. L. *The handbook of psychotherapy and behavior-change.* New York: Wiley, 1971.

6. CAMPBELL, D. A counseling evaluation study with a better control group. *J. counsel. Psychol.*, 1963, 10:334–339.
7. CARTWRIGHT, ROSALIND, & VOGEL, J. S. A comparison of changes in psychoneurotic patients during matched periods of therapy and no therapy. *J. consult. Psychol.*, 1960, 24:121–127.
8. CROSS, H. J. The outcomes of psychotherapy: a selected analysis of research findings. *J. consult. Psychol.*, 1964, 28 (5), 413–417.
9. EYSENCK, H. J. *The handbook of abnormal psychology.* New York: Basic Books, 2nd Ed., 1973.
10. EYSENCK, H. J., & BEECH, R. Counterconditioning and related methods. In Bergin, A. E., & Garfield, S. L. *Handbook of psychotherapy and behavior change.* New York: Wiley, 1971.
11. FAIRWEATHER, G. W. (Ed.). *Social psychology in treating mental illness: an experimental approach.* New York: Wiley, 1964.
12. KRASNER, L. An operant approach in behavior therapy. In Bergin, A. E., & Garfield, S. L. *The handbook of psychotherapy and behavior change.* New York: Wiley, 1971.
13. KRUMBOLTZ, V. D., & THORESON, C. E. (Eds.). *Behavioral counseling.* New York: Holt, Rinehart, 1969.
14. LEARY, T., & HARVEY, J. S. A methodology for measuring personality changes in psychotherapy. *J. clin. Psychol.*, 1956, 12:123–132.
15. MERENDA, P., & ROTHNEY, J. W. Evaluating the effects of counseling—eight years after. *J. counsel. Psychol.*, 1958, 5 (3), 163–168.
16. PATTERSON, C. H. Matching vs. randomization in studies of counseling. *J. counsel. Psychol.*, 1956, 3:262–271.
17. ROGERS, C. R., & DYMOND, ROSALIND F. *Psychotherapy and personality change.* Chicago: University of Chicago Press, 1954.
18. ROSENMAN, S. Changes in the representation of self, other, and interrelationship in client-centered therapy. *J. counsel. Psychol.*, 1955, 2:271–278.
19. ROTHNEY, J. Counseling does help. *Voc. Guidance quart.*, 1957, 6:15–19.
20. SHLIEN, J. M., MOSAK, H. H., & DREIKURS, R. Effect of time limits: a comparison of two psychotherapies. *J. counsel. Psychol.*, 1962, 9:31–34.
21. TEUBER, N. L., & POWERS, E. Evaluating therapy in a delinquency prevention program. *Proc. Assoc. Res. nerv. ment. Disorders*, 1953, 31:138–147.
22. TRAVERS, R. W. M. A critical review of techniques for evaluating guidance. *Educ. Psychol. Measmt.*, 1949, 91:211–225.
23. TYLER, LEONA. Minimum change therapy. *Personnel Guidance J.*, 1960, 38:475–479.
24. VOLSKY, T., MCAGOON, T. M., & HOYT, D. *The outcomes of counseling and psychotherapy.* Minneapolis: University of Minnesota Press, 1965.
25. WILLIAMS, J. E. Changes in self and other perceptions following brief educational–vocational counseling. *J. counsel. Psychol.*, 1962, 9:18–28.

RECOMMENDED READINGS

BERGIN, A. E., & GARFIELD, S. L. *Handbook of psychotherapy and behavior change.* New York: Wiley, 1971.
GOLDSTEIN, A. P., & DEAN, S. J. *The investigation of psychotherapy.* New York: Wiley, 1966.

15

THE DEVELOPMENT OF THE DEVELOPMENTAL COUNSELOR

Much has been written in the preceding pages about human development. The aspect of development that is of most vital concern to the counselor-in-preparation is that of his own personal and professional growth. What are the kinds of growth and change that are involved in becoming an effective counselor?

Unfortunately, too often in counselor education programs, all too little time and energy is devoted to this problem of personal development. Courses and curricula are packed with facts and principles that seem to relate to the needs and development of others. Little time is focused upon the needs of the developmental counselor.

The graduate school settings, which are typically the locus of counselor education programs, are hardly ideal developmental milieu for counselors to grow or perhaps for that matter for anyone to grow in balanced ways. The emphasis is almost always on evaluation and competition. The climate is hurried and impersonal. Little attention seems to be given to the development of growth-accelerating relationships with staff or among students.

Although the picture painted above seems bleak, real progress has been made in very recent years in recognizing the need for growth-producing experiences among counselors in training. Increasing awareness of the nature of group processes and the building of developmental groups into counselor educational programs has moved somewhat to overcome the problems inherent in graduate education in counseling.

The development of the counselor requires that he comes to understand himself, his values and attitudes, and the quality of his interpersonal relationships before he can operate effectively. Students in counseling must be given opportunities to acquire new understandings and attitudes about themselves and their interpersonal relationships. At least three kinds of such experiences seem vital to the developmental counselor. These include:

1. *Group counseling and laboratory experiences.* An essential part of a counselor's experience is an exposure to group situations that provide opportunity for "feedback" about his own characteristic ways of interacting with and relating to others. Such experiences are best obtained within a closely knit and secure group committed to understanding themselves and the reactions that they evoke from others. When such a group is secure enough to develop trust and confidence in each other and time is available for the process, it can create real opportunities for personal and professional growth of members.

2. *Supervised counseling experiences.* The most crucial phase of any counselor's preparation is the counseling practicum. This is an experience that gives the counselor an opportunity to experience counseling relationships and interviews and then to convert these into the raw materials for learning to understand and control his own behavior. Counseling practicum can be threatening to many students. When it occurs within a network of relationships with supervisors and fellow students in which the accent is on development rather than evaluation, it can be extremely rewarding.

3. *Professional seminar experiences.* Counselors-in-preparation are budding professional persons. One important aspect of their identity structure involves feelings of belongingness and affiliation with their chosen profession. In professional seminars, counselors-in-preparation can work through many of the professional issues of role, ethics, and

relationships with other groups that can contribute to a clearer identity. Contacts with counselor educators and practicing counselors on warm and close rather than formal and impersonal levels can sharpen feelings of identification and belonging.

When the kinds of experiences described above are available to students, opportunities for real growth exist. The attitude by which the student approaches such opportunities is often the crucial determinant of their value. When those opportunities are approached with attitudes of openness to change, willingness to examine self, and courage to reveal self, they can be maximally growth-producing.

COMPETENCIES OF THE DEVELOPMENTAL COUNSELOR

Becoming a counselor is not solely a matter of personal growth and awareness, although that is undeniably a major aspect of counselor education. Functioning in the wide variety of situations and interventions described in the preceding chapters requires a very considerable body of understandings, skills, and attitudes.

Below is a set of basic learning outcomes associated with the functions of a developmental counselor.

The list is long and may be intimidating for the beginner to examine. It is not meant to threaten, but to help the counselor in preparation for the building of a framework to think about his own professional development and consequently to gain some control over the directions and distances of his own growth.

Not all counselors will be equally proficient or mature in terms of any of these competencies. Some competencies will have greater immediate relevance and importance for any individual counselor than others. Not all will be learned within the context of a formal preparation program. Some competencies will mature over many years of professional experience. For others, high degrees of competence may have been developed long prior to entering a formal program!

Since the purpose of the list*is self-awareness and self-direction, it may be useful to consider where one is on each competence in terms of the unitary scale described in Chapter 8. It runs as follows:

Panic	Inertia	Striving	Coping	Mastery

* This list is heavily based upon a set of learning outcomes compiled by the counselor education staff at Florida State University to whom the author served as a consultant.

Counselor Competencies

1. The counselor explicates a personal value structure.
2. The counselor identifies the primary components of the value systems of others.
3. The counselor differentiates areas in his personal value structure which deviate from the value structures of various identifiable groups.
4. The counselor applies principles of effective communication in interactions with students, parents, faculty, administrators, and other personnel.
5. The counselor establishes and maintains positive helping relationships with students, teachers, administrators, and parents.
6. The counselor responds to and interacts with others in a way that demonstrates his awareness of his own thoughts and feelings, his openness about them, and his sensitivity to the thoughts and feelings of others.
7. The counselor exhibits openness, flexibility, compassion, and tolerance in professional interactions and continues to evidence a concern for personal growth and development in himself and others.
8. The counselor exhibits self-direction and individuality in professional interactions.
9. The counselor manifests in a variety of settings (for example, rap sessions, encounter groups, classes, informal interactions, and counseling sessions) a sensitivity and tolerance to human feelings.
10. The counselor evidences commitment for continuing professional growth in a variety of settings and activities.
11. The counselor actively seeks out and interacts with allied professionals and their literature (for example, social welfare, clinical psychology, developmental, social, and educational psychology, and other behavioral sciences).
12. The counselor explicates and applies a personal theory of counseling (based on his experience of himself and relevant literature).
13. The counselor develops (and is continuing to develop) a model of human effectiveness and relates this current model to his professional and personal life.
14. The counselor demonstrates the ability to discuss relationships between and among his theory of counseling and theories of personality, learning, and psychological assessment.
15. The counselor demonstrates varying methodologies and rationales for initiating the counseling process and dealing with client concerns.
16. The counselor acknowledges variables in his own personality which affect his counseling.
17. The counselor distinguishes among component forces operative in subcultural contexts, for example, economic factors, political pressures, value orientations.

18. The counselor identifies psychological dynamics operative in varying subcultural contexts, for example, motivation, anxiety, defense systems, reinforcement contingencies.
19. The counselor describes sociological dynamics operative in varying subcultural contexts, for example, family mores, status, ethnic traditions, religious "taboos," language idioms.
20. The counselor establishes interpersonal professional relationships with persons of varying subcultural backgrounds.
21. The counselor understands implications of contemporary social issues (for example, drugs, race, homosexuality) for counselor behavior.
22. The counselor demonstrates an open-minded and professional attitude in working in areas of social concern and conflict.
23. The counselor demonstrates awareness of difficulties he would encounter in relating as a counselor to persons involved in contemporary social issues (for example, a drug user, a homosexual, a person of another race).
24. The counselor identifies environmental factors which contribute toward the development of positive mental health.
25. The counselor effects changes in policies and procedures of institutions (for example, schools, agencies, etc.) that would enhance opportunities for the development of members.
26. The counselor demonstrates an understanding of formal and informal organizational patterns of diverse social systems.
27. The counselor identifies feasible ways in which a social system could be improved.
28. The counselor intervenes successfully in social systems as a "change agent."
29. The counselor establishes his professional priorities.
30. The counselor organizes his activities in accordance with his articulated priorities.
31. The counselor defines his role in relation to his given situation (school, agency, etc.)
32. The counselor demonstrates an understanding of theories of human development.
33. The counselor describes relevant developmental features of individual counseling problems.
34. The counselor describes the interactive effects of differing developmental problems in group relationships.
35. The counselor communicates to clients the behavioral implications of developmental stages.
36. The counselor discusses with lay groups the developmental problems often associated with specific age ranges.
37. The counselor describes the counseling process in terms which are non-technical and understandable to the client.
38. The counselor restates a counselee's problem in a way which is acceptably accurate for the client.

39. The counselor selects and supports his selection of the following actions, given a client's presented problem:
    a. Continuance of counseling and choice of a particular counseling strategy
    b. Referral to a non-counseling resource
    c. Referral to another counselor
    d. Discontinuation of counseling
40. The counselor demonstrates such learning principles as selective reinforcement, extinction, etc., by setting up basic learning situations for particular clients.
41. The counselor applies a course of action when presented with a problem of resistance, silence, hostility, indifference, lack of motivation, unresponsiveness, and dependency.
42. The counselor applies a counseling style comfortable for him with a particular client.
43. The counselor defends his choice of counseling approach (given a particular case) on the basis of his own experience and knowledge of the literature.
44. The counselor responds appropriately to client expressions of feeling.
45. The counselor criticizes his own counseling for strengths and weaknesses in techniques and methodology by hypothesizing results which could have come from his behaving differently with the client.
46. The counselor demonstrates the following in response to a group member's problems:
    a. Empathic understanding of the member's problem-feeling expressions
    b. Increasing the member's awareness of his feelings and how they influence his behavior
    c. Increasing a member's understanding of the current bases for these feelings
47. The counselor demonstrates appropriate risk-taking as a group leader and as a member in several kinds of groups.
48. The counselor analyzes in non-technical terms group processes in response to a member's inquiry.
49. The counselor conducts group guidance activities to convey personal, educational, and vocational information.
50. The counselor criticizes his own group leadership for strengths and weaknesses in techniques and methodology by hypothesizing results which could have come from behaving differently in the group.
51. The counselor selects and defends a strategy comfortable to him, given a particular group problem.
52. The counselor facilitates growth in vocational decision making with different-aged clients by means of (a) providing relevant vocational and education information and (b) applying a theory—personal or otherwise—of human development.
53. The counselor understands the nature of study skills problems and develops appropriate strategies for their remedy and/or prevention.

54. The counselor describes several situations in which consultation is an appropriate behavior.
55. The counselor outlines the parameters of a consultative relationship.
56. The counselor reports at the appropriate level to a variety of consultees about specific situations.
57. The counselor explains methods or procedures for follow-up in the consulting role.
58. The counselor identifies correctly the technical criteria and resources that can be used in comparing and synthesizing the most appropriate assessment tools for group or individual appraisal.
59. The counselor identifies aptitude, achievement, and personality tests appropriate for use in a school or agency given the characteristics of the individual or population to be served.
60. The counselor demonstrates an ability to administer standardized test instruments in a manner consistent with accepted standards and cognizant of factors affecting test-taking behavior.
61. The counselor analyzes, organizes, and synthesizes test results obtained on standardized tests (identified by the counselor education faculty) in verbal and/or written language appropriate for the recipient.
62. The counselor relates standardized test results to the goals, aspirations, abilities, and environment of the client.
63. The counselor collects and synthesizes client or population information utilizing non-test assessment techniques (questionnaires, case studies, anecdotal records, individual interview procedures).
64. The counselor identifies reference resources that counselors in the field can use in designing relevant research strategies.
65. The counselor identifies basic professional references that counselors can use to keep abreast of current trends, research, and professional activities in the field.
66. The counselor analyzes published research studies on counseling, identifying hypotheses, assumptions, limitations, and conclusions.
67. The counselor designs an action research study, identifying the characteristics of such research and the use that will be made of the results.
68. The counselor demonstrates a knowledge of the professional areas in which there is a need for research in the counseling and guidance profession.
69. The counselor develops one or two alternative research strategies that could be applied, given an identified problem for investigation.
70. The counselor develops a rationale of the relevance of research strategies to the professional and personal development of the counselor as well as the relevance to the functioning role of the counselor.
71. The counselor translates research results into "practical" implications.
72. The counselor acts in a manner consistent with personal ethical-value system and professional codes of ethics in professional relationships.

73. The counselor exhibits a knowledge of legal standards and procedures relevant to his work setting.
74. The counselor identifies professional limitations, formulates and acts upon strategies of consultation.

The above list was taken from a very comprehensive set of learning outcomes compiled by counselor educators and students at Florida State University. It may not be completely suited to all counselors but what is important is that each counselor does have in his own mind a set of competencies for professional practice and goals for professional growth that are tailored to his own needs and responsibilities.

Below is a statement of a very sensitive and capable student in a professional program that did provide some of the kinds of experiences and competencies discussed above. This student was able to approach the challenges and opportunities presented with openness and courage.

It is a challenging assignment to try to put down on paper the ways in which my life has been altered by the past year. It fills me with a certain excitement and pleasure, and yet I wonder how adequately I can really tell about what has happened to me.

Before the present time I had been a student for sixteen years, and although I paid attention and did my work, I was not even aware that the most important part of my education was lacking. By this I mean becoming aware of myself and from this, developing a deeper awareness of the various human beings with whom I come in contact.

The crux of the matter comes when one must take the intellectualized abstractions and the theories learned so carefully before and bring them home to bear on one's own feelings about self and about others. This is a confrontation which can be frightening, perhaps painful, but in its resolution can give a feeling of satisfaction, a change in relationships with other people and a thirsting for more knowledge about the workings of mankind, oneself in particular.

I think I have learned to be more honest. I have sat with a friend over coffee and we have shared our fears that the other might see our weaknesses and then think less of us. What we discovered was that to share our weaknesses as well as our strengths endeared ourselves to each other not encouraged contempt.

I have learned to have more courage. I have told someone whom I greatly respected that I was afraid to be myself with him because of strong, uncomfortable feelings I had for him. Our chance to talk this over did not lead to a refusal of friendship, but to an altered relationship which was more satisfactory for our courage to face each other.

I have learned to listen better. I have sat in small rooms with other human beings and allowed them to speak out about the joys and fears which meant very much to them without attempting to make them hear what I would do, how I have suffered or how I have been made happy.

I have learned to receive criticism, given with skill, insight and kindness, and not be crushed, but rather which filled me with a determination to redirect my actions in a more helpful manner. I still have much to learn about giving criticism that repairs, not injures, but it is a goal for me to work toward.

I have learned to be inquisitive about the way that others see things, and so I can look upon their statements as raw material for understanding their worlds better, not as ammunition for a war of words.

I have learned to recognize the pleas for understanding which come in many ways disguised and waiting for a sign that it was all right to feel emotions and give them expression. I have heard someone for whom I felt respect whisper, "I'm lost," and not blush, or joke or turn away to hide the reality of the moment. To recognize this sign in others seems to me like learning a new word. Before I never knew it was, and now I hear it everywhere.

To sum it up, I am learning to be myself. And it has paid dividends. Because I am behaving in ways more honest, more courageous and more concerned, I have found that I can know others more completely. I hope to become a counselor in the profession soon. But if I never hold a job as such, it really would not matter, I can be one anywhere.

For this student, the process of counselor education was a vital and valued experience in personal and professional development. This is the kind of experience that can help counselors become true facilitators of human effectiveness, including their own.

RECOMMENDED READINGS

HENDRICKSON, D. E., KRAUSE, F. H. (Eds.). *Counseling and Psychotherapy training and supervision.* Columbus, Ohio: Charles Merrill, 1972.

PARKER, C. A. (Ed.). *Counseling theories and counselor education.* Boston: Houghton Mifflin, 1969.

16

A SYSTEMATIC ECLECTIC MODEL FOR DEVELOPMENTAL COUNSELING

In Chapter 1 we examined the goals and assumptions of developmental counseling and pointed out an emerging role for professional practice based upon an essentially ecological view of human development. Such a view, we noted, has emerged from models described as community mental health or outreach approaches, and has appeared in the literature for a number of years (1)(5)(8).

From an ecological perspective the overriding goal of the developmental counselor is to facilitate the kind of interaction between the client and his environment that will yield optimal growth for the client in the directions that are goal-oriented for him. In a broader social sense the developmental counselor is also vitally concerned with the maintenance of a network of positive learning environments within family, school, and community that will support and enhance the human growth and development of all members. Many of the learning environments that exist in our present institutions are not those that enhance the full growth and development of human beings. Critics of modern education, for example, have asserted that the typical school child will never again be as psychologically whole and healthy as he is on the day he enters formal school (6)(9).

At times, then, it seems clear that the developmental counselor will be functioning within the client's milieu as an agent of environmental change (7). The developmental counselor thus functions as an applied social scientist using the tools afforded him by social and developmental psychology to facilitate positive changes in those human systems that affect his clients (1)(3). Many of the considerations involved in such roles have been described in Chapters 6 and 12.

Within the ecological framework, as we noted in Chapter 1, the client may be seen as either a single individual or as a larger social system such as an entire family, peer group, classroom, or even a complete school or community organization. Because of the wide range of problems and situations that are identifiable within an ecological framework, it seems obvious that the developmental counselor, to be effective, will employ a variety of approaches. These include consultation techniques, small group work, organizational development skills, and direct teaching methods, as well as the more traditional individual counseling approaches. At given times developmental counselors may be engaged in consulting with teachers about classroom management problems, teaching parent or teacher effectiveness courses, running interpersonal skill, vocational decision-making, or academic improvement groups for students, or be involved in running staff or organizational development workshops with school administrators or community leaders. This is *not* to say that developmental counselors will cease to engage in one-to-one counseling sessions with a variety of clients. Indeed, many of the other opportunities the developmental counselor has to work with larger systems will arise directly out of his success and skill in individual counseling.

As we saw in Chapter 3, a major problem in the counseling field has been the proliferation of competing and conflicting theories. Many of these theories have evolved out of essentially restricted clinical or experimental settings, and have been tested on relatively small, narrowly selected groups of clients or subjects. Indeed, many of our counseling theories have really been based upon a limited set of presenting problems brought to the clinic by white, middle-class, adult neurotics.

The ecologically oriented counselor is presented with a much wider range of situations. He is interested, for example, in facilitating the struggle to grow of systematically oppressed ghetto children, he is concerned with the vocational and educational development of people across the entire life span, he is concerned with his own professional growth and that of others who work with his clients. He is actively involved in parent education and community development activities.

Few of our existing theories can be stretched to cover this wide-ranging cluster of settings and situations. For several years, leaders in the field have called for the development of "systematic eclectic" approaches that will provide the flexibility needed to apply the kinds of specific help that have proven effective for the spcial needs of particular clients and situations (2)(4). The profession has finally begun to abandon its search for panaceas and super-theories (2).

In this final chapter we are attempting to pull together much of the material discussed in earlier chapters to describe a unified, systematic eclectic model for developmental counselors. The model is eclectic in the sense that it draws upon a variety of sources of gain which may be modulated to provide optimal "loadings" for particular types of clients and situations. It is systematic in that it provides a framework for making decisions about such loadings and suggests an optimal sequence for employing them.

In Chapters 4 and 5 we examined several developmental frameworks in terms of their usefulness in understanding the needs, problems, and potentialities of clients. These factors are all defined, of course, by the interaction of the client and his environment.

As the developmental counselor works with people, then, he becomes in a sense a consultant about, and designer of, growth-producing experiences and environments. The developmental counselor, in other words, has available a variety of resources that he can employ to assist his client. These resources are all aimed at facilitating constructive interaction between the client and his physical, social, or psychological worlds. Indeed, the relevance of the developmental framework lies in its usefulness in helping the counselor and client to choose among the resources available to enhance the client's growth at a particular point in time and space.

As these available resources are brought to bear in the life of the client, the counselor may operate in one of two basic modes. He may work *directly* with the client within the medium of a deeply personal face-to-face relationship in individual or group counseling (see Chapters 9 and 10). He may, however, in many situations find that his most effective choice involves utilizing the relationship resources that already exist elsewhere in the environment of his client. In such situations, the developmental counselor will find himself working in an *indirect* mode through one or more *consulting* relationships with significant people in the client's life space. In this way the counselor joins closely with teachers, parents, peers, or other professionals to create a relationship network through which appropriate help can be delivered to the ultimate client. In previous chapters, we examined concepts of milieu therapy and behavior modification that exemplify the indirect mode of counselor functioning.

The very wide range of situations to which the developmental counselor must address himself would represent an impossible level of complexity if there were no set of common elements to bring together. As we saw in Chapter 3, however, there are several major sources of gain that are common to most counseling approaches.

COMMON ELEMENTS IN DEVELOPMENTAL COUNSELING

Relationship Factors

First, most important human learning experiences occur within the context of a network of interpersonal relationships. Significant human behavior patterns are generally complex. They involve integrated patterns of thinking, feeling, and acting. Generally they involve social interaction. We now know (see Chapter 9) that people tend to change, grow, and learn in terms of these significant behavior patterns when they are touched by relationships characterized by warmth, empathy, congruence, and positive regard. In some theories these elements are described as therapeutic conditions, in others they are considered merely as factors that allow social reinforcement to operate.

However they are described, they represent very important sources of gain in almost any learning situation. Little evidence exists to support the notion that only a few select or specially gifted people can provide these relationships. On the contrary, for optimal human growth and development to occur, every human being should be touched by such relationships throughout his life.

The developmental counselor, then, does not view himself merely as a dispenser of such relationships, but rather as a *facilitator* whose knowledge of human relations—and skills in training and consultation

—are such that he can enhance the relationship network in a variety of social systems to enrich the environments of his clients.

Communication Processes

A second common element in counseling that is closely related to relationship conditions involves communication processes. Indeed, relationship conditions are really operationalized through communication processes. Counselors are virtually always concerned with creating open, broad band channels of communication with, around, and within client systems. The opportunity for human beings to learn and grow is enhanced when they are able to exchange direct, clear, and honest messages about their feelings, needs, and aspirations. As relationship and communication elements begin to bridge the social psychological distances that separate people of differing ages, sexes, races, values, and backgrounds, they are able to learn from each other and so enrich their environments in terms of stimulation and opportunity.

When these kinds of honest, trusting, and self-revealing patterns of communication are opened, the possibilities for growth are multiplied. The T group model of group counseling is built around group processes that build trust and open up communication (see Chapter 11). Familiar techniques in individual counseling such as reflection and clarification are similarly designed to open communication (see Chapter 10).

Much of the work of the developmental counselor in the indirect mode is aimed at improving communication patterns between parents and children, teachers and students, teachers and parents, or other sometimes conflicting groups. The developmental counselor then functions as a kind of communication specialist or linkage person who creates temporary communications systems to accomplish particular tasks, or helps to improve the communications patterns in permanent systems such as families or schools to enable them to function in self-renewing and self-enhancing ways.

Cognitive Processes

A third common element in developmental counseling processes is cognitive change. Most developmental learning experiences involve new ways of thinking about self, others, or the world. Generally, these experiences entail acquiring, organizing, integrating, and applying new ideas and information. They lead to new ways of construing old experiences and new ways of relating to present and future events. George Kelly described this aspect of counseling as acquiring new personal constructs. Such constructs determine goals, values, and aspirations as well as self-esteem.

The very process of relating to reality, coping with stress, and mastering a complex environment is heavily determined by the cognitive maps or conceptual frameworks by which individuals analyze, understand, and predict the significant events in their own lives.

Behavior Change Processes

A fourth common element in developmental counseling processes involves change in overt behavior. Just as all counseling theories are "client-centered" in lower-case letters, so are all counseling approaches "behavior modification" theories in a general sense. Much of the intactness or wholeness in a human life derives from an integration among elements of thinking, feeling, and acting or behaving.

For people to develop in fully human ways they must learn to behave overtly in effective, purposeful, and humane patterns. We know that much of a human being's overt behavior is influenced by stimulation coming directly from his environment. We as counselors, in fact, have no way of reaching out to help him except by being part of that environment. Counselor knowledge of techniques involving shaping of overt behaviors, desensitization, the use of social modeling, and effects of particular schedules of reinforcement are all elements that can be utilized to help people grow into full actualization of their human potentials.

We are no longer comfortable in the belief that change in thinking or "insight" is invariably accompanied by appropriate changes in overt behaviors. One of the major deficiencies in our educational institutions is precisely the over abstraction and intellectualization of human experiences. What we know about the transfer of learning tells us that it is unlikely to occur unless provision for it is carefully built into learning experiences. Developmental counseling processes hence stress task assignments or "homework," or tryouts of new behaviors that are aimed at insuring the transfer of verbally defined goals into action plans that eventuate into new and more appropriate overt behavior.

Wherever possible, specific behavioral or performance objectives are used as success indicators in evaluating counseling outcomes.

A SYSTEMATIC ECLECTIC MODEL

The common elements that have been described above can be integrated into a systematic model to guide the developmental counselor in his professional practice. The model has the advantage of serving as a kind of cognitive map that the counselor can use as he approaches the very wide range of situations presented by an ecological approach.

Within this model he is able to utilize both direct and indirect interventions, employ sources of gain represented by relationship conditions, communication processes, cognitive restructuring, social learning, and operant shaping, and function in group or individual counseling, or consultation formats.

The systematic eclectic model is described in Figure 16–1. We can further discuss and explain the processes involved as we elaborate upon each step.

The systematic eclectic model assumes that the first step in the total process of developmental counseling begins with the counselor himself and with the values, goals, and commitments that define his professional identity. It is considered essential that the counselor clearly understand his own goals in relation to the needs and perceptions of his potential clients and employing institution *before* he begins to intervene with his client's systems. This principle may be expressed in a basic postulate of the systematic eclectic model:

Postulate One: The developmental counselor understands himself and the systems within which he operates before he intervenes actively.

The developmental counselor next scans the relevant learning environments or developmental milieu with which he works to find opportunities to advance his professional goals. He operates from a pro-active rather than a reactive stance, reaching out to create or seize opportunities to enrich the growth-producing qualities of the environment. From this pro-active stance the counselor assesses the needs of client populations and actively plans projects that will be addressed to those needs. Such projects may involve the counselor with parents, teachers, administrators, extracurricular activities, student organizations, or community action groups. He is not confined to walk-in contacts in his office, although he by no means ignores them.

This step may be summed up in a second basic postulate:

Postulate Two: The developmental counselor actively reaches out to create opportunities that will maximize his basic professional goals. He maintains positive controls over his expenditure of time and resources, assessing needs of client populations and investing resources in terms of feasibility and payoff within his professional priorities.

As the developmental counselor identifies groups and situations that represent potential opportunities to facilitate growth in key human systems, he begins by building communication and relationship networks that will allow open, honest, and important messages to be transmitted in many directions. The communication and relationship network developed in this process is characterized by empathy, trust, caring, and congruence.

This phase of the systematic eclectic model may be summarized in a third postulate:

Postulate Three: The way to begin to help any human system is to listen to it and help it to listen to itself within the context of an empathic, trusting, and caring network of relationships.

After the communication and relationship network has been successfully established, the next phase of the model involves negotiating openly and directly with the client system to arrive at a mutually defined and agreed upon developmental contract or action program. It is obvious that this kind of negotiation and goal clarification process can only occur when the communication and relationship conditions have been established.

It is vitally important that this negotiation phase really represents a mutually involving collaborative process rather than a slick selling job in which the counselor actually imposes his goals, needs, and values on the client system. The key outcome of this stage is *mutual commitment* on the part of the counselor and the client system to a set of quite specific and, if possible, behaviorally defined goals. This phase is summarized in Postulate Four:

Postulate Four: Growth in human systems occurs most readily when goals are clearly and mutually agreed upon and when public commitment is obtained in an explicit and contractual way.

Upon completion of the negotiation phase, a whole–part–whole learning sequence is initiated. First the client system is helped to obtain the new information or concepts needed to understand fully both the means and ends involved in implementing the developmental contract. We note that new information and ideas are only presented *after* they become relevant to the client systems' needs via the developmental contract. Sound teaching procedures are employed in presenting the new cognitive material in small, clear, carefully sequenced steps and obtaining frequent feedback from the client system to insure that understanding occurs. The counselor may use short, direct verbal presentations and dialogues or utilize carefully selected reading materials or employ audio-visual materials in this phase. He always allows, however, for active client participation and discussion.

After the understandings and concepts have been acquired by the client system, the counselor next arranges for modeling of new complex target behaviors that are involved in the client systems developmental contract. The counselor may model new interpersonal skills directly in the counseling process, he may arrange for the client system to observe or interview someone performing at a high level, or he may utilize audio-visual aids. An important consideration is that the target behaviors be modelled by someone perceived by the client system as reasonably similar, high in status, and that the model is recognized as having been rewarded for a high level of performance. Again adequate opportunity for discussion and involvement during the modeling phase should be provided.

The complex target behaviors should now be broken down into manageable parts and a shaping or discrimination and error correction learning process initiated. The client system should have an opportunity for adequate practice of specific skills and for reinforcement of successively improved performances. This step may be accomplished by short role playing or role reversal sessions, brief tryouts of specific new behaviors (as, for example, study skills) or may employ feedback from a significant other person such as parent, teacher, or group member.

The complex behaviors are now put back together in a simulation situation. Such a situation might represent role playing, active practicing of new interpersonal behaviors with friends (as in a fixed role assignment, for example, to be more assertive or more sensitive) or might be a more formalized practice of study skills or test-taking techniques. It is essential that simulation be accomplished in a safe, low-risk situation where opportunity for non-threatening feedback about the overall quality of performance can be obtained. Often such opportunities occur quite naturally and spontaneously within group processes or interview situations.

This sequence is more elaborate and complex than the others described in the systematic eclectic model. It is summarized in Postulate Five:

Postulate Five: Human systems learn new complex behavior best when presented with clear, explicit cognitive frameworks and role models, followed by discrimination training and shaping procedures, followed by supervised practice in safe settings.

The next sequence of activities is aimed at transfer of learning and the maintenance of the new learning in the actual environment where it must be used. The counselor follows up the client system as it attempts to respond to real problems in new ways. He also attempts to arrange for the new behavior to be supported and encouraged by significant other individuals or subsystems. The basic postulate here follows:

Postulate Six: The help-giving process is not complete until the client system has successfully utilized its learning in the real situation and has experienced rewards for doing so.

The final sequence involves evaluation and is shown in Figure 16–2. Basically, it entails computing success ratios for specific treatments with specific client outcomes and populations and using this information to improve performance and goal-setting. (see Chapter 14). The final postulate is simple:

Postulate Seven: Professional practice can only improve where accurate and immediate feedback about results is available.

The preceding discussion of this systematic eclectic model for counseling practice is necessarily rather brief and abstract. It seems at first very complex and perhaps cumbersome. It has been employed successfully, however, in many practical counseling situations. Below are some examples of its use drawn from the experience of a counselor with an ecological orientation as she actively entered the learning environment represented by a junior high school.

The following job description was the result of this counselor's effort to define clearly areas of expertise and general professional goals with consideration for her needs and the needs of the educational institution she was about to enter. Administrators, other counselors, teachers, and parents used this outline as a stimulus for further negotiation and clarification of goals for the school and the counselor during the counselor's entry into the system (Step 1, Figure 16–1).

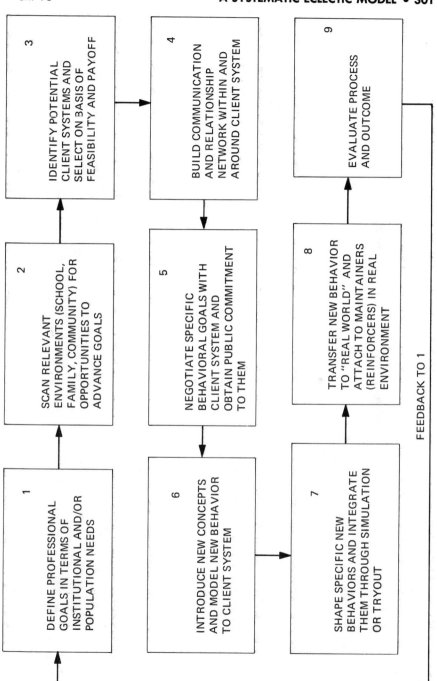

Fig. 16-1. Facilitating change in human systems.

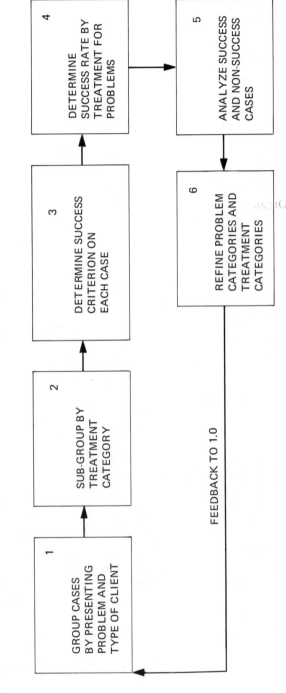

Fig. 16–2. Breakdown of evaluation procedures.

I. *Expertise in staff development and consulting with teachers in the following areas:*
   A. Group Dynamics
   B. Communications skills
   C. Decision-making skills
   D. Study skills
   E. Student development
   F. Individual differences
   G. Vocational development
   H. Parental and/or family counseling
II. *Training and expertise in consulting with staff and administration concerning problems of:*
   A. Human relations
   B. Organizational development
   C. Curriculum development
III. *Expertise and experience in organizing and conducting:*
   A. Academic improvement groups
   B. Interpersonal skills groups
   C. Vocational–educational planning groups
IV. *Skills in individual counseling with students who have special needs and concerns.*
V. *Ability to perform assessment and diagnostic activities in regard to the following types of problems:*
   A. Learning difficulties
   B. Special referral problems (personality disorders and learning dysfunctions)
   C. Vocational aptitudes and interests

Example 1

An example of how this systematic eclectic approach can be implemented is described in this counselor's consultation with a first year teacher. The counselor indicated a desire to help new teachers with any problem they might have (Step 3, Figure 16–1). General dissatisfaction with what was happening in one of her classes brought the young teacher to the counselor. After trust and understanding were established in their relationship (Step 4, Figure 16–2), the teacher invited the counselor to visit her class and observe the classroom interaction.

Before agreeing to enter the classroom, the counselor asked the teacher to define some specific behaviors that she wanted the counselor to observe during the process observation (Step 5, Figure

16–1). A set of group rating scales was used as a basis for negotiation in this particular case because the teacher had some difficulty in defining these specific behaviors (3). Having the behaviors written down and explicitly agreed upon, the teacher and the counselor decided on the day and the time of the classroom observation (Step 5, Figure 16–1). Throughout this preparation period the counselor was very much aware of the relationship she was trying to establish with this teacher. Her goal at this point was to insure the continued flow of expressive, instrumental, positive, and negative communication between the two (Step 4, Figure 16–1). This climate needed to be well established *before* the results of the process observation were given to the teacher.

Sensing that the teacher was nervous after her classroom presentation, the counselor moved back to Step 4 and tried to help her stay with some of the feelings she was experiencing (Step 4, Figure 16–1). With the communication open once more, the two studied the results of the observation and again negotiated until they agreed upon a plan of action (Step 5, Figure 16–1).

During the ensuing two sessions the counselor introduced her client to new ways of thinking about her students and herself, reinforced the teacher's attempts at new behaviors, and played the role of a student as the teacher tried out some personally difficult behaviors in the counselor's office (Step 7, Figure 16–1). The counselor was invited back into the classroom for a follow-up observation (Steps 6 and 7, Figure 16–1). Afterwards, at the end of feedback in their session, the counselor asked the teacher if there were any one person on the staff whom she liked and respected; someone she could talk to about the skills she was trying to acquire. This teacher's closest friend turned out to be a veteran teacher in another department. In a joint meeting the counselor served as a facilitator in insuring that goals were feasible and clearly defined and that the communication between the two teachers working on this was direct and open (Step 8, Figure 16–1). Before terminating that session, the counselor and the new teacher once again reviewed the value of this particular approach and mutually agreed upon another time to re-evaluate the situation (Step 9, Figure 16–1).

Example 2

Six students whose goal was to increase their study skills in an Academic Improvement Group provided another example of the use of the systematic eclectic model. During the individual intake interviews conducted before the first group meeting, the counselor clearly defined her goals for the group and decided with each student if his goals were appropriate for this particular group. Once this was determined, the counselor requested that the potential group members publicly declare their behavioral objectives to the group in the first or second sessions, commit themselves to assisting other members in the group, and let the group know of any decision to leave should they find the group inappropriate for their needs after the first two meetings.

Even before the counselor met with the group as a whole, she showed evidence of following the first three postulates in that she knew her own goals, tried to secure the right people for the right group, and obtained an oral commitment to individual and group goals. Once the group convened, it was necessary to redefine, with all the members present, the group's objectives through the sharing of expectations. During the negotiation of group and then later of individual goals, the counselor modelled the honest communication she wanted the students to be using with each other. She also reinforced personal and relationship statements emitted throughout all the group sessions. Students were paired up at the end of each meeting to draw up a learning contract for the week with their partners. Each co-signed the other's written agreement (Steps 4 and 5, Figure 16–1). Specific study techniques were introduced, discussed, and modelled in the group (Steps 6 and 7, Figure 16–1).

Group members were soon able to congratulate each other on successes—no matter how small—and confrontations especially between partners over unfulfilled contracts were common (Steps 7 and 8, Figure 16–1). At the last session the counselor had the students draw a picture of the group in terms of how they saw each member's participation and the group's movement toward its goals. This served as a departure point for a general evaluation and feedback session to the entire Academic Improvement Group and for the counselor (Step 9, Figure 16–1).

Example 3

Knowing of her special interest in conducting in-service training for the staff, the principal called upon this counselor to design a workshop for ten teachers during the summer. This eight-day workshop which ran for four hours daily had several objectives: (a) to help the teachers to meet the community members with some degree of ease; (b) to compile a community resource directory for the school; (c) to devise a plan that would assist these workshop teachers in attracting other teachers in the school to make community contacts and to add to the community resource directory.

Having heard the principal's institutional goals defined, the counselor met with the teachers to obtain their professional and personal objectives for this project (Steps 1, 2, 3, Figure 16–1). In these discussions, the counselor functioned as a group facilitator in carefully listening to what was being said and helping the members listen to each other (Step 4, Figure 16–1). Once the professional goals in terms of institutional needs were clearly defined, specific behavioral goals were agreed upon, both in the large group of ten teachers and between those pairs who decided to work together (Step 5, Figure 16–1).

Group members as well as the counselor introduced new concepts and practical skills to each other (Steps 6 and 7, Figure 16–1). This allowed the group to draw on the expertise of all of its members. Simulated task sessions coupled with a sharing of the previous day's field work experiences gave each member a chance to evaluate how well he was personally progressing, and he could then serve as critic and reinforcer for others (Steps 7, 8, 9, Figure 16–1). Members were constantly asking each other for advice and the typical class session would begin with "let's find out where everyone is," followed by a setting up of the goals they wanted to achieve for that meeting.

On days when some teachers were meeting with community members, the counselor remained in the school for the purpose of keeping communication open and getting to know each staff member in the workshop better. This also proved to be an excellent opportunity for re-teaching small units involving concepts and skills on an individual basis. Another aspect of having some free informal time for the teachers came in the form of having the occasion to encourage and reinforce those relevant behaviors that had just been practiced in the community (Steps 7 and 8, Figure 16–1). The counselor reinforced the teachers, and the teachers in a very short time were reinforcing each other.

At the closing session of the workshop, members reviewed their original goals to evaluate their progress, modified their project guidelines, and appointed a committee to organize the information obtained from more than one hundred community contacts. They committed themselves to a jointly determined strategy for introducing and teaching their skills to the rest of the faculty. This strategy included having each project member identify one other member as a support system as he went back to his department to make an input about this project. After filling out an evaluation questionnaire, members shared their evaluation of the entire workshop. Personal feedback was given to every member of the group with communication open enough by this time for expressive, critical, and positive messages to be given and received (Step 9, Figure 16–1).

This counselor found all of the steps in the systematic eclectic model necessary for effectively working with a variety of human systems. Although she had performed some of the steps intuitively before being introduced to the model, the conceptual framework provided her with a cognitive map with which to analyze her progress. This proved especially helpful when resistance and opposition appeared to be blocking further advancement of goals. She was then forced to study the sequenced steps and retrace some when necessary before proceeding.

We have described the systematic eclectic model from its theoretical frame and have also attempted to illustrate through the use of examples how the model is used in the daily functioning of a developmental counselor. The model described provides a systematic conceptual framework flexible enough to be used in a wide range of situations and interventions including individual and group counseling as well as consultation and organizational development. The model also draws upon sources of gain in facilitating behavior change that include relationship conditions, public commitment, cognitive learning, social modeling, and operant shaping and reinforcement. The model also attends to problems of transfer and maintenance of behavior usually ignored in therapeutically oriented systems.

One point that must be made clear is that the model is not a rigid or confining framework used in mechanical ways. Rather, it is a cognitive map which the counselor utilizes to ask important questions, define important problems, and make professional decisions as he proceeds with each case.

For example, the counselor can carefully consider the sources of gain built into his approach to a particular client, plan a sequence of activities, move ahead or retreat as he meets with success or resistance, and carefully evaluate the outcomes of his efforts.

It is obvious that each counseling case will differ in the amount of attention or "loading" given to each step in the model. An alienated, unhappy youngster with very low self-esteem may require a very heavy loading in the relationship and communication stages and once these basic conditions have been established, the succeeding stages may be accomplished very quickly.

A vocational–educational planning situation with a healthy, optimally developing youngster may need only minimal attention to relationship and communication conditions and very heavy emphasis on cognitive change processes as the client seeks to explore and understand himself and the world of work. Cases involving acquisition of specific study habits or social skills may require extensive modeling, shaping, and transfer procedures before they can be made part of the client's general behavior patterns.

In every case, the client's needs as revealed in the examination of life stage, life space, and life style factors determine the final directions and distances to be traveled with the systematic eclectic model serving as the map that aids navigation.

REFERENCES

1. BERDIE, R. F. The 1980 counselor: applied behavioral scientist *Personnel Guidance J.*, 1972 (30), 451–456.
2. BERGIN, A. E., & STRUPP, H. H. New directions in psychotherapy research. *J. of abnorm. Psychol.*, 1970, 75.
3. BLOCHER, D. H., DUSTIN, R. E., & DUGAN, W. E. *Guidance systems.* New York: Ronald Press, 1971.
4. CARKHUF R., Counseling research, theory and practice, 1965. *J. counsel. Psychol.*, 1966 (13), 467–480.
5. DANSKIN, D., KENNEDY, C. E., & FRIESEN, W. S. Guidance—the ecology of students, *Personnel Guidance J.*, 1965 (45), 130–135.
6. FRIEDENBERG, E. Z. The modern high school: A profile. *Commentary*, 1963 (36), 373–380.
7. McCULLY, H. The counselor: instrument of change. *Teachers College Record*, 1965 (66), 105–112.
8. SHOBEN, J. Guidance: remedial function or social reconstruction. *Harvard Educ. Rev.*, 1962 (32), 430–443.
9. SILBERMAN, C. E. *Crisis in the classroom.* New York: Random House, 1970.

RECOMMENDED READINGS

COOK, D. *Guidance for education in revolution.* Boston: Allyn & Bacon, 1971.
SPRINTHALL, N. *Guidance for human growth.* New York: Van Nostrand, 1971.

NAME INDEX

SUBJECT INDEX

Accomplishment roles, 79
Acculturation, process of, 117
Achievement, 73
  cultural values, 117
  motivation for, 122–23
  need for, 122–23
Adaptability, 93
Adolescence
  authoritarian coercion, 239
  early (ages twelve to fourteen), 71–73
    coping behavior, 72–73
    developmental tasks, 72
    social roles, 71
  heterosexual roles and relationships, 248
  later, 74–75
    coping behaviors, 75
    developmental tasks, 74
    social roles, 74
  psychosocial moratorium, 248–49
Affiliative behaviors, 84
Affluent society, 136
Alienation, 12
Alternatives, selection of, 125–26
  game theory, 123–24
  value inquiry, 125–26
Ambiguity, controlled use of, 52, 81, 189
Ambivalence, sociological, 107
"Anomie" or deviant behavior, 106
Anthropology, 114–20
  areas of, 114–16
  cultural, 116–17
    discontinuity, 117–20
    values, 116–17
Authoritarian patterns of coercion, 239
Automation, effects of, 131–32

Behavior
  development of effective human, 61–84
Behavioral counseling model, 53–56
  counseling implications, 56–59
Behavioral science, 102–27
  anthropology and counseling, 114–20
  definition, 102

economics, 126
influence on development, 102–3
political science, 126–27
preferential behavior studies, 123–26
research in, 103
social psychology, 120–23
sociology and counseling, 104–14
Belongingness, need for, 51

Career choosing, 74, 76
Case-centered model, group counseling, 216–17
Change, 130–44
  awareness of inevitability, 82
  counselor's role, 227–29
  economic, 131–33
  in education, 141–44
  in family life, 139–41
  human growth and development and, 3
  in occupations, 132–34
  in population, 138–39
  in values, 135–38
Changes in human rights, 135
Child-rearing processes, 118
Childhood
  early (ages three to six), 68–69
    coping behaviors, 69
    developmental tasks, 68–69
    social roles, 68
  later (ages six to twelve), 69–71
    coping behaviors, 70–71
    developmental tasks, 69–70
  social roles, 69
Classical conditioning, 57
Client systems, 23
Clients
  college students, 249–51
  dependency, 180
  developmental relationships, 122, 171–82; see also Relationships, developmental; Humanistic psychology
  initiating contracts with, 262
  resistance of, 180–81

311